THUMPIN' IT

THUMPIN' IT

*The Use and Abuse of the Bible
in Today's Presidential Politics*

Jacques Berlinerblau

Westminster John Knox Press
LOUISVILLE • LONDON

Unless otherwise indicated, Scripture quotations are from The New King James Version, copyright © 1979, 1980, 1982 Thomas Nelson Inc., Publishers. Used by permission.

Book design by Sharon Adams
Cover design by designpointinc.com

First edition
Published by Westminster John Knox Press
Louisville, Kentucky

This book is printed on acid-free paper that meets the American National Standards Institute Z39.48 standard. ⊚

PRINTED IN THE UNITED STATES OF AMERICA

08 09 10 11 12 13 14 15 16 17 — 10 9 8 7 6 5 4 3 2 1

Library of Congress Cataloging-in-Publication Data

Berlinerblau, Jacques.
    Thumpin' it : the use and abuse of the Bible in today's presidential politics / Jacques D. Berlinerblau. — 1st ed.
        p. cm.
    Includes bibliographical references and index.
    ISBN 978-0-664-23173-6 (alk. paper)
    1. Christianity and politics—United States.   2. Bible—Use.
  3. Evangelicalism—Political aspects—United States.   4. Presidents—
Religious life—United States.   I. Title.   II. Title: Thumping it.
    BR526.B46   2008
    261.70973—dc22   2007034480

*Pour le petit Emile
Chou!*

Contents

Acknowledgments

This book would have never come into existence had Georgetown University not invited me to visit and then to stay. Prior to my arrival in Washington, DC, American politics was something I only observed from a distance, like an audience member sitting in the back of a theater. Yet once I started teaching at the School of Foreign Service (and exchanging downtown New York for the nation's other capital) I was afforded a much closer glimpse of the stagecraft, if you will. From this vantage point I was permitted to indulge one of my lifelong obsessions. For beyond the good and the evil of things, beyond the left and the right, beyond the red and the blue of it all, I have always been preoccupied with form, style, "technique"—how things get *done*, be it in literature, music, or now, electoral politics.

When I arrived at Georgetown, I was not equipped with the experiential or emotional tools to understand why graduates of this (or any other) university were so passionately devoted to their alma mater. Why is it, I asked in my first few months, that everyone here "bleeds Hoya blue"? I have come to learn why that is, and suffice it to say that Georgetown is a very special place.

I owe a tremendous debt of gratitude to President Jack DeGioia, Provost Jim O'Donnell, and Dean Robert Gallucci for the extraordinarily warm welcome they extended to me. My colleagues in the bourgeoning Program for Jewish Civilization have turned the past few years into an intellectual thrill ride. I salute Professor Robert

Lieber, Rabbi Harold White, and the irreplaceable Melissa Spence for jointly forging a vision of substance.

I lost many good men and women during the frenzied writing of this book and the incessant shuttling between cities. Permit me to mention the names of those (I hope) I still have with me: Tom Banchoff, Jorunn Buckley, Bob Burkett, Erin Carter, James Crossley, Joe DiGiacinto, James Eisenberg, Sondra Farganis, Warren Frisina, Charles King, Barbara Lekatsas, Sabine Loucif, Cynthia Ozick (to whom I owe an explanation), and Camala Projansky. My redoubtable research assistant Cynthia Pekron (SFS '07) was my little bibliographical sun.

Philip Law was the editor who first saw merit in this project. His comments and advice were, to borrow a phrase from President Bush, of "matchless value." Mr. Law and the idea-loving folks at Westminster John Knox Press are as gifted as they are honorable. May all writers work with a press such as this one.

As usual, Laurette and Rubin are to be extolled, as are Patsy and Pasquale. My previous book was dedicated to my grace-full wife Ippolita and my son Cyrus, who excels in spectacularity. But this one is for Emile. He has made it through his two-year trial period; the three of us have decided to keep him.

Washington DC
August 10, 2007

Introduction

"The Bible Is Raw Power"

Never before has God given American Evangelicals such an awesome opportunity to shape public policy.
National Association of Evangelicals, "For the Health of the Nation: An Evangelical Call to Civic Responsibility"

Once, when I was a younger, completely unknown scholar of the Bible, I had the great good fortune to go pubbing with some older, extremely well-known scholars of the Bible. This happened at one of those yearly academic conferences where experts in sacred Scriptures convene to share the fruits of their research, exchange ideas, and— as the reader might have gathered—forgo various counsels of the Good Book. Among our party was a highly respected professor from a storied European university. After a few hours of active and enthusiastic participation in our revelries, he seemed to grow distant, sullen, disoriented. By all appearances he was oblivious to the loud (and not exceedingly coherent) conversation raging around him.

What were his inebriated colleagues "discussing"? Homosexuality. We were disputing whether the Bible really opposes homosexuality. In an effort to clinch the argument, each participant triumphantly cited verses from Scripture, only to be contradicted (and interrupted) by another who often used the exact same lines to draw precisely the opposite inference. Along the way, more than a few took the opportunity to hurl invective at the Bible itself. I seem to recall the phrase "civilizational biohazard" being tossed around a good bit. This document, it was claimed, had created unimaginable human suffering.

1

Some riposted by pointing to the role it had played in antislavery campaigns, the social gospel movement, and the civil rights activism of the sixties. (There is something endearing, is there not, about those who slur their speech as they stake the moral high ground?)

Just as the debate lurched to its noisy climax, the great scholar suddenly raised his head from the napkin upon which it had been resting and interjected, "Don't you understand, the Bible in and of itself is neither good nor evil. It can be used for both. It says everything. It says nothing. The Bible is just raw power!" He then face-planted upon the table, landing with the muffled concussive thud that signals a lesson (or anecdote) is over.

❧❧❧❧❧❧

"The Bible is just raw power!" Just beyond the halfway course of my life I recognize this as the most profound insight I have ever absorbed about my subject matter. If it were possible, I would chisel these words on the façade of the Washington Monument (vertically, as with Chinese lettering, though using English characters, of course). My reasons for wanting to inscribe this cryptic revelation on a cryptic national icon will become clear in time. But presently, I would like to introduce the theme that energizes this book: the Bible's "raw power" is surging into American politics with an intensity perhaps not equaled since the nineteenth century.

Some of the nation's most contentious public debates now feature participants who claim biblical warrant for their views. Appeals to Scripture are evident in controversies over the environment, immigration, abortion, stem cell research, gay rights, public school curricula, the treatment of the poor, and foreign policy, to name but a few. These appeals are typically made by religious special interest groups. *"It's in the Bible!"* they exclaim. And if it's in the Bible, so goes the logic, then local, state, and federal lawmakers must take swift and immediate measures.

In the secular-liberal mindset, those who subscribe to this line of reasoning are categorized under the catchall rubric of "red-state people": Republicans, right-wingers, megachurch congregants, NASCAR aficionados, Jesus freaks, guys in Montana with guns strapped to their backs, "anachronistic ding dongs," and so forth.[1] Yet the truth is that a surprisingly large number of blue-state types have identified an actionable liberal agenda on the pages of Scripture. Such was the case, for instance, when the interfaith group Network of Spiritual Progressives recently took out a full-page advertisement in the *New York Times*. There they demanded that the nation's leaders put an end to the war in Iraq, apologize to the United Nations, and "confess wrong-doing" in the spirit of 2 Chronicles 7:14.[2] Their intervention stands in a long American tradition of Bible-based, left-wing advocacy.[3]

Intriguing as well is the tendency of high-profile politicians to incorporate Scripture into their rhetoric. Our own outgoing commander in chief provides a sterling example. "No other President," writes Jeffrey Siker, "has so clearly perceived his calling in such epic biblical terms."[4] Consider that George W. Bush quoted from the books of Psalms, Matthew, and Romans in the immediate aftermath of 9/11. It is reported that with Bible in hand he once exclaimed, "This is the only handbook you need. This handbook is a good go-by."[5] Upon being asked to name his favorite philosopher or thinker, the future forty-third president famously responded "Christ, because he changed my heart."[6] With his coded scriptural rhetoric and uncanny ability to wink subtly to his conservative Christian base, Bush has carried two national elections.

This is not to say that all politicians who cite the Bible ride her winged words to glory. In the coming chapters we will have a chance to survey the wreckage that results from ill-considered, high-speed thumping. Former House majority leader Tom DeLay probably wishes he hadn't mentioned that God was using him to "stand up for biblical worldview." Sharing a few impromptu reflections on the book of Job is something Howard Dean will never do again. John Kerry could just as well have cited *The Fortunes and Misfortunes of the Famous Moll Flanders* for all the good that his scriptural references did him in 2004. The lesson is clear: when the entire national press corps is on duty, harness the Bible's energy at your own risk.[7]

The mention of Dean and Kerry calls attention to a point of considerable significance for our inquiry. The use (and abuse) of the Bible in politics is no longer a predominantly Republican undertaking. Emboldened by the triumphs of faith-on-their-sleeve-wearing candidates in the midterm elections of 2006, Democratic presidential frontrunners are letting the Scriptures sing out. Determined not to repeat the mistakes of 2004, they invoke the text more confidently and creatively than their GOP counterparts. Senator Barack Obama, for one, may just have the best Scripture game in town. So polished is

Obama that he can arrogate to himself the ombudsman-like role of distinguishing proper from improper citation. In a 2006 address he chastised those on the right who advanced sectarian and simplistic readings. "So before we get carried away," he asserted cheekily, "let's read our Bibles. Folks haven't been reading their Bibles."[8]

Having a good Scripture game is no longer optional for Democrats. One high-profile political consultant advises her liberal clients to incorporate "recognizably biblical language" and to steer clear of the phrase "separation of church and state."[9] Recently, a former press secretary for Bill Clinton made the following recommendation: "If Democrats and progressives truly wish to reach the faithful voters of America with arguments and messages that resonate, they will need to dig deep into scripture and find first how the eternal word of God speaks to them."[10] This is consonant with the request that a handler made of Senator Mark Pryor of Arkansas before his successful run: "Mark, I never want you to give a speech in Arkansas without quoting the Bible, okay?"[11]

Senator Hillary Clinton of New York, for her part, will never give a major speech in Arkansas or anywhere else her campaign takes her without quoting the Bible or rehearsing her narrative of faith. An indication of things to come was offered in March 2006 when she lambasted Republican immigration legislation with the memorable words, "It is certainly not in keeping with my understanding of the Scriptures. This bill would literally criminalize the Good Samaritan and probably even Jesus himself."[12] While ruminating on the implications of this remark, David Klinghoffer concluded that "2008 will likely prove to be the Year of the Bible."[13]

The Rise

The Bible is *back*! This statement, as we shall see, is laced with ironies, paradoxes, and cunning misdirection. And this statement—when taken at face value—elicits deeply emotional and not entirely rational responses from American voters. Conservative Christians in particular are positively overjoyed by the good news. Others see this as sufficient cause to apply for Canadian citizenship.

As far as the overjoyed Christians and others are concerned, the Bible is back from involuntary exile. In their opinion, it had been banished, held captive, placed in a choke hold by the profane, tattooed, secular arms of the judiciary, liberal media, and professorate. At last, through the Herculean efforts (and prayers) of Bible-believing folks, it has been freed. God's sacred writ stands ready to guide the nation again. But there is so much more work to be done.

Although imperfect, this narrative of a liberated Scripture has some merit. By its very obstreperous presence in public life, the Bible is, in fact, testifying to the declining power of state- and court-sponsored godlessness. The resurgence of the Good Book provides undeniable evidence that conservative Christians have made tangible electoral and judicial strides in the past few decades. It also points to a truth that has been discussed far less frequently: during the same period, political secularism in this country has stagnated woefully.

One of the subplots in this book concerns the divergent fortunes of two parties associated with two divergent constituencies. The Republicans prospered handsomely because they understood how to communicate with and mobilize those citizens who made the Bible's public resurrection possible. The Democrats, on the other hand, were slow to read the signs of the times. They clung tenaciously to certain secular presuppositions about the nature of the republic. Only lately have they begun to accord the Good Book and those who treasure it their proper due. Only lately have they begun to rethink their relations with the nonbelievers and strict church/state separationists who form part of their base.

In order to better understand Scripture's historical drama of public exile and restoration, as well as the triumph of the Christians and the trauma of the secularists, a brief historical overview is in order. For, yes, it might very well be "the Year of the Bible" again (see above and below). But by this logic we could also claim that the period from the landing on Plymouth Rock in 1620 to the Revolution was "the Century and a Half of the Bible." It would be hard to exaggerate how central a role the Scriptures played in the political thought of the Pilgrims and Puritans. They arrived with a fondness for the Old Testament—a fondness which, by the standards of a later age, would appear to verge on the obsessive or the talismanic. It was in the translations of those Hebrew Scriptures where they found justification for nearly every imaginable component of their existence.

"The Pilgrims," write Joseph Gaer and Ben Siegel, "made scripture a political and religious guide, deciding their social organization should be modeled as closely as possible after Israel's twelve tribes under Moses."[14] Along with the Puritans they conceived of themselves as a "New Israel." They crossed a "Red Sea" that was the Atlantic Ocean. They sojourned in order to arrive in "Zion," and they did this while fleeing "Pharaoh," who was James I.[15]

Their abhorrence of King James, and English absolutism in general, provides a perfect illustration of how their readings of Scripture informed their politics and ideology. With its frequent denunciations of the monarchy, the Bible served the Puritans as an antikingmaker, if you will. Did not the prophet Samuel enumerate a litany of reprehensible things that kings are wont to do (1 Sam. 8:11–18)? Did not even David, the anointed one of the Lord, err spectacularly (2 Sam. 12)? The headstrong Puritans, of course, downplayed contradictory biblical passages—passages that seemed supportive of monarchy and passive obedience to rulers in general (e.g., Rom. 13:1–7; 1 Pet. 2:13–14).[16] It is a peculiarity of the Good Book that it elicits in its readers the strong conviction that it unequivocally supports their strongest convictions.

With the onset of the revolutionary period, Scripture lost none of its symbolic cachet. To get a sense of the esteem in which it was held by the nation's political elite, consider the following. In 1776 Benjamin Franklin, John Adams, and Thomas Jefferson suggested that an image of Moses leading the Israelites through parted waters (and being pursued in vain by a *crowned* Pharaoh) be adopted as the national seal.[17] According to legend, biblical Hebrew was once proposed as a substitute for English by members of the revolutionary Congress.[18]

Historians Mark Noll, Nathan Hatch, and George Marsden have observed that "nearly every important person in America's early political history had extensive experience with Scripture."[19] Yet these writers go on to make an observation of the utmost importance. Few of the leaders of that storied generation actually believed that "the Bible was a unique revelation from God."[20] Given the highly unorthodox worldviews of some of the founders, this makes a great deal of sense.

One need look no further than Thomas Jefferson. It was he who cut and pasted for himself an abridged version of the Gospels, *The Life and Morals of Jesus of Nazareth*, which separated the good bits from the bad. In Jefferson's words, the worthy teachings of Jesus were "as distinguishable as diamonds in a dunghill."[21] How far we have come from the Pilgrims and Puritans who venerated every jot and tittle of Scripture! Jefferson—reverently designing a national seal with scriptural allusions and industriously butchering the Gospels—embodies a contradiction about the Scriptures that remains with us until this day.

The Holy Bible is a symbol. It is the grandest and most revered symbol of the nation's collective faith. The scholar Martin Marty has referred to it as an "icon," arguing that America "has more than the Declaration of Independence and the United States Constitution enshrined in a vault in its archival heart; The Bible also is there."[22] But to the consternation of traditional Protestants since the founding of the republic, *the Bible functions as little more than an icon*. Its ability to directly influence public policy is severely constrained.

And the founders are largely to blame. It was all well and good to honor the text ceremoniously. George Washington did as much when he kissed it upon taking the oath of office.[23] John Adams did likewise when he exulted, "The Bible is the best book in the world."[24] But this did not mean that they wanted "the best book in the world" to directly impact the young nation's political fate. Recall that the Declaration of Independence and the Constitution are bereft of explicit biblical references—a staggering truism that itself merits being carved on a national monument.[25] Whether explicitly or not, the Scriptures were being put in their place, and their place was not in the charters of the new republic.

By conjuring up the separation of church and state, the founders, in the words of Garry Wills, "made the United States a new thing on the earth."[26] It became the type of thing that was structurally built to prevent the Good Book from playing any official, unmediated role in the business of the state. This innovation provided a built-in check and balance on the ability of the sacred text to directly and substantively influence American politics. In a country of competing and often antagonistic denominations, no one sectarian interpretation of the Scriptures would be made into law by Congress. The Establishment Clause of the First Amendment may just be the most effective

Bible repellent created in the history of Christian polities. Church/state separatists have sprayed this repellent liberally, so to speak. The symbolic prominence of the Good Book did not diminish in the nineteenth century. Andrew Jackson was doing what all American leaders do when he called the Bible "the rock upon which our republic rests."[27] The abolitionists, as my drunken colleagues correctly recalled, made much use of the Scriptures. In order to validate their opposition to slavery they eagerly invoked divine texts. What will be of interest to us later on is that *their adversaries did precisely the same thing*. When Abraham Lincoln bent over to kiss the King James Version while taking his second oath of office, he was giving the Bible its proper ceremonial respect.[28] But, again, the contradictions between symbol and substance are striking. Historian Louis Weeks, who looked at the relevance of the Bible in nineteenth-century America, concludes that "the Bible meant little in political affairs."[29]

The Fall

The United States underwent a process of secularization so thoroughgoing in the first three quarters of the twentieth century that even the Bible's *symbolic* salience was threatened. What it came to represent for an emerging elite was not authority and timeless wisdom, but obscurantism, irrationality, and premodern mumbo jumbo.

First, there were the storm clouds of European biblical criticism that came wafting across the Atlantic in the late nineteenth century. Now as never before, the Bible's accuracy and even integrity were called into question. Did Moses write the first five books, or did the so-called J, E, D, and P schools identified by the German professors stitch it together? Did the flood really occur, or was it a myth conjured up by prerational minds unencumbered by any understanding of environmental processes? With the advent, if not apotheosis, of secular knowledge, the credibility of the Scriptures was severely undermined.[30]

But the most severe blow to the Bible's prominence was dealt by the so-called Scopes Monkey Trial of 1925. It was here that Scripture's most vocal champions were shamed into silence. This was a constituency that never doubted the propriety of bringing the Bible into political deliberation, and this was a constituency that was about to get rolled. Douglas Sweeney remarks, "Nothing symbolized the defeat of mainline Protestant fundamentalists like their 'victory' at the Scopes trial."[31] "By 1930," writes John Green, "fundamentalists and many other evangelicals had withdrawn into their own religious circles and largely detached themselves from public affairs."[32] While those who wanted Scripture to play a central role in the nation's public life went into a state of prolonged political hibernation, a new group arose to fill the void. Let's call them "the secularists." We should not assume, however, that they were atheists or agnostics. They were secular in a different sense: they supported the strict separation of church and state. Many, if not most, were Protestants, Catholics, and Jews (with Jehovah's Witnesses playing a starring role in the courts).[33] Each group had its own motives for wanting to exclude (Protestant) religion, and by extension the Scriptures, from America's political life. The promulgation of nonbelief was not foremost among them.

In the half century after the Scopes Trial the labors of the secularists were to change America dramatically. The wall of separation dividing church and state was lengthened, fortified, coated with flame retardant materials, and equipped with surface-to-air missiles. The years 1925 to 1973 might be described as the Golden Age of American Secularism. Justice Black set the tone in 1947, and thus "revived Jefferson's metaphor," when he commented, "The First Amendment has erected a wall between church and state. That wall must be kept high and impregnable. We could not approve the slightest breach."[34]

The period in question was the era of landmark court cases such as *McCollum v. Board of Education* (1948, prohibiting religious instruction in public schools), *Engel v. Vitale* (1962, prohibiting school prayer), and *Abington Township School District v. Schempp* (1963, prohibiting Bible reading in public school). It was the age which gave us that eternal nemesis of the religious right: the Lemon Test with its somewhat baffling three-pronged criteria of Establishment dos and don'ts. Those who pined for a greater place for the Scriptures in political life felt the weight of one particular reading of the Constitution bearing down on them with unprecedented force.

The Golden Age accelerated into the sixties with the explosion of an immense counterculture. These were the days of free love, the exploration of Eastern religions, and the mass proliferation of recreational drugs of decent quality. Not far behind was the women's movement and imported post-Marxist ideologies that had come to the United States to howl deafeningly before they died.

Save for the civil rights movement, the Bible's power to substantively impact the life of the nation had reached an all-time low. Those for whom the Good Book was just another book were swelling the ranks of the elite universities, law schools, and media. They carried with them a sophisticated worldview that brooked no contact between the affairs of the state and the interests of any church. As one fundamentalist later put it, "A new religion of secularism was evolving [that] threatened the existence of Judeo-Christian values."[35]

Christianity's proper place in this worldview was either to privatize itself completely or, in more extreme versions, to go away. To my mind, the Golden Age aurally culminates in John Lennon's "Imagine," the unofficial national anthem of secularism. The song asks us to imagine a world without religion, concluding: "Imagine all the people, living life in peace, Yoo hoo oo woo woo!"

The Comeback

The precise moment when the Bible started to make its comeback is difficult to pin down. As far as conservative Christians are concerned, it was the *Roe v. Wade* case of 1973 that ignited their activist fires.[36] That verdict did, in fact, mark the zenith of a secular political and judicial worldview that had gradually become an orthodoxy in the half century since Scopes. When Justice Blackmun concluded that the decision to terminate the life of the fetus prior to the first trimester "must be left to the medical judgment of the pregnant woman's attending physician," he conveniently left God out of the consultation.[37] To hear evangelicals tell it, Blackmun virtually sent out his clerks to kick the shins of every good Christian in the country.

It seems, however, that the initial outrage over Roe was mostly expressed by small groups of *Catholics*.[38] Eventually, an irate constituency of traditional Protestants dedicated itself to grassroots and national political mobilization around this and other issues. It is often forgotten that these Protestants were initially excited and galvanized by the candidacy of the Southern Baptist Jimmy Carter. Ultimately, the president from Georgia disappointed them (and so many others). He did, however, succeed in awakening "the sleeping giant of evangelical Protestantism."[39] The rest is, well, American history.

Casting aside their traditions of political quietism, conservative Christians played a significant role in the 1980 presidential election. It was there that the ambiguously evangelical Ronald Reagan trounced the incumbent liberal evangelical Jimmy Carter (and, for good measure, the evangelical John Anderson).[40] Reagan went so far as to proclaim 1983, with the approval of the Congress, the "Year of the Bible."[41] "Of the many influences that have shaped the United States of America into a distinctive Nation and people," he declared, "none may be said to be more fundamental and enduring than the Bible." Sensing they had a chum in the High Office, conservative Christians helped reelect the Great Communicator in 1984. The fragrantly secular and liberal duo of Walter Mondale and Geraldine Ferraro was sent packing. It was also during these years that conservative Christians hit upon "secular humanism" as a new scapegoat to accompany communism.

The part played by the Moral Majority in the Reagan Revolution is undeniable. As Susan Harding observes, Jerry Falwell's coalition managed to reunite "two things that had been kept apart for much of America's mid-twentieth century—routine public activism and aggressive Bible-believing Protestantism."[42] Falwell's legacy will be debated for years. Yet the recent suggestion that his enterprise precipitated "the biggest voter realignment" in modern American history seems highly plausible.[43]

Growing increasingly confident and politically sophisticated, conservative Christians eventually signed on to the candidacy of George H. W. Bush in 1988. His adversary, the ultrasecular, liberal, northeastern Democrat Michael Dukakis, had no discernible Scripture game whatsoever. But neither did George H. W. Bush. To stabilize his shaky reaching-out gestures to the Christian right, the services of a certain born-again Texas businessman by the name of George W. Bush were called upon. It was in this effort that the younger Bush gained experience and forged contacts that would serve him well twelve years later.[44]

Bill Clinton—an "Arkansas 'good old boy'"—had no fatal weaknesses among evangelical religious voters in 1992 and 1996.[45] As we shall observe, he showed considerable dexterity with constituencies of faith. Such dexterity was not evident in the feckless campaigns of Mondale, Dukakis, and John Kerry. This brings us to George W. Bush—arguably the most outwardly religious president in the nation's history.[46] His eight years in office may just coincide with the dawn of a new conservative Christian century. Or millennium, perhaps.

The Evangelicals

The dust has settled. What some are calling "the Fourth Great Awakening" is hitting its stride. The Promethean evangelicals are everywhere—red states, blue states, right, center, left, this coalition, that coalition, the *New York Times,* the *Southeastern Idaho Plains Dealer.* They strike fear in the hearts of secularists, like the Vandals descending on Rome.

Evangelicals constitute one of the most dynamic social movements in recent American history. In the past decade they have emerged as an electoral kingmaker in their own right. Evangelicals alone comprise a hush-inducing 20–25 percent of the entire American electorate, estimated to encompass between 50 and 80 million people. Described as the "religious mainstay" of the Republican Party, 78 percent of them cast their ballots for George Bush in 2004 (40 percent of all those who voted for him were evangelicals).[47] Yet as we shall see, some are casting come-hither stares in the direction of obliging Democrats.

Having mastered the art of ecumenical coalition building, evangelicals have also learned how to form strategic alliances with other political groups. The more politically conservative ones refer to this as "co-belligerency," and their most reliable co-belligerents have been traditional Catholics, Mormons, and a smattering of politically conservative Jews.[48] All have expressed concern over the moral drift of American culture. The culprit is "secularism," of course. It is to be blamed for abortion on demand, homosexual lifestyles, indecency in the arts and media, and the nation's impressively robust porn industry.

Nonbelief, for its part, stands in marked contrast to all of this evangelical dynamism. Politically speaking, this type of secularism is a study in stasis: a picture of a picture of a potted plant. Consider the following examples of immobility and crisis. There appears to be exactly one out-of-the-closet nonbeliever out of 535 representatives in the House and Senate (Congressman Peter Stark of California). This lack of representation is exacerbated by the inability of nonbelievers to forge effective political partnerships (especially, and most puzzlingly, with mainline Protestants, liberal Catholics, and Jews).

And it gets worse. Under George W. Bush's watch, the balance of the Supreme Court has been ideologically tipped. That numerous accomplishments of the judicial Golden Age will soon be undone seems to be a foregone conclusion. The Democratic Party, meanwhile, has undergone a conversion to "faith and values" rhetoric. With the judiciary and the legislative bodies abandoning them, American secularists, like potential victims of a nuclear bomb, are faced with a grim choice: radiation or blast?

No one is enjoying the fallout more than our peripatetic evangelicals. And before moving forward I should note that defining precisely who they are is notoriously difficult to do. The complexities are attributable to the astonishing heterogeneity of the movement. As Richard Kyle observes, "Evangelicalism is tremendously diverse—nearly defying definition."[49] Allen Hertzke refers to it as "a vast, rather complex, decentralized, entrepreneurial world."[50] Confusing matters more is that evangelicals overlap in terms of theological and political beliefs with other Bible-centered Protestant groups. These include fundamentalists, charismatics, and Pentecostals.[51]

As with all these groups, the evangelicals place an immense practical and doctrinal premium on Scripture. In their estimation, the Bible is the "inerrant word of God," the paper pope, so to speak.[52] "Evangelicals," jokes Martyn Percy, "believed in a different Trinity to the rest of Christendom: Father, Son and Holy Scripture."[53] Roger Olson observes that for evangelicals the Bible is "God's uniquely inspired and authoritative book; for them it is the supreme source and norm for Christian faith and practice."[54] As evangelicals consolidate their demographic power and sprout their political wings, it is no surprise that the Scriptures soar with them. Why is the Bible back in American politics? The simplest answer is: because evangelicals are back.

The esteem of the evangelicals for the Good Book does not differ significantly from their Puritan ancestors. Neither does their thinking about the Bible's proper place in America's political life. And this is where the tensions that inform this study arise. Today's dynamic,

Bible-toting evangelicals are not content to have the Good Book function as some sort of national mascot. In their view, the Good Lord did not gift us with the Holy Text in order for it to serve as an icon. On the contrary, it is to be a "good go-by" for the nation's priorities, a substantive shaper of domestic and foreign policy. Conservative Christian leader Gary Bauer put it bluntly when he warned, "The last thing America wants or needs is more symbolic God talk to religious people as a pet constituency."[55]

Articulating this desire to shift the Bible from grand symbol of the nation's faith in God to grand shaper of domestic and foreign policy is a remarkable document released by the National Association of Evangelicals in 2004. Entitled "For the Health of the Nation: An Evangelical Call to Civic Responsibility," it is nothing less than a full-blown party platform. The preamble declares that "the bias of aggressive secularism is the last acceptable prejudice in America." The statement continues: "As Christians committed to the full authority of Scripture, our normative vision must flow from the Bible and from the moral order that God has embedded in his creation."[56]

"For the Health of the Nation" ends with a plea for Christians to vote, to "communicate biblical values to their governmental representatives," and to "encourage our children to consider vocations in public service." A progressive evangelical group advocating for environmental issues phrases it with a little more edge: "*Whether* we will enter the public square and offer our witness there is no longer an open question. We are in that square, and we will not withdraw."[57]

With a pivotal national election upon us, the motivations of our cast of characters are clear. The evangelicals want biblical substance. The secularists want biblical irrelevance (and not to get rolled). The liberal Catholics and mainline Protestants want to stake out some middle ground. The Democratic and Republican presidential aspirants want to get elected. This is where our inquiry begins.

✯✯✯✯✯✯

My fellow Americans, when you cast your votes for president this coming November, I regret to say that I will not be joining you. I am sitting this election out (my role model being Zachary Taylor, our twelfth president, who did not vote, not even for himself).[58] This act of electoral abstinence must not be interpreted as a form of protest or as a lack of patriotism. If it is any consolation, I fully intend to be present at the inauguration of our forty-fourth commander in chief on January 20, 2009. I will bring the kids, put the three-year-old on my shoulders, so that he may soak in the pageantry, and let the six-year-old wander about in the massive crowd and hope for the best. No! I withhold my ballot in order to achieve critical distance. Any personal investment in the candidates I will be writing about would arouse my sweatiest, clarity-befogging passions. Ideally, my ambivalence will lessen the reader's suspicions that the analysis and opinions expressed here correspond to a party line or agenda. This is not a profession of objectivity. Rather, it is a pledge to try and be as evenhanded as possible.

In what follows, I hope to avoid the paroxysms of partisanship that characterize discussions of faith and politics, especially among the American professorate. Few things molest our (already limited) powers of impartiality like our own faith and our own politics. "Bad air!" as Nietzsche would say. In order to avoid all that, a conscious attempt will be made to subject all political interest groups and all politicians to a relentlessly mistrustful gaze. So, let me warn the reader in advance: if you are looking for an endorsement of your own beloved candidate or cherished opinion, chances are exceedingly high that you won't find it here.

In what follows, politics will be construed as a form of theater, albeit one with grave implications. I am interested in understanding the roles the "actors" are playing, the technique they bring to their craft, the way they deliver their lines, and so on.

Let the theologians assess the morality of the performance. It is a cynical business, politics is. It becomes no less so when public servants and interest groups get it into their heads that God himself provided proof-texts for their policy initiatives two thousand years ago.

PART 1 The Bible and Public Policy

Chapter 1

The Bible in American Politics

A Primer

Both [sides] read the same Bible and pray to the same God, and each invokes His aid against the other.
Abraham Lincoln, Second Inaugural Address

And even if we did have only Christians in our midst, if we expelled every non-Christian from the United States of America, whose Christianity would we teach in the schools? Would we go with James Dobson's or Al Sharpton's? Which passages of Scripture should guide our public policy? Should we go with Leviticus, which suggests slavery is okay and that eating shellfish is abomination? How about Deuteronomy, which suggests stoning your child if he strays from the faith? Or should we just stick to the Sermon on the Mount—a passage that is so radical that it's doubtful that our own Defense Department would survive its application?
Barack Obama, "'Call to Renewal' Keynote Address"

*O*f the three hundred or so people who turned up to hear Tom DeLay's speech at the First Baptist Church of Pearland, Texas, on April 12, 2002, it is safe to surmise that at least one of them was not a big fan of the majority whip. For a few days later the advocacy group Americans United for Separation of Church and State leaked a secretly taped recording of the Republican congressman's remarks to the *Houston Chronicle.*

DeLay's comments at the "Worldview Weekend" gathering were quotable, to say the least. There was a discussion of the ungodliness of Baylor and Texas A&M Universities. There were testimonials to the support that the Lord had offered DeLay during his efforts to impeach Bill Clinton. There was a good deal of Christian triumphalism on display as well. "Only Christianity," said the congressman, "offers a way to live in response to the realities that we find in this world."[1]

As regards my interest in "thumping" and thumping-related activities, however, the most relevant item was his insistence that God had used him to promote "biblical worldview." In his own memorable locutions, DeLay announced, "He [God] has been walking me through an incredible journey, and it all comes down to worldview. He is using me, all the time, everywhere, to stand up for biblical worldview in everything that I do and everywhere that I am. He is training me, He is working with me."[2]

It is by no means unusual for a politician to declare that he or she is acting on behalf of Scripture and, by extension, God. Nor is the declaration of fealty to biblical principles a uniquely Republican conceit. Senator Edward Kennedy, for one, has been known to crack out his Bible every now and then. In expressing his reservations about the war in Iraq he declaimed, "The Book of Proverbs in the Bible teaches us that, 'Pride goes before destruction, and a haughty spirit before a fall.' It's time for President Bush to swallow his pride."[3]

Senator Barack Obama of Illinois also grounds opinions in Scripture. Notice how he craftily takes a proreligion position without in any way undermining his support for a woman's right to choose: "My Bible tells me that if we train a child in the way he should go, when he is old he will not turn from it. So I think faith and guidance can help fortify a young woman's sense of self, a young man's sense of responsibility, and a sense of reverence that all young people should have for the act of sexual intimacy."[4]

In American politics it is not unhelpful to assert that one's policies have biblical sanction. Come to think of it, I cannot recall a single case in which the opposite holds true. I have never heard a seeker or holder of office utter something to the effect of, "*The policy that I am advocating has no biblical warrant. It flies in the face of the words of Scripture. It is diametrically opposed to the teachings of our Lord and Savior Jesus Christ. Thank you. May God bless America.*" Insofar as a majority of the electorate is Christian, political figures risk little when they make vague claims about the symmetry between their own views and those in the Good Book.

Let this serve as a reminder that use of the Bible in American political discourse is light not heavy, theatrical not substantive, and rhetorical as opposed to policy oriented. A public servant can thump away about "biblical worldview" or what "my Bible tells me" without being expected to supply any rationale or supporting evidence for these broad assertions. Ted Kennedy's remark illustrates that appealing to Scripture is not a labor-intensive activity; as we shall observe throughout this book, the average length of a typical citation made by an American politician is exactly one verse. Aligning one's positions with the Good Book is inexpensive, demanding no vast stock of erudition or debating prowess.

There are many explanations for the absence of profundity in our nation's God-talk. Here are a few: (1) the representatives of our government, bless them all, do not usually possess advanced degrees in theology; (2) the very thought of jousting with civil liberties groups is enough to prevent most public servants from delivering the extended homily that they know they have in them; (3) the American electorate—I speak here as a patriot—rarely demands intellectual depth and scholarly precision from its leaders.

But in this chapter I wish to focus on another reason that accounts for the superficial manner in which Scripture is employed by our politicians. This involves certain peculiarities of the Bible itself.

Scriptural Dueling Banjos

Using the Bible to think about the complex issues that confront the American people is a difficult task. For starters, the ancient Scriptures are often singularly uninterested in the complex issues that confront the American people. Two evangelical Christian commentators hit the nail on the head when they observe, "The Bible doesn't mention nuclear energy, the Internal Revenue Service, or global warming."[5] I concur and would politely add that it does not say a whole lot about homosexuality or abortion either.

This may come as a shock to those who have watched these issues nearly overrun domestic policy discussions in recent election cycles. As I have discussed elsewhere, verses that explicitly deal with same-sex relations are exceedingly infrequent.[6] In chapter 3 we will observe that the Scriptures say very little about abortion. This is not to say that the Good Book is "pro-gay" or "pro-choice" but that it offers us scant resources for formulating credible opinions on these issues. But even when the Scriptures speak at length about concerns of relevance to us, clarity is elusive. It has often been noted that the Bible devotes a great deal of attention to the poor. This argument has been popularized and retrofitted for blue-state deployment by Jim Wallis. America's best-known religious man of the Left remarks: "I'm an evangelical Christian, and I'm bound to a Bible where there are 3,000 verses on the poor. . . . The issue the Bible talks about most often, over and over again," he continues, "is how you treat the poorest and most vulnerable in your society. That's the issue the prophets raise again and again, and Jesus talks about it more than any other topic, more than heaven or hell, more than sex or morality."[7]

Let's call this the "hermeneutics of emphasis." It is an interpretive principle whose basic rule could be described this way: the more the sacred text says about an issue the more that issue stands as one of its moral priorities. It's a simplistic but effective argument, and one that can neutralize certain commonly heard conservative Christian articles of faith. Jesus, after all, said not a word about homosexuality or the rights of the unborn. To dwell on such issues while pushing for tax breaks for the wealthy, charges the shrewd Democratic operative, is to callously restructure Jesus' social agenda and ignore his concerns for the indigent.

Rhetorically speaking, this approach is a winner, and Democratic frontrunners are using it liberally (see chapter 6). But were someone to delve into the scriptural fine print, the matter would become considerably more opaque. Upon closer inspection, it is evident that the Bible does not have one worldview on the question of poverty. I find it significant that when God wishes to reward mortals, He often rewards them with *riches*. Job's prize for speaking the truth about God (or praying on behalf of his friends) is to receive "twice what he had before" (42:10). Material prosperity is lavished on the patriarch Abraham by the deity (Gen. 24:35). It is the Lord, we are informed, "who gives you the power to get wealth" (Deut. 8:17–18). Wealth, then, can be something of a divine dispensation. Poverty, by contrast, is attributed in the Book of Proverbs to laziness and sloth (20:13; 24:33) or a lack of discipline (13:18).[8]

In the New Testament Jesus reminds us, "For you have the poor with you always, and whenever you wish you may do them good; but Me you do not have always" (Mark 14:7). All this might ignite the imagination of a mischievous, sociologically minded interpreter. She or he might deduce from this that poverty is a structurally inherent, divinely sanctioned component of any social system. If the poor will always be with us, then why tinker with God's inscrutable designs?

I have just performed the exegetical equivalent of a House filibuster. That is, I have adduced Scriptures that can bog down antipoverty Bible thumpers, such as Jim Wallis, with countless contradictory passages suggesting that his reading is not faithful to the sacred writ. And like any good congressperson I have not necessarily done this because it corresponds with my most sincere personal convictions. I have no doubt that a theologian could effectively challenge every one of my arguments. In the process he or she would undoubtedly accuse me of irresponsibly wrenching sacred words out of their original contexts. Guilty as charged. But I am no guiltier than the theologian who tries to align ancient documents with the precepts of modern political liberalism.

Leaving questions of culpability aside, the previous example illuminates a truism about Scripture-centered political debates: they quickly devolve into He-(God) said, He-(God) said shouting matches. The Bible can always be cited *against itself*, no matter what the issue. If this seems unduly hypothetical or absurd, let it be stressed that biblical proof-text warfare has been part of American culture for centuries. In colonial America, debates on English absolutism led both sides to scour the Scriptures for verses that supported their positions. Those who abhorred the idea of monarchy could invoke the scathing assessment of kingly flaws found in 1 Samuel 8.[9] Their opponents countered with the New Testament text 1 Peter 2:13–14: "Submit yourselves to every ordinance of man for the Lord's sake: whether it be to the king, as supreme; or unto governors, as unto them that are sent by him for the punishment of evildoers, and for the praise of them that do well" (KJV).

In the nineteenth century—the golden age for protracted public squabbling about what Scripture says—lengthy arguments ensued about national Sabbath laws. As Louis Weeks notes in his survey of the controversy, "Both proponents and opponents employed the

Bible." As the debate dragged on, however, "Americans became wary of such an ambiguous source of authority."[10] Perhaps no other political controversy featured as much biblical back-and-forth as the question of slavery. The story of how abolitionists *and* proslavery figures appealed to the Bible is well known and need not be rehearsed here.

A few quick observations about that debate, however, are instructive in helping us contemplate the interface between sacred writings and politics. First, those who alleged that the Bible condones and even encourages slavery did not lack for a significant docket of verses proving their point. It could even be said that the case *for* slavery in Scripture is more substantive and explicitly framed than the case against it. As one commentator puts it, "An objective observer can only conclude that the Southerners had Scripture on their side."[11] The second point is that after years in the trenches many antislavery leaders who once grounded their argument in Scripture came to doubt the text's efficacy in this debate. James Brewer Stewart refers to "an emphatic shift away from Scripture as the primary authority for abolitionists."[12]

In other words, these deeply religious activists came to view appeals to Scripture as useless.[13] Once the nation itself came to understand that the Bible could not resolve the quandary, the next logical phase was violence. As Mark Noll describes it, "It was left to those consummate theologians, the reverend doctors, Ulysses S. Grant and William Tecumseh Sherman, to decide what in fact the Bible actually meant."[14]

The cacophony of scriptural dueling banjos has been heard again and again in American history. The fact that diametrically opposed camps can both find warrant for their views in the same book (or the same verses) demonstrates the hazards, if not the futility, of bringing Scripture alone into serious political deliberation. For most of the twentieth century such battles played a limited part in American political discourse. Now they are about to return. As two evangelical writers put it, "Only if we allow a biblical worldview and a biblically balanced agenda to guide our concrete political work can we significantly improve the political order."[15]

The Bible Is an Anthology: Forty Authors or a Thousand?

The question arises as to why the Bible gives so many political groups the impression that it supports their views. My answer, prefaced with a booming glissando so as to alert the reader to its importance, is as follows: the Bible is an *anthology*. It is a collection of discrete documents written by different people, with different perspectives, living at different times, and beholden to completely different worldviews. This is what makes Scripture such a rich, profound, inconsistent, volatile, and maddening source for political thought and action.[16]

One of the greatest challenges that a college professor of Bible faces is getting his or her bewildered charges to *not* think of the Bible as they would a modern book. A contemporary novel or work of nonfiction is almost always written by one person. Given the average life span of a member of the species, a modern author will write a book over the course of a year, or a decade, or, for those suffering from debilitating writer's block, half a century.

The Bible's process of composition could not have been more dissimilar. The scrolls that comprise it were not written across one person's lifetime. Scripture was not created in mortal time but civilizational time. Its books—especially those in the Hebrew Bible/Old Testament—were written and rewritten, and edited and reorganized together across centuries. The many far-flung contributors to the final, two-testament product lived in periods as varied as the Davidic monarchy in the tenth century BCE, the Assyrian Empire in the eighth century, the Persian restoration of the sixth and fifth centuries, and the Hellenistic and Roman periods. Let's say that the conjectured "author" of the earliest text in the Hebrew Bible lived around the tenth or ninth century BCE and that the last book of the New Testament was written somewhere in the early second century CE. If this is the case, then the earliest and latest contributors to the Bible stand as far apart from one another as we do from Charlemagne (who lived in the eighth century CE).

This would account, in part, for the jarring inconsistencies, puzzling contradictions, and thematic tensions found in the finished product. Here are a few for you to contemplate. On the matter of intermarriage, do the writers of the books of Ezra and Ruth seem like kindred spirits? Do those responsible for the erotically charged Song of Songs appear to be the type of folks that the prudish Paul would have gotten along fabulously with? Does the theology of the Gospel of John mesh seamlessly with that of the Gospel of Matthew?

Here are a few statistics to bear in mind. A standard Hebrew Bible (roughly approximating what Christians call the Old Testament) was originally a collection of some 24 scrolls that are now divided by Jews into 39 books. The New Testament adds another 27. That makes 66 books in all. (The Catholic Bible, with its inclusion of the deutero-canonical books, has a total of 73.) A Bible, then, is a massive, sprawling, multifaceted thing. It consists of over 30,000 verses and nearly 1,200 chapters.

Why is this relevant to politics? Because the peculiar way in which the Good Book was layered into existence across time and space has resulted in its having bequeathed to posterity multiple worldviews. Its complex, transhistorical process of composition has freighted it with a broad array of messages for its loyal readership. Think of it as a vast repository of potential positions, to be championed by generations of Christians and Jews.

The foregoing opinions, I will be the first to admit, will not strike all Americans as gospel truth. Few might disagree more passionately with my conclusions regarding the Bible's political impracticality (and compositional history) than fundamentalist and evangelical Christians. Prior to contrasting the differences for the reader, I must underscore that conservative Protestants are a large and varied group.[17] As will become apparent throughout this book, there are differences of opinion among them on questions of belief, practice, politics, and so on. These divergences become increasingly conspicuous among that large, vibrant, electoral prize know as the evangelical community.

But if there is one broad, doctrinal common denominator that binds all the parts together, it would be an extraordinarily high regard for the Bible.[18] A platform statement of the centrist National Association of Evangelicals articulates this point clearly: "As Christians committed to the full authority of Scripture our normative vision must flow from the Bible and from the moral order that God has embedded in his creation."[19] Evangelical scholar Bruce Waltke remarks, "The Bible in all its parts is the word of God, it is unified and consistent with itself. . . . Scripture is its own interpreter."[20]

For conservative Protestants, the entire text stems from a single divine Author. This Author worked through, or inspired, a small number of mortal writers (as opposed to the thousands of anonymous workers that I envision). A glance at fundamentalist and evangelical Web sites suggests that they have settled on the idea that "forty men" wrote the entire Bible.

Since God is infallible, the text He gave us must be in perfect harmony with itself; all 66 books and all 31,000 verses of the Bible are completely synchronized with one another. For most conservative Christians, then, there are no dissonances in Scripture. No contradictions. No unsolvable enigmas. The oft-heard refrain "Scripture interprets itself" speaks to the belief that all the seeming contradictions or ambiguities in the text can be reconciled *by consulting other parts of Scripture.* The implication of such a belief is startling, namely, that the well-known divergences of opinion regarding what the Bible says testify to the inadequacies of the interpreters, *not* those of the sacred document being interpreted.[21] A true Christian knows the Scriptures have one Author and one worldview.

Pertinence and Opposing Views

We now come to the key question of how *relevant* the Scriptures are to contemporary political problems. Nonbelievers, it goes without saying, will respond to this question in a flash: "Not in the least bit relevant!" But leaving them aside for the moment, it must be noted that there is considerable disagreement among Christians as to how to answer this question.

Unlike certain types of Catholics and mainline Protestants, most evangelicals and fundamentalists maintain that every word of Scripture speaks to our lives today. Some, such as activist David Barton, insist that *all* of our distinctly modern issues are addressed by the Good Book:

> There is no issue that the Bible doesn't address. . . . Did you know that the Bible takes a very clear position on capital gains tax? It takes a very clear position on income tax. The Bible takes a clear position on the estate tax, and takes a position on minimum wage. All these are economic issues that we should be able to shape citizens' thinking on because of what the Bible says.[22]

For other evangelicals, the Bible does not speak to contemporary policy disputes with this level of wonkish specificity. The National Association of Evangelicals, for example, acknowledges that the Scriptures may not *explicitly* engage all modern concerns. By no stretch of the imagination, however, does this obviate or diminish the Bible's usefulness in political deliberation. Instead, it compels evangelicals to seek out general principles, or what they have referred to as "the normative vision" of Scripture. The general principle could be something like the "God-given dignity of human beings."[23] Therefore, when confronted with an issue not explicitly addressed in the Good Book, they can turn to the general principle for guidance. The question of cloning, for instance, is not referenced in Scripture. But the overarching theme of the sanctity of life teaches that this must be wrong.

How different this approach to Scripture is from views generally held by mainline Protestants! For them the Bible must be read—this is the key phrase—*in context*.[24] The Good Book bears witness to the acts of God at a particular ancient time and ancient place. Accordingly, it cannot be expected to proffer comprehensive answers to complex modern political problems and issues. Further, mainliners do not usually ascribe infallibility to the Bible, as do evangelicals. The text, they happily concede, makes mistakes and may even say things that are factually inaccurate and morally inappropriate.

This is not God's fault, mind you. Rather, the blame lies with the human secretaries who transmitted his revelation—mere mortals with mortal flaws. The Bible in liberal Christian theology is often a problematic document. It is looked at with awe, but that awe is daubed in mistrust, apprehension, and even embarrassment.

In a very important article about the role of the Scriptures in American life, the Episcopalian L. William Countryman notes that his mainline denomination is "less inclined to treat the Bible as its sole authority."[25] Countryman is adamant that conservative Christians have stifled the Bible's "ability to surprise and transform" by reading it as a document that defends the conservative political status quo.[26] He goes on to note:

> The Bible does not, in fact, afford simple, clear blueprints for social order. Only by ignoring large portions of it can anyone claim that it does. The more carefully people read the Scriptures, the more evident this becomes. The Bible is an ongoing conversation in which one writer counters another. What is assumed as inevitable in one text is discounted in another.[27]

This approach is strikingly similar to that of J. Leslie Hoppe, a liberal Catholic commentator. In a piece entitled "Don't Bully People with the Bible," Hoppe explains, "Experience has taught us that the Bible is not always a satisfactory source for immediate principles of conduct. The moral compass that the Bible offers is found more in its more general values such as freedom, community, responsibility, forgiveness and love of God and neighbor."[28]

Liberal Protestants will freely acknowledge that their beloved Bible can sometimes be irrelevant, incomprehensible, or just plain wrong. When confronting political problems they will gladly supplement the text with other sources of wisdom. The recent remarks of Hillary Clinton capture this tendency to be awed by Scripture, all the while not getting too overwrought: "The whole Bible gives you a glimpse of God and God's desire for a personal relationship, but we can't possibly understand every way God is communicating with us. I've always felt that people who try to shoehorn in their cultural and social understandings of the time into the Bible might actually be missing the larger point."[29]

Such doubts and ambivalences do not afflict conservative Protestants. For them there is a "right" reading of Scripture—and lots of wrong ones too! What results is a psychological/exegetical orientation not often seen among mainline Protestants and Catholics (whose approach to Scripture and politics we will look at in chapter 3). Conservative Protestants go "in" to the Bible *and the Bible alone* fully assured that they will come "out" with a clear, internally consistent teaching on a given political dilemma. From there they endeavor to apply the scriptural injunction to the social body writ large. Evangelical activism is the attempt, through political and legislative initiatives, to impose these biblical teachings on society as a whole. Looked at in reverse, it is an effort to avoid subjection to the types of non–biblically based worldviews that emanate from secular America.

This willingness to use the government as a means of promulgating or imposing biblical truth is something of a novelty for conservative Protestants. It is interesting, and an affirmation of my argument above, that less than half a century ago, many evangelicals and fundamentalists *specifically renounced the political sphere.* And this was because the Bible told them so! Nearly all were beholden to a completely different conception of the types of political engagement that their sacred Scriptures demanded of them.

As John Green observes, for most of the twentieth century, evangelicals practiced "quiescent politics." He defines this as "a deliberate detachment from political institutions as a matter of principle."[30] Among fundamentalists an identical impulse could be seen. It is often forgotten that no less a public figure than the late Jerry Falwell advocated an apolitical ethos. In 1964, with the civil rights movement shaking America to its foundations, he famously intoned, "Preachers are not called to be politicians, but to be soul winners. . . . I feel that we need to get off the streets and back into the pulpits and into the prayer rooms."[31]

In those apolitical days, the politically passive Reverend Falwell could certainly have corroborated his quietist stance with passages from the Good Book.[32] Romans 13:1–4 furnishes us with one of the most profound meditations on the relation between Christians and their government:

> Let every soul be subject to the governing authorities. For there is no authority except from God, and the authorities that exist are appointed by God. Therefore whoever resists the authority resists the ordinance of God, and those who resist will bring judgment on themselves. For rulers are not a terror to good works, but to evil. Do you want to be unafraid of the authority? Do what is good, and you will have praise from the same. For he is God's minister to you for good. But if you do evil, be afraid; for he does not bear the sword in vain; for he is God's minister, an avenger to execute wrath on him who practices evil.

As is well known, later in his life Jerry Falwell had a change of heart. It should come as no surprise that he found biblical proof-texts to justify his shift away from quietism and into the whir of political combat. "We have tended to develop," he wrote in 1987, "the attitude that our only obligation is to preach the Gospel and prepare men for heaven. We have forgotten that we are still our brother's keeper and that the same spiritual truths that prepare us to live in eternity are also essential in preparing us to live on this earth."[33]

The Scriptures can furnish justification for *both* the quietist and the activist iterations of conservative Protestantism seen in the past century. We are now in a period where the activist reading has gained ascendancy. Many evangelicals, therefore, are not satisfied with the symbolic Scripture citation that prevails in the American theater of politics. They want the Good Book to function more profoundly in the nation's political life. In doing so, they forget that it rarely yields clear and unambiguous political counsel.

Conclusion: The Department of Scriptural Affairs

Why doesn't the United States government have a Department of Scriptural Affairs? It has a Department of Transportation. It has a Department of Education (or at least it did at the time of the printing of this book). It even has a Department of Housing and Urban Development, with its somewhat gruff-sounding acronym. But no Department of Scriptural Affairs. Why?

One surefire way of answering this question is to speculate as to what the mission statement for the DSA might look like. To my way of thinking its responsibilities would include (1) establishing a canonical (American) English language translation of the original Hebrew and Greek Scriptures to be called *The Official Bible of the United States of America*,[34] (2) distributing copies of the aforesaid Bible to all of the nation's citizens, (3) identifying correct interpretations of the OBUSA as befits the public good (and by extension adjudicating between competing readings of the divine writ), (4) performing routine "quality control" inspections to ensure that the Bible is being invoked, cited, and interpreted properly in houses of worship across America.

The DSA that I have conjured up might conceivably be the most disturbing Leviathan of government that an American could ever imagine. But as a tool for pondering the interplay between the Bible, politics, and a very diverse religious America, my hypothetical agency performs swimmingly. Functioning as a bureaucracy *cum* national church, the DSA would run roughshod over all of our cherished constitutional protections and civil liberties. Secularists would surely become unhinged at this inexcusable breach of separation.

Yet what the secularists sometimes fail to grasp is that they are not the only ones outraged by infringements on civil liberties. Their reactions would be muted when compared with the maelstrom that the

DSA would elicit among conservative Protestants. They would probably regard the agency as a malevolent, if not a quasi-satanic, administrative entity. Its very mention would dredge up traumatic historical memories of state persecution they experienced in the Old World and in the colonial period.[35] More importantly, the DSA would invariably, ineluctably, make decisions about "correct interpretations" that would infuriate large segments of evangelical and fundamentalist America. And this would come to pass even if the administration of the department was composed entirely of graduates of Jerry Falwell's Liberty University, Bob Jones University, and Pat Robertson's Regent University.

How can I make this claim with such certainty? The examples from American history cited above provide one line of evidence. In all due respect to Tom DeLay, the Scriptures are the incubator of *multiple*, often irreconcilable, worldviews. Consensus building is not the Bible's strong suit. But assume for a minute that the traditionalists are correct, that the Good Book does, in fact, contain one, unequivocally correct reading on homosexuality, abortion, and all other issues. Assume that one could discover this reading through diligence, faith, intelligence, and assistance from the Holy Spirit. Even if this were theologically true, *it would be politically irrelevant.*

This is because not only the American experience but two thousand years of biblical interpretation have demonstrated again and again (and often accompanied by the most disturbing possible physical evidence) that no empire, no society, and rarely even one denomination has ever been able to agree on what the Bible says. Put differently, even if there were one "right" reading of the Bible, we have yet to find a social body that has achieved agreement to what it might be.

Chapter 2

The Bible and the Environment

Evangelicals Discover Climate Change and Democrats Discover Evangelicals

Thus says the Lord:
"Heaven is My throne,
And earth is My footstool."
                    Isaiah 66:1

When a total stranger starts speaking to you on the streets of Manhattan, the rules of etiquette are clear. It is, of course, acceptable to respond to him or her politely. But if you desire to be dismissive, snide, or rude to this person then—and this is understood by every single resident of New York City—you are fully entitled to do so. I, for example, was often solicited by young pamphleteers who accosted me as follows: "Hi. My name is Howard. Would you like to help save the environment?" Cognizant of local customs, I would reply, hands quivering protectively in front of my face: *"The environment? Oh God, Howard. I hate, I mean, I just hate the environment! It's an awful thing!"*

This scene from my long career in absurdist street performance draws a revealing contrast with American political theater. No sane politician can publicly profess hatred for, or even indifference to, the environment. One can be antiabortion or anti–death penalty, but one can never, ever claim to be antienvironment. In their rhetoric all public servants must declare that they are enthusiastically *for* the environment. And they must do this no matter how many times they voted in favor of relocating PCBs to the local playground's sandbox.

The Bible too, in the estimation of many, is *for* the environment. This is a theme that a few evangelical groups have recently affirmed.

Some have even started interpreting the Good Book with a "tree hugging" sensibility. In so doing, they advocate stances on concerns such as global warming that have clear affinities with those of secular, liberal environmentalists. This has not escaped the attention of more right-leaning evangelicals. They worry that their coreligionists have tacked to the far left and gone off the deep end. Nor has this escaped the attention of Democratic strategists. Thanking their lucky stars for the vibrancy and heterogeneity of evangelical America they are—as we speak—positioning their nets to catch this electoral windfall.

Faster than you can say "wedge issue," the question of Scripture's view on the environment is emerging as important to the 2008 election. Naturally, I would like to raise the possibility that Scripture's *views* on the issue are a bit less clear and consistent than the participants involved in this debate are likely to realize.

Democrats and Evangelicals

Why would the sudden emergence of "green" evangelicals hold any interest whatsoever for the Democrats? After all, this is a party traditionally, though perhaps mistakenly, seen as a champion of secular constituencies (see chapter 6). In order to answer this query, a little historical background is required.

In the run-up to the 2004 presidential election, Democratic contenders were urged to both acquaint and ingratiate themselves with evangelical voters. Acquaintance was necessary because liberals clearly did not understand much about this constituency—a constituency that comprised one-quarter of the electorate. As far as most blue-staters were concerned, evangelicals were right-wing, religious fanatics, swaying in their garish megachurches to saccharine hymns intoned to a homophobic, gun-toting, sweet Jesus.[1]

Blue-staters correctly ascertained that the majority of today's evangelicals steadfastly voted Republican.[2] What they failed to recognize, however, was that the minority did not. And the minority was not inconsequential. In some estimates it comprised as many as ten million people. Commentators in 2004 made much of the electoral potential of these "swing" or "freestyle" evangelicals.[3]

This is where the part about ingratiating themselves to these voters came in. Given George W. Bush's impossibly narrow margin of victory in 2000, a few million votes (or 537 votes) were not to be taken for granted. Recent history, moreover, suggested that Democrats should reach out to evangelicals. In the last forty years only two non-Republicans have sat in the White House. One (Jimmy Carter) *was* an evangelical, and the other (Bill Clinton) was fluent in their spiritual-political dialect.[4] Some speculate that had Al Gore campaigned harder among freestyle evangelicals in a few states in 2000, he would have subsequently had far less free time to appear on *Saturday Night Live,* grow a beard, make movies, or engage in other sorts of inane runner-up activities. (Bob Dole, I feel compelled to mention, starred in Viagra ads during Clinton's second term.)[5]

As the 2004 election hit its stride and as pollsters came to comprehend the wonder-working power of the evangelical ballot, front-runners such as Howard Dean and John Kerry made increasingly conspicuous—and in some cases unsightly—efforts to establish their religious street credibility (see chapter 5). Nothing worked. A few months after the loss Jim Wallis, the official go-to guy for all media queries about progressive evangelicals, offered this rather unmerciful eulogy: "There are millions and millions of moderate evangelicals and moderate Catholics who are simply not in the pocket of the religious right. And yet Democrats haven't got a clue as to how to speak to them. They have no idea! And Kerry gave them nothing to vote for."[6]

Determined to give them something to vote for in 2008, the party is trying to reconnect with this constituency. When a few million votes are up for grabs, good politicians know how to let ideological bygones be bygones. Only this truism can explain why Howard Dean—once dubbed "one of the most secular candidates to run for president in modern history"—appeared on Pat Robertson's *700 Club* in May 2006.[7] There he affirmed that the Democrats "have an enormous amount in common with the Christian community, and particularly with the evangelical Christian community."[8] In June 2006, Barack Obama phrased it this way: "If we don't reach out to evangelical Christians and other religious Americans and tell them what we stand for, Jerry Falwells and Pat Robertsons will continue to hold sway."[9]

Dean's party is searching desperately for policy product lines to roll out for Christian conservatives. If only an issue could be found that lures the swing evangelicals back to the Democratic fold. (Prior to the seventies, evangelicals had been a reliable Democratic constituency.) If only an issue could be found that would loosen the Republicans' viselike grip on 25 percent of the nation's voters.

The Evangelical Mainstream and Climate Change

Enter, as if on cue, the Evangelical Climate Initiative. In February 2006 this group issued a declaration called "Climate Change: An Evangelical Call to Action."[10] Among its eighty-six signatories were college presidents, academics, and the occasional megachurch pastor.[11] "Christians must care," it states, "about climate change because we love God the Creator and Jesus our Lord, through whom and for whom the creation was made. This is God's world, and any damage that we do to God's world is an offense against God himself (Gen. 1; Ps. 24; Col. 1:16)." Not one of the three cited verses remotely implies that God takes offense at human destruction of his world. So when Scripture is cited in political debate, one ought to suppress any instinctual desire to shout "Amen!" until all references have been thoroughly checked.

The ECI's statement focuses on global warming, drawing an association between the latter and poverty. "Millions of people," it claims, "could die in this century because of climate change, most of them our poorest global neighbors." This declaration touched off something of a firestorm within the evangelical community. Yet this was not the first time that a green consciousness had surfaced among conservative Christians.[12]

One of the signers of the document was the Reverend Jim Ball, CEO of the Evangelical Environmental Network. The Web site of that group contains the following statement: "EEN is a unique evangelical ministry whose purpose is to 'declare the Lordship of Christ over all creation' (Col 1:15–20)."[13] EEN is best known for its glib 2002 campaign "What Would Jesus Drive?"[14] Prior to that it released a statement signed by roughly five hundred prominent evangelicals

entitled "On the Care of Creation." After a citation from Psalm 24:1—
"The Earth is the Lord's, and the fullness thereof"—the document
opens thusly: "As followers of Jesus Christ, committed to the full
authority of the Scriptures, and aware of the ways we have degraded
creation, we believe that biblical faith is essential to the solution of
our ecological problems."[15]

Those looking for sophisticated analysis of Scripture—or any
analysis of Scripture—will not find it here. "On the Care of Creation"
never stops to probe the linguistic or interpretive complexities of the
verses adduced. Biblical citations appear at the end of sentences, acting as a form of shorthand whose meaning seems to be, "*This proves
that the preceding statement is true*." Here is a representative sample
of the EEN's "exegesis": "The Creator's concern is for all creatures.
God declares all creation 'good' (Gen. 1:31); promises care in a
covenant with all creatures (Gen. 9:9–17); delights in creatures which
have no human apparent usefulness (Job 39–41); and wills, in Christ,
'to reconcile all things to himself' (Col. 1:20)."

This reading could just as soon have come from a middle school
student in one of the nation's less competitive districts. In fairness to
EEN, however, its analytical approach does not much differ from that
of even the headiest of political actors (see below).

Groups like the ECI and EEN are *not* on the leftist fringe of the
evangelical movement. Rather, they are decidedly centrist and mainstream. The same could be said sevenfold about an even larger and
more influential group with whom they overlap: the National Association of Evangelicals, which has 45,000 affiliated churches. In my
introduction I discussed the major policy statement that the NAE cir-
culated in 2004, "For the Health of the Nation: An Evangelical Call
to Civic Responsibility." The declaration's seventh and final "Principle of Christian Political Engagement" certainly turned some heads:

> We affirm that God-given dominion is a sacred responsibility to
> steward the earth and not a license to abuse the creation of which
> we are a part. . . . Our uses of the Earth must be designed to con-
> serve and renew the Earth rather than to deplete or destroy it. The
> Bible teaches us that God is not only redeeming his people, but is
> also restoring the whole creation (Rom. 8:18–23). Just as we show
> our love for the savior by reaching out to the lost, we believe that

we show our love for the Creator by caring for his creation. Because clean air, pure water, and adequate resources are crucial to public health and civic order, government has an obligation to protect its citizens from the effects of environmental degradation.[16]

All of these manifestos would seem to amount to good news for Democrats. As one journalist remarked, these initiatives create "an odd alliance between the goals of evangelical Christians, who are often conservative in their political views, and traditional environmentalists, who tend to bend toward the left."[17] The opinion was shared by certain liberal commentators, who gleefully concluded that the rise of green evangelicals seems to have exposed a "small crack in the conservative movement."[18] At the very least, it points to one of those coveted wedge issues that could drive some Christians to abandon the Grand Old Party in 2008.[19]

Is this the opportunity that so many Democratic strategists have wished for? There are clearly affinities between secular liberal views and those associated with the "creation care" model of conservative Christians. It seems to me, however, that the likelihood of centrist evangelicals joining hands with Democrats is still remote. Let us not forget that "creation care" is neither the only nor the most important concern of green evangelicals. Notice the priorities mentioned on the homepage of the Web site for the Evangelical Climate Initiative: "The same love for God and neighbor that compels us to . . . protect the unborn, preserve the family and the sanctity of marriage, and take the whole Gospel to a hurting world, also compels us to recognize that human-induced climate change is a serious Christian issue requiring action now."

The amount of bridging required to get the Democrats' secular base to find common ground with pro-life, anti-same-sex-union evangelicals is substantial.[20] Nor does it seem that evangelicals are much enamored of the secular Democratic base. Take the case of the Reverend Richard Cizik of the NAE. Cizik, a confirmed Reaganite and a pro-Bush conservative, shocked many in 2004 when he came out openly for the environment. "We are commissioned by God the Almighty," he opined in an interview, "to be stewards of the earth." Elaborating upon some of the criticisms he received from his brethren, Cizik explained, "There are still plenty who wonder, does advocating this agenda mean we have to become liberal weirdos? And I say to them, certainly not. It's in the Scripture. Read the Bible."[21]

The Evangelical Right Unleashes a Counter–Wedge Issue

I will leave it to Democratic higher-ups to figure out how they will convince evangelicals to make common cause with liberal weirdos. For now I wish to point to the real divisions that are waiting to be exploited by strategists working on behalf of the party of the latter.

Shortly after the ECI released "Climate Change" in February 2006, an internal evangelical scrum broke out. The National Association of Evangelicals voted to take no official position on the question of global warming.[22] According to published accounts, the group had been pressured by prominent conservative religious figures such as James Dobson of Focus on the Family and Richard Land of the Southern Baptist Convention. They reasoned that since "Global Warming is not a consensus issue" within the community, it should not carry the imprimatur of the NAE.[23] Even the affable Richard Cizik did not lend his signature to the document, in order to display "an accommodating spirit" to coreligionists who did not agree with him.[24]

A much more pointed attack on "Climate Change" has come from an ecumenical group with a large number of conservative evangelicals. The Interfaith Stewardship Alliance has challenged environmentalists, be they religious or secular, for years.[25] In their most recent activism, they have deployed that most devastating of political weapons: the counter–wedge issue. If environmentalists insist that God loves the environment and the poor, then the ISA responds that the types of solutions to global warming they offer up will impact disastrously upon the underprivileged.

As a challenge to the ECI, the ISA released in July 2006, yes, a declaration. (As the reader may have figured out by now, declarations and statements seem to be the garrulous evangelicals' preferred mode of political expression.)[26] *A Call to Truth, Prudence, and Protection of the Poor: An Evangelical Response to Global Warning* is twenty-five pages long, coherently argued, professionally written, and save for one oversight (about which more anon), quite media savvy. It is almost completely bereft of any biblical citation, save the cryptic

Matthew 24:25. This is unusual, since evangelicals virtually exhale scriptural passages. Lacking any reference to sacred writ and lacking any pronounced theological framework, the text reads like a position paper from a secular, pro-big-business think tank.

A Call to Truth does not contest the reality of global warming per se. Instead, it calls into question the charges that humans are responsible for it and its results will be catastrophic. Further, it challenges the specific remedies proposed by the Evangelical Climate Initiative and others. Such proposals, according to the ISA, "would be both economically devastating to the world's poor and ineffective at reducing global warming."[27] By supporting a raise in energy prices the ECI will be "condemning the world's poor to slower economic development."[28] The indigent, they write, "are much better served by enhancing their wealth through economic development than by whatever minute reductions might be achieved in future global warming by reducing CO2 emissions."[29] The cure prescribed by the ECI, the document continues, "will rob the poor of the very thing they most need if they are to be able to adapt not just to catastrophic global warming, but to *any* future catastrophe: wealth."[30]

It is very hard to tell what specific *theological* concerns might have prompted evangelicals in the ISA to compose this declaration, but here are some possibilities. Evangelicals are known to dislike the types of broad, heavy-handed governmental solutions that environmental policies usually require. Salvation for them occurs when an individual comes to Christ, not when massive socio-structural changes are enacted. Further, global problems require transnational cooperation, and perhaps some are weary of cooperating with non-Christian polities. A classical monotheistic aversion to excessive esteem for nature can also be detected. Reading through evangelical literature, one often gets the sense that they equate environmentalists with witches and wizards frolicking naked around phallic maypoles.

While the theological reasons motivating this disdain of global warming are obscure, the political concerns are clear. The ISA is adamantly pro-capitalism, pro–big science, and pro–big business.[31] And here is where *A Call* makes an uncharacteristic rhetorical misstep. Its authors do not convincingly address their own reasons for involvement in this project. It is, quite honestly, difficult to fathom why a group of religious intellectuals would get *so* worked up over the Kyoto

Protocols. For a media-savvy operation, the ISA seems not to have anticipated the most obvious objection to their enterprise. Is there any Washington stereotype more well-known (and reviled) than that of the well-credentialed lobbyist hired out by energy corporations to neutralize environmentalist concerns?

I do not have any fresh evidence indicating that this is the case with the ISA.[32] But in the absence of full disclosure and in the absence of *any* compelling theological argumentation, one must read the ISA's otherwise slick manifesto with a good deal of skepticism.

The Bible's Dark Side

An instructive (and entertaining) sidebar to the spate of declarations, statements, and internal debates chronicled above might be called the "Watt/Moyers affair." It is an obscure incident to be sure. Yet it calls attention to a biblical conception of nature that none of the evangelical Christians we have encountered so far, be they progressive or conservative, seem to have considered. It also underscores a point I made in chapter 1 about the Bible's lack of dependability in political debate.

In December 2004 the liberal journalist Bill Moyers accepted the "Global Environmental Citizen Award" from Harvard University's Center for Health and the Global Environment. Meryl Streep was on hand in New York City to present him with the honor, and Moyers proceeded to deliver an address that contained the following remark:

> Remember James Watt, President Reagan's first Secretary of the Interior? My favorite online environmental journal, the ever engaging *Grist*, reminded us recently of how James Watt told the U.S. Congress that protecting natural resources was unimportant in light of the imminent return of Jesus Christ. In public testimony he said, "After the last tree is felled, Christ will come back."[33]

Moyers might consider canceling his e-subscription to the ever engaging *Grist*, for the citation he based his argument on was erroneous. After learning of the speech, Watt protested: "I never said it. Never believed it. Never even thought it. I know no Christian who believes or preaches such error. The Bible commands conservation—that we as Christians be careful stewards of the land and resources entrusted to us by the Creator."[34] I believe that James Watt never said this. So does Moyers, who later apologized for the error.[35] So does *Grist* magazine, whose editors printed a retraction. Yet with all due respect to the former secretary, there certainly are Christians who believe "such error."[36]

Here is one who comes very close. Paul Chesser writing in the *American Spectator Online* accuses signers of the Evangelical Climate Initiative of having "been duped by environmentalist liberals." He continues:

> I hope the ECI endorsers didn't overstrain their eyes searching those Scripture references for evidence of God's anger at human abuse of earth. Instead, they would do well to recall some other biblical citations that emphasize what the real goals of Christian ministry should be in relation to the planet. They should remember that the apostle Paul disdained those "who set their mind on earthly things. For our citizenship is in heaven, from which we also eagerly wait for the Savior, the Lord Jesus Christ" (Philippians 3:19–20).[37]

Chesser closes his essay with what sounds like a threat: "God has some serious global warming of his own planned (2 Peter 3:10). Christian leaders ought to be warning people about that rather than looking for ways to mitigate the questionable effects of the current heat wave." The verse cited reads, "But the day of the Lord will come as a thief in the night, in which the heavens will pass away with a great noise, and the elements will melt with fervent heat; both the earth and the works that are in it will be burned up."

The implications of Chesser's reading of his proof-text are startling. They suggest that human destruction of the environment is but a secondary concern in light of the (eagerly anticipated) apocalypse. At best, a legislator who shares such opinions will be apathetic to the plight of the ecosystem. At worst, she will use her political clout to expedite its collapse. Bloggers and pundits on the left are convinced that such views are normative among conservative Christians. As they see it, the latter are heartened by the site of slushy polar ice caps and perplexed polar bears. Moyers himself spoke of "millions of Christian fundamentalists" who believe that "environmental destruction is not only to be disregarded but actually welcomed—even hastened—as a sign of the coming apocalypse."[38] It strikes me, however, that while the apocalyptic mentality is real, it is presently a marginal phenomenon in contemporary Christianity.[39]

But even though it is still a minority opinion, it does not lack for scriptural warrant. Chesser's interpretation taps into a persistent scriptural theme, one that readers often overlook. In some sections of the Bible it is exceedingly clear that *God does not much fancy the earth*. He does not have too sanguine a view of its future either, if only because He intends on obliterating it at some later point in time. While the New Testament reminds us that neither we (nor the earth) have long to go, Yahweh of the Old Testament/Hebrew Bible symbolically or literally brutalizes the natural world.

He does this, often enough, to teach a painful lesson to His chosen people, or to their enemies, or to His own mythological adversaries. He has every right to engage in such activities because, as one theologian aptly put it, "the earth is his property."[40] Throughout the Bible the deity treats the earth like an object—a means to a really spectacular end. In the process, He displays an obsessive desire to trumpet his superiority to the very world he brought into being.

God, the writers of the Bible want us to know, is terribly strong. How terribly strong? So strong that he repeatedly shows nature the back of his immense and powerful hand. In the Old Testament much is made of Yawheh's ability to degrade and humiliate the earth, the seas, the heavens, the stars, the sun, the moon, and so on. At points the prophets boast that Yahweh frightens the earth and heaven, or physically shakes them.[41] He overturns mountains, roughs up valleys, dries up rivers.[42] Darkness and destruction are repeatedly inflicted upon the planet. Isaiah reports that the deity promises to "make the earth a desolation," to dim the sun, stars, and moon.[43] In fits of rage God lays the planet bare and pulverizes the land of various offending nations.[44]

There are passages that show the earth to be a *temporary* domicile, a planet that will one day "wear out like a garment."[45] Psalm 29 is a veritable eco-nightmare. It is replete with scenes of God splitting cedar trees, macerating Lebanon, "convulsing the wilderness," and obliterating forests. By the final verse one can almost hear the deity cracking his knuckles with satisfaction. As one commentator put it, this "tauntlike psalm" is intended to demonstrate "God's sovereignty in nature."[46] If there are Christians out there who are not *for* but *against* the environment, let it not be said that they completely mis-read their own Scriptures.

Conclusion: Cite and Run

In his bestselling 1992 book *Earth in the Balance*, Al Gore set out to investigate "the very nature of our civilization and its relationship to the global environment."[47] Gore, a committed Christian though not an evangelical, occasionally cites Scripture when trying to demonstrate that responsible stewardship is a religious obligation.

The former vice president spent some time in his youth studying at Vanderbilt's Divinity School, and that training has clearly left its mark. His prose is clear and compelling. His ability to integrate popular science with theological and philosophical concepts is impressive. The sweep and breadth of his knowledge belie his image as a robotic policy wonk. Yet for all of his erudition Gore's use of Scripture and his rather narcissistic conception of its message do not differ much from any of the figures encountered above.

In terms of using the Bible to prove a point, Gore employs what I call "the cite-and-run method." This is more complex than another popular technique which I refer to as "the Generic." The latter involves a politician who simply mentions "the Bible" in the same breath as his or her preferred policy position. Tom DeLay's reference to "biblical worldview," or Richard Cizik's exclamation, "It's in the Scripture. Read the Bible," are typical examples of generic citation.

Cite-and-run operations, by contrast, require more finesse. Here one must demonstrate that one's particular policy position neatly corresponds with this or that biblical citation. Political actors who deploy this technique (as well as the Generic) share a self-important assumption that seems to be, *"The Bible agrees with me."* Never in history has a text so readily conformed to its admirers' political opinions.

Brevity is the essence of the cite-and-run method. Under no circumstances is the politician in question to engage in any sort of analysis of those biblical texts that allegedly validate his or her position. *Make the damn reference and get on with it!*—that's the rule of thumb. By devoting as little time as possible to a discussion of the allegedly corroborating verse, the speaker achieves two strategic goals. First, he or she gives the impression that the point just made and seemingly echoed in Scripture is so obvious that it scarcely requires explanation. Somehow, political actors who cite the Bible have come to the conclusion that it's a singularly transparent document. Gore, for instance, states that the Bible's message on the environment is "clear" and consistent with his own.[48]

Second, by avoiding any discussion of the texts, the speaker avoids getting bogged down in the word-and-thought-defying complexity of the Old and New Testaments. Gore interprets Joseph's warning to Pharaoh of "seven lean years" as evidence that an ecological consciousness existed in biblical times.[49] He reads Hosea's "They have sown the wind, and they shall reap the whirlwind" (Hos. 8:7) as a prophecy about the greenhouse effect.[50] Is he correct? Did an eighth-century seer really have uncanny premonitions about global warming? Did Hosea know carbon dioxide emissions from hellfire? Of course not. But it is, admittedly, a cute reading.

Gore, prudently, does not follow up his citation of Hosea with a discussion of the meaning of the verse in its original Hebrew. He does not comment on how the passage has been interpreted across two millennia. He does not provide the context that may help us ascertain what the prophecy might have meant to early Jewish and Christian communities. Nor does he call attention to contradictory lines from Scripture.

In truth, not one of the commentators mentioned in this chapter was able to acknowledge that the Bible's stance on the environment is equivocal, elliptical, complex. In the case of the evangelicals, at least, one wonders how a group as biblically literate as they are could possibly *not* know about those Scriptures that contradict their cherished worldviews. As we shall now see, this is not the only example of them making poor and tendentious readings.

Chapter 3

The Blastocyst and the Bible

Stem Cell Research, Abortion, and the Silence of Scripture

> *For not only did God take human form, he did so in the form of a blastocyst, as an early embryo.*
>
> Nigel M. de S. Cameron, "The Sanctity of Life
> in the Twenty-First Century: An Agenda
> for *Homo Sapiens* in the Image of God"

*I*t is July 26, 2006, and Senator Edward Kennedy is letting the president have it, and have it good. One week earlier George W. Bush, for the first time in nearly six years of holding office, vetoed a bill. Kennedy dutifully reminds his listeners that the president refrained from vetoing tax breaks for the wealthy.[1] He refrained from vetoing cutbacks to Medicaid. He refrained from vetoing massive reductions for student loans. But on July 19 he did not refrain from nixing H.R. 810, the Stem Cell Research Enhancement Act (Castle-DeGette Bill) which would have lifted Bush's 2001 ban of federal funding for the study of human embryonic stem cells.[2]

Kennedy wraps things up with an unexpected rhetorical flourish: "Last week, Congress made the right choice on stem-cell research, and I am deeply saddened that the president made the wrong one. Hope cannot be extinguished or destroyed—but it can be delayed. In the Bible, the Book of Proverbs tells us, 'Hope deferred makes the heart sick.'"[3]

Did the liberal senator from Massachusetts just do a cite-and-run on Proverbs 13:12? Yes, yes he did! And he did so with sass.[4] In fact, Kennedy added a twist by employing a move—a classic, really—that I like to call "biblical transvaluation."

More on that later, but for now let us look at how Orrin Hatch addressed the same piece of legislation. Hatch, a Mormon bishop, once introduced a constitutional amendment banning abortion. One might, therefore, expect that the positions of the pro-life senator from Utah would differ dramatically from the ardently pro-choice, score-a-NARAL-rating-of-100, Kennedy. Yet after mentioning that he had consulted the Bible (i.e., the generic citation) as well as other unspecified texts, Hatch averred: "I do believe, very strongly, that it is possible to be both anti-abortion and pro–embryonic stem cell research."[5]

Jerry Falwell, for his part, was apt to demur. Starting from the premise that medical research must be "biblically correct," Falwell exclaimed, "I believe life begins at conception. Therefore, for the same reason I oppose abortion, I oppose stem cell research."[6] Falwell is anti-choice and anti–stem cell research. Kennedy is pro-choice and pro–stem cell research. Hatch is antichoice and pro–stem cell research. Surely Democratic strategists somewhere are pondering the deeper (electoral) relevance of Hatch's position.[7] True, Utah's senior senator, who has recorded numerous albums, has always had a quirky streak (might I recommend his 1997 album *Jesus' Love Is Like a River*).[8] Yet his political instincts are spot-on: his position harmonizes with polls that show roughly 60 percent of Americans favor federally funded study of embryonic stem cells.[9]

Aside from calling attention to another prime Democratic wedge issue in 2008 (albeit one the Democrats tried, and failed, to exploit in 2004), this chapter will point to a peculiarity and vulnerability of the type of conservative Protestantism that informs the thought of Falwell and others.[10] When these Christians launch themselves into political battle they brandish just one theological weapon. But packing the Bible, *and the Bible alone*, as we are about to see, does not make for convincing, let alone flexible, public policy initiatives.

The Blastocyst

Our goal here is to understand how interpretations of the Bible surface in public policy discussions regarding stem cell research. In order to do so, we need to familiarize ourselves with a few biological basics. Insofar as the writer of this book—whose brain tissue, if cross-sectioned and analyzed upon his death, would surely unlock the mysteries of scientific imbecility—is no embryologist, the following exposition will be brief.

Upon the union of sperm and ovum, after the moment of fertilization, a single cell known as a zygote forms. After one day the zygote becomes a two-cell embryo. After two days it becomes a four-cell embryo. On the fourth day of cleavage a *morula*, or little mulberry-like ball (Lat., *morus*), develops that consists of a few dozen cells. Between the fifth through seventh days, a hollow cell known as a blastocyst emerges. Situated in the fallopian tube and smaller than a grain of sand, this cell is prepared to embark on its fateful sojourn to the uterus. Of course, if this blastocyst was cultivated through the process of in-vitro fertilization it won't be embarking on any fateful sojourns. Not unless, that is, a physician removes it from its petri dish and implants it via catheter in the uterus.

Aside from having one of the most percussive names in all of biology, the blastocyst is an astonishing piece of work. It contains what is known as the inner-cell mass (ICM), described as "perhaps the most extraordinary cells ever discovered."[11] Scientists refer to these cells as "pluripotent," meaning that they can "give rise to virtually all of the tissues of the human body."[12] In 1998, James Thomson and his team at the University of Wisconsin–Madison announced in the magazine *Science* that they had managed to isolate the ICM of a cultured blastocyst.[13] This was a development that raised intriguing and, for some, deeply disturbing new possibilities.

Within the uterine environment the ICM has a specific role to play. Once it performs that function it quickly differentiates "to other cell types with a more restricted developmental potential." But when these cells are extracted and placed in a culture dish they are no longer able to perform their natural role. Freed from traditional responsibilities and encouraged by scientists to cut loose in the laboratory, they can now "proliferate and replace themselves indefinitely."[14] Thomson marvels at the "remarkable developmental plasticity" of the ICM. In theory, they "maintain the developmental potential to form any cell type."[15]

It is conceivable now that a revolutionary chapter in the history of regenerative medicine can be written. As one biomedical entrepreneur puts it, the significance of human embryonic stem cell research "would be to broaden the definition of medical therapy from simply halting the progression of acute or chronic disease to include restoration of lost organ function."[16] The new technology could one day address ailments such as Alzheimer's disease, Parkinson's disease, coronary heart failure, cancer, type 1 diabetes, and spinal injuries.[17] Maybe it could even tamp down the national debt and put an end to rampant grade inflation. By some estimates, upwards of over 100 million Americans are affected by conditions that might be alleviated if human embryonic stem cell research achieves its considerable promise.[18]

Others, however, are somewhat less sanguine about the possibilities. Four general types of criticisms are heard. The first is that the newfangled technology is in its inchoate stages and thus unproven and potentially dangerous.[19] Next, some insist that there are better options to be explored, such as adult stem cells and umbilical cord blood.[20] Third, it is argued that to devote so many resources to an experimental technology that would most likely benefit the wealthy while so many Americans lack basic health care is ludicrous.[21] Last, there is a vexing moral conundrum. In order to grow stem cell lines, the blastocyst must be broken open and the ICM removed. For the research possibilities to come to life, the spare laboratory embryo must die.

Enter Christian conservatives, the most vociferous opponents of human embryonic stem cell research in the United States. Their objections have been couched, almost without exception, in the language of pro-life politics.[22] As theologian Karen Lebacqz puts it, "The stem cell debate has become rather hopelessly entangled with the abortion debate."[23] Notice, for example, the use of pro-life buzzwords (in italics) in President Bush's rationale for vetoing the Stem Cell Research Enhancement Act:

> This bill would support the taking of *innocent human life* in the hope of finding medical benefits for others. It crosses a moral boundary that our decent society needs to respect, so I vetoed it. . . . We must also remember that embryonic stem cells come from human embryos that are destroyed for their cells. Each of these human embryos is a *unique human life* with *inherent dignity* and *matchless value*. . . . America was founded on the principle that we are all created equal, and *endowed by our Creator with the right to life*.[24]

What must be stressed is the following: for conservative Christians and others, *the zygote is a human being.*[25] Reckoned as part of the living community, it is endowed with all of the dignity and moral status conferred upon the living.[26] The derivation of ICM from a blastocyst, then, is construed as an act of murder. No matter how noble the motivations of scientists might be, the procedure violates the sanctity of life. This view impacts upon how conservative Christians think about so-called spare embryos. During the in-vitro process many eggs are collected and fertilized, but only a few are actually implanted. This has resulted in an immense surplus. Sitting peacefully in the freezers of fertility clinics across America are perhaps hundreds of thousands of extra embryos suspended at, or around, the blastocyst stage.[27] As one scholar helpfully points out, these embryos "don't seem to go bad or get freezer burn like a steak."[28] They can be adopted by new parents who would bring a so-called snowflake baby into the world (this is the possibility favored by Christian conservatives). Conversely, the refrigerated blastocysts can be thawed out and destroyed. There is another possibility: with the consent of the donors, the extra blastocysts can be handed over to scientists who will extract the ICM and get to work on studying its therapeutic powers.

In fact, any researcher with enough financial backing and the donor's consent is free to do precisely this. Human embryonic stem cell research is *legal* in the United States.[29] The present national debate concerns whether federal funds can be used for the investigation of this problem. On August 9, 2001, President Bush called for a freeze, as it were, on government funding for any newly developed stem cell lines. The president did, however, permit federally funded research to continue on roughly sixty existing stem cell lines harvested prior to this date. This decision has always puzzled one of the most ardent supporters of stem cell research. As Senator Tom Harkin put it, "I've often wondered aloud . . . why is it that embryonic stem cells derived prior to 9:00 p.m. August the 9th, 2001, are moral?"[30]

Evangelicals and the Bible Alone

Some might be wondering about how a one-cell zygote can be endowed with the same rights and moral standing as, let's say, a three-

year-old child munching on cheddar bunnies. How do pro-lifers justify such a view? Opponents of stem cell research who speak as Christians, be they Catholic, Protestant, or Greek Orthodox, almost always
invoke the Bible when making their case. They often cite the same
small set of verses and make the same confident assertions about what
those verses mandate for national bioethical policy.

Yet not all Christians place the same emphasis on scriptural
writ. Evangelicals and fundamentalists typically let the Bible (and
by this I mean, of course, their readings of the Bible) override all
other available sources of information when thinking about this
issue.[31] This is because they have an almost unparalleled faith in
Scripture's ability to definitively explicate ethical dilemmas, political controversies—in fact, anything at all. For them, the document
is held to be authoritative, inspired, inerrant, and infallible. It towers
above all other texts as a resource for policy decisions. Roger Olson,
author of the excellent *Westminster Handbook to Evangelical Theology*, phrases it as follows: "Evangelical theologians agree that
inspired Scripture is uniquely authoritative for religious belief and
practice, because it is in a sense unparalleled by any other book—
God's word in written form. This high regard for the Bible is a hall-
mark of Evangelicalism, and no evangelical theologian has dared
call it into question."[32]

In this sense evangelicals and fundamentalists are somewhat
unique. So much so that from the perspective of other religious
groups, their adoration of Scripture looks something like bibliolatry.
Mainline Protestants, as we saw earlier, do not cling so tenaciously
to the idea of the Bible's centrality, authority, and infallibility. Nor do
Catholics or Jews. None of the aforementioned imagine themselves
to be relying on "just the Bible" when translating their religious convictions into social action.[33]

I would like to suggest that this elevation of Scripture to the status
of "master proof-text" among evangelicals and fundamentalists is
something of a political liability. First and foremost, the Good Book
often fails to address in any direct, explicit, coherent, and consistent
manner many of the public policy concerns that are so dear to them.
Take, for example, the issues discussed in this chapter. Abortion is
never mentioned in the Old Testament. It is never mentioned in the New
Testament.[34] To this let me add—does it even need to be said?—that

the entire Christian Bible from Genesis to Revelation is silent on the question of ICM and blastocysts.[35]

As a result, conservative Christians cannot point to any unambiguous, unequivocal, clinching proof-texts. Instead, they scour the Scriptures for passages that speak about the womb and then read them with as much of a pro-life spin as possible. Since no Scriptures speak of embryos, they must look for verses that point to broader values— values they believe subsume within themselves a divine repugnance for any sort of medical intervention that harms the unborn. Typically, they try to show that all prenatal life has a God-ordained dignity. Going even further, they argue that the Creator recognizes, knows, and even "bonds" with the individual embryo and/or fetus.

These are somewhat roundabout ways of proving that the dignity accorded to a full-fledged human being should be granted to a one-week-old embryo. What results are somewhat strained interpretations of biblical passages—passages that appear to have no direct relevance to the issues at hand. The silence and ambiguity of Scripture on this issue also render conservative Protestants vulnerable to the most damning of accusations—namely, that their politics do not spring from their readings of the Bible but that their readings of the Bible spring from their politics. In order to explore this point, let us first turn to the Scriptures they invoke in debates about stem cell research.

The Embryonic Verses

Biblically based pro-life rhetoric just wouldn't be the same without Genesis 1:27. The famed *imago Dei* passage is something of an obligatory starting point for all Christian contestations of abortion and human embryonic stem cell research. Evangelical bioethics provides no exception to the rule.[36] In their official statement on the issue, the Southern Baptist Convention declares:

> The Bible teaches us that human beings are made in the image and likeness of God (Gen. 1:27; 9:6) and protectable human life begins at fertilization. . . . We call upon the United States Congress to maintain the existing ban on the use of tax dollars to support research which requires the destruction of the human embryos; and

Be it further resolved, that we call upon those private research centers which perform such experiments to cease and desist from research which destroys human embryos, the most vulnerable members of the human community.[37]

The verses cited here do indeed say that we are created in the image of God.[38] But the arguments about "protectable human life" beginning at "fertilization" are nowhere to be found. In Genesis 1:27 we read that God created humankind (Heb. '*adam*) in his image. I have come to understand that conservative Christians hear this verse as follows: "God created *individual human beings* in his image *from the moment of conception.*" The italicized words represent sentiments that are not in the original Hebrew, though they seem implicit in evangelical and fundamentalist interpretations of this verse. The possibility that God formed the *species* in his image, as opposed to each individual member of the species, is never explored. This would change the tone of the passage considerably.[39]

Another commonly cited text is a short, difficult section from Psalm 139:13–16. My translation reads as follows:

> Indeed, it was You who created my kidneys[40]
> You sheltered me in my mother's womb.[41]
> I praise You
> for I am awesomely, wondrously made;
> Your work is wonderful;
> I know it very well.
> My bones were not concealed from you[42]
> when I was being made in a hidden place
> knitted together in the depths of the earth.[43]
> Your eyes saw my *golem*;[44]
> they were all inscribed in your book;
> in due time they were formed.
> (translation mine)

Evangelicals believe that this text, allegedly composed by King David, clearly repudiates any sort of prenatal tampering. Of this passage, J. Kerby Anderson writes, "The Bible does not speak of fetal life as mere biochemistry. The fetus in his mother's womb was not a piece of protoplasm that became David. This was David already being cared for by God while in the womb."[45] "It is abundantly clear," remarks John Jefferson Davis, "that God, the divine 'parent,' has already 'bonded' with the child that he is making."[46] In line with standard evangelical readings, these interpreters take the passage to say that God knows us in the womb. If this is so, then fetal life must be sacred to Him.

In order to clinch this interpretation, they often read the Hebrew word *golem* as "embryo." Hence they translate: "Your eyes saw my embryo." The curious term *golem* appears only once in the entire Old Testament and the translation "embryo" is not widely accepted by most scholars.[47] Moreover, those who oppose embryonic stem cell research tend to overlook a signal curiosity of this passage. Verse 15 rather clearly suggests that the deity fashioned David "in the depths of the earth." Perhaps this is figurative usage, but the Hebrew implies, however inconclusively, that human formation occurs in a nonuterine region. This would mean that God crafts mortals *outside* of the womb. His workshop is in-vitro, so to speak, and for these reasons this passage would not seem germane to any of the concerns mentioned above.[48]

A few other texts are typically adduced as evidence that embryos and fetuses are fully fledged persons. Jeremiah 1:5 reads:

> Before I formed you in the belly, I knew you[49]
> and before you departed the womb I consecrated you.
> (translation mine)

Similarly Isaiah 49:1 reports:

> Yahweh from the womb called me;
> from the innards of my mother he pronounced my name.
> (translation mine)[50]

The last of these womb passages occurs in the New Testament, in Luke 1:41. Mary, mother of Jesus, happens upon Elizabeth, mother of John the Baptist, and the following ensues: "And it happened, when Elizabeth heard the greeting of Mary, that the babe leaped in her womb; and Elizabeth was filled with the Holy Spirit" (NKJV).

The claim that the unborn John "pays homage to his unborn Lord" is hard to verify.[51] None of these womb passages seem to conclusively rule out scientific exploration of the blastocyst. That God knew famous prophets in the womb does not seem tantamount to saying that all embryos must live. As D. Gareth Jones comments, "The personal history of God's servants is, principally, the personal history of God's servants. To make this into a general principle relating to the status of all embryos regardless of their relationship to a community of faith requires reference to extra-biblical concepts."[52]

Evangelicals in the United States have shown themselves to be creative and talented builders of initiatives, consensus, and communities. Organizationally speaking, they are the essence of dynamism. Yet their interpretations of the Good Book are often static, forced, unoriginal, and simplistic. By way of digression, scholar Mark Noll devoted an entire book to the subject of anti-intellectualism among conservative Protestants, entitled *The Scandal of the Evangelical Mind*. A reader of that book gets the impression that the "'Bible-only' mentality" that Noll describes has contributed largely to the anti-intellectualism that he has identified.[53] This same mentality, I wish to stress, renders them vulnerable to counterattack on strictly theological grounds.

To their credit, some within the movement are willing to acknowledge the shortcomings. I consider the following remark of two evangelical thinkers to be indicative of a growing willingness to be self-critical: "Evangelicals do not have the kind of sustained, theologically grounded reflection on social and political issues that shapes some other Christian traditions."[54] Aside from indicating that evangelicals are far less blinkered than their critics imagine, this remark, as we shall now see, happens to be true.

Catholics and Interpretive Space

It emerges from this that the Bible presents no clear teaching regarding abortion and stem cell research. Most conservative Protestants have nevertheless adopted the position that both are expressly forbidden. Of course, conservative Protestants are no less endowed with a capacity for dissent than any other American religious group, and it seems perfectly reasonable to expect that some will reject the party line. Momentarily, I will point to a fairly obvious way that a Bible-toting evangelical with a contrarian streak could challenge prevailing interpretations.

Among Catholics, by comparison, there is already an affluence of lively disagreement on the question of human embryonic stem cell research. Catholic bioethicists, whose numbers are apparently legion, have staked out every imaginable position on the issue. As Scott McConnaha observes, "Not all Catholic moral theologians agree . . . on the moral status of the embryo. Some are hesitant about affording it all the rights that come with full personhood and are thus wary of placing an absolute ban on the use of ESCs [embryonic stem cells]."[55] McConnaha proceeds to make an exceptionally important observation: "It is irrational to think that our Christian scriptures, the most recent parts of which were written some two thousand years ago, can speak directly about contemporary ethical issues."[56]

It certainly is irrational to make such an assumption, and contemporary Catholics, in large part, steer clear of this pitfall. I attribute this not to any innate Catholic intellectual superiority but to a difference in the size of their interpretive canon and their thick, age-old traditions of hermeneutical inquiry. Not doctrinally incarcerated within the funhouse/madhouse of ancient Scripture, Catholics simply have more resources at their disposal, more biblical interpretations to examine, and more authoritative opinions *not* predicated on the Bible to take into consideration.[57]

A Catholic trying to make sense of a complex modern issue need not restrict herself to the seventy-three-book canon of Scripture approved by the Synod of Laodicea in the fourth century. She could consult Augustine, Basil, and Tertullian. She could ponder sundry medieval philosophers—not least of whom would be Thomas Aquinas (whose belief that ensoulment sets in after forty days for boys and even later for girls would seem to undermine claims about the blastocyst's human status).[58] She could scrutinize a running record of papal encyclicals. And let us not forget the possibility of personal consultations with her parish priest, the kindly Jesuit down at the seminary, and Sister Rosemarie (who prior to joining the order did graduate course work at a Catholic-affiliated medical school).

Catholics do not—cannot—live by the Bible alone. Recent church documents have even repudiated an "excessively literalistic approach to the Bible."[59] Let me put it more starkly: Catholics cannot delude themselves into thinking that they live by the Bible alone. With so much more interpretive space at their disposal, their readings are far more diverse and nuanced than those of fundamentalists and evangelicals. Indeed, what often emerges in Catholic bioethical thought is a range of opinion as varied and complex as the sources regarded as authoritative for Catholics. Perhaps this is why Catholic elected officials advance opinions on this issue as distinct of those of Rick Santorum and Sam Brownback on one side, and John Kerry and Edward Kennedy on the other. Reviewing contemporary Catholic positions on stem cell research and abortion would necessitate its own seventy-three-volume set and will not be tried here. What must be noted is the fairly free and tolerant interplay between popes who unambiguously oppose stem cell research and many Catholic thinkers who don't. John Paul II, addressing George W. Bush on July 23, 2001, spoke of the evil of "proposals for the creation for research purposes of human embryos, destined to destruction in the process. A free and virtuous society, which America aspires to be, must reject practices that devalue and violate human life at any stage from conception until natural death."[60]

Yet many Catholics seem willing and able to challenge the pontiff's view. Margaret Farley, reiterating a sentiment mentioned above, states that "growing numbers of Catholic moral theologians . . . do not consider the human embryo in its earliest stages (before development of the primitive streak or implantation) to constitute an individualized human entity with the settled inherent potential to become a human being." "I myself," she continues, "stand with the case for embryonic stem cell research, and I believe this case can be made persuasively within the Catholic tradition."[61]

Also important is the way the tradition provides Catholic thinkers with the tools to arrive at subtleties in their policy positions *even when they adamantly oppose stem cell research*. Edward Furton believes "human embryo destruction is moral evil."[62] Yet displaying a sort of analytical flexibility notably absent in evangelical treatments, he offers an intriguing proviso to his argument. "Catholic health care facilities, Catholic physicians, and Catholic patients alike," he writes, "should be able to make use of therapies that derive from embryonic stem cells despite their immoral origins."[63]

Jesuit scholar John Langan also disapproves of ICM derivation, arguing that Catholic institutions ought not conduct such research. Still, he commendably allows that "Catholics should be prepared to tolerate the carrying forward of such research by those committed to it, even while raising crucial questions about it."[64] How different this is from the statement of the Southern Baptist Convention quoted above, which essentially endeavors to impose its reading of Scripture on both the federal government *and* the private sector.

Conclusion: Transvaluation

For maybe three decades now, the same complaints have been hurled at politically engaged conservative Protestants. They go something like this: Their readings of the Bible are tendentious and hypocritical. Their actions are not animated by lofty spiritual goals but a creaturely urge for political gain. They cloak a lust for power in the frocks of scriptural writ. Later on, I will defend evangelicals and fundamentalists from these charges. But first I want to expand the indictment a bit.

Lending more credence to the aforementioned accusations is the fact that there exists an obvious way to cite biblical citations *in favor* of embryonic stem cell research. One would expect a religious group with such a high degree of biblical literacy to acknowledge that Jesus spent a great deal of his earthly time curing extremely sick (or dead) people. As Stevan Davies phrases it in his book *Jesus the Healer*, "No fact about Jesus of Nazareth is so widely and repeatedly attested in the New Testament gospels as the fact that he was a healer of people in mental and physical distress."[65] There are, actually, far more verses that speak unequivocally about the importance of healing than those that speak of prenatal life. Luke 7:21–22 provides a fairly generic example:

> And that very hour He cured many of infirmities, afflictions, and evil spirits; and to many blind He gave sight.
>
> Jesus answered and said to them, "Go and tell John the things you have seen and heard: that the blind see, the lame walk, the lepers are cleansed, the deaf hear, the dead are raised, the poor have the gospel preached to them."[66]

The positive valuation attached to mending the sick might lead one to ask: Isn't the real message of the Bible about alleviating suffering? Isn't there more evidence of Jesus' concern for the ill than for the rights of the unborn? Wouldn't Jesus himself in a white lab coat extract the ICM in the name of curing those who suffer from debilitating diseases?

I do not wish to argue that the biblical evidence recommends precisely such conclusions. Rather, my interest lies in demonstrating that whenever Scripture is dragged into the political arena, it lends itself to a devastatingly effective political tactic I call "transvaluation." When a person transvalues the Bible she effectively redefines its moral center. She says it's not about *this* but *that*. She re-hierarchizes (what someone else believed to be) the moral priorities of the text in a way that conforms to her own moral priorities.

For example, the mainline Protestant body the United Church of Christ approves of stem cell research because "Jesus set an example, by his ministry of healing and caring for the sick and disabled, challenging us to follow his example by supporting the healing and caring ministry in our own day."[67] Senator Kennedy above insisted the Bible is about hope. Karen Lebacqz performs a similar act of transvaluation when she elevates concern for the living over concern for the embryo. She dares her fellow Protestants to follow Jesus' example and "break many rules of 'cleanliness' in order to heal and save on the Sabbath." "Morally speaking," she declares, "what matters most is not whether my hands are clean but whether life is served. . . . I argue that the direct killing of the blastocyst in stem cell research is not wrong."[68] In each instance the assertion is made that one's opponents have misunderstood the "real" values of Scripture.

Transvaluation is a devastatingly effective political tool. It places one's opponents on the defensive, because it insinuates that they have completely misread their own sacred texts. And it is easy to do because the Bible, like the ICM, is pluripotent. Its astonishing plasticity permits political actors to identify virtually all of the positions necessary for the advancement of their preferred policy initiatives.

Chapter 4

The Bible and International Relations

A Foreign Policy in Christ?

I pray that God may guide all your proceedings, especially in the putting forth of a fearless warning that we are in the awful end of the Times of the Gentiles, with no hope for humanity except in the personal return of the Lord in glory.
Cyrus Scofield, Letter to the Philadelphia
Prophetic Conference, 1918

The left must try at long last to understand the American religious scene. The first requirement is to calm down.
Leo Ribuffo, "George W. Bush and
the Latest Evangelical Menace"

*I*magine an intersection in Washington, DC. Imagine that this intersection stands at the junction of three roads. One is called "American Foreign Policy Avenue," another goes by the name of "Bible Boulevard," and the last is called "West Religion Place."

Up until a few years ago, almost nobody would have been standing at our hypothetical junction. Save for a few stragglers, it would have been dark and empty—like most intersections in drab, dull, dead-after-7-p.m. DC.

By conjuring up this unhappy little street scene, we come to understand a truism about the nation's foreign policy prior to September 11, 2001. In the waning decades of the twentieth century, Judeo-Christian religious concerns, let alone scriptural concerns, did not figure significantly in the American government's thinking about its international affairs. It is hard to name, for example, one secretary of state in recent memory who seemed excessively motivated by faith-based considerations. "Serving the Lord" would not seem to accurately characterize the public service (and self-perceptions) of Henry Kissinger, or Cyrus Vance, or George Shultz, or James Baker III, or Warren Christopher, or Madeleine Albright, or Colin Powell.[1] As Albright recently put it, "I cannot remember any leading American diplomat . . . speaking in depth about the role of religion in shaping the world."[2]

As for the Washington international relations establishment, it has traditionally shown far more interest in realism than revelation. James Lindsay, vice president of the influential Council on Foreign Relations, admits that when it comes to religion, "we are not used to thinking about the topic."[3] Indeed, one does not easily envision folks at many of the prestigious think tanks in Washington reciting psalms to themselves as they draft op-ed pieces about destabilizing unfriendly regimes on their shiny Macs.[4] To quote the *Economist*, "America's foreign-policy elite is . . . one of the most secular groups in the country."[5]

Yet secular pundits and policy makers no longer have the luxury of remaining religiously illiterate. Reading through post-9/11 foreign policy analyses, one encounters an incredulous sigh of *"What were we thinking?"* Assorted wonks, scholars, and public servants now lament that they did not take religion (and by this they usually mean radical Islamic religion) seriously. In retrospect, everything from the Iranian Revolution, to the Rushdie affair, to the first World Trade Center attack, pointed to Muslim extremism as a significant geo-political variable.

Understanding the beliefs of others, it is now conceded, has national security implications. Possessing a basic knowledge of what people across the world think about the hereafter, or the ethics of warfare, is tantamount to intelligence gathering. Even more sobering for secular elites has been the realization that many Americans want religion (and by this they usually mean conservative Protestant religion) to be factored into their own government's approach to international relations.

And there they are *again*! The spry evangelicals. Their own non-governmental organizations have been dealing with grim global issues for years. In the words of Allen Hertzke, "This movement is filling a void in human-rights advocacy, raising issues previously slighted or insufficiently pressed by secular groups."[6] They have called attention to (and tried to alleviate) the AIDS crisis in Africa, the practice of human sexual trafficking, and the persecution of Christians around the world. Of course, their authentic social concerns and good works are fused with pragmatic considerations: Africa, South America, and Asia are emerging as tremendous growth markets for Christian souls.

In a recent article in the journal *Foreign Affairs*, Walter Russell Mead identifies two major ways that evangelicals are exerting influence in the sphere of international relations.[7] In terms of humanitarian aid and human rights, as we just saw, various Christian NGOs have a long and not undistinguished track record of helping others in less fortunate lands.[8] The Bush administration, as is well known, has taken steps to facilitate their work.

Mead goes on to observe that evangelicals have also "deepened U.S. support for the Jewish State."[9] Not averse to granting religion a place at the table and generally optimistic about its potential contributions, Mead concludes, "Evangelical power is here to stay for the foreseeable future, and those concerned about U.S. foreign policy would do well to reach out."[10]

In the opinion of others, however, there is no need to reach out: evangelical power has gotten way out of hand. As far as secular Americans are concerned, the intersection of religion, Scripture, and foreign policy mentioned above is an open-air megachurch teeming with Bible thumpers and Jesus freaks. Every blue-stater knows that the executive branch is overrun by right-wing Christian ideologues. Every blue-stater knows that President Bush factors the Bible into his "thinking" about America's international priorities. And every blue-stater knows that the nation's foreign policy in the Middle East has gone hopelessly "Christey."

In this chapter I will focus on one popular variant of the latter critique. This will help us better gauge Scripture's influence, or lack thereof, on American statecraft. It will also give us a sense of the hyperbole that accompanies discussions of the Bible's place in the nation's politics.

Jihadized Evangelicalism

Writing on the op-ed page of the *New York Times* in 2002, Nicholas Kristof pointed to "a broad new trend that is beginning to reshape

American foreign policy: America's Evangelicals have become the newest internationalists."[11]

That evangelical beliefs are shaping, if not outright dictating, the Bush administration's Middle East agenda is a commonly heard reproach. Those making this claim often concentrate on a reading of Scripture known as "premillennial dispensationalism." This theology, they charge, has hijacked the nation's foreign policy priorities. The sheer volume of this allegation is astonishing, as is its pervasiveness across diverse liberal, secular, Democratic, and radical subcultures. Let us begin by looking at the allegations themselves.

Christian Zionists, according to many, have the Bush administration's ear. Writing in *Tikkun*, Tony Campolo wonders if dispensationalist theology has "permeated the thinking" of the president himself. "Religious leaders who espouse these beliefs," he contends, "such as Falwell, Robertson, and Franklin Graham are among his closest spiritual advisors."[12]

Offering evidence for the charge that policy makers in Washington are actually consulting religious extremists is Rick Perlstein. Citing a leaked memo, he sounds the alarm: "We're not supposed to know the National Security Council's top Middle East aide consults with apocalyptic Christians eager to ensure American policy on Israel conforms with their sectarian doomsday scenarios." Perlstein refers to an alleged March 25, 2004, meeting between the Pentecostal minister Robert Upton and Elliot Abrams, then the NSC's Near East and North Africa Affairs director (and now deputy national security advisor). Perlstein charges that Bush has been "eager to work with apocalyptics." The president, he concludes, "is discussing policy with Christians who might not care about peace at all—at least until the rapture."[13]

Such accusations are fairly subdued when compared with a much more strident critique. Here it is held that Bush and his advisors do not merely pander to the base by granting audiences to apocalyptic Christians. Instead, they personally share the base's convictions. Washington strategists, according to Tony Judt in the *New York Review of Books*, are possessed by an "eschatological urge to tear down a frustrating international order and remake it in their image."[14] Michael Ortiz Hill claims that "the Commander in Chief of the most powerful military force in human history has located American foreign policy within a biblical narrative that leads inexorably toward . . . the battle of Armageddon."[15]

Lawrence Davidson, a professor at West Chester University, refers to "the persistent Christian Zionist belief that American foreign policy is destined to help pave the way for Christ's second coming and the apocalypse."[16] As with most of the commentators mentioned in this section, Davidson maintains that Bush and his backers "have effectively blocked any substantive American Government support for a Palestinian state or the trading of land for peace."[17]

The most popular rehearsal of these themes was advanced by Kevin Phillips, author of *American Theocracy: The Peril and Politics of Radical Religion, Oil, and Borrowed Money in the 21st Century*. Phillips served in the Nixon administration, and in an age where the phrase "secular Republican" sounds like an oxymoron, his screed comes from an unfamiliar quarter. Referring to the present GOP as "the first religious party in U.S. history," Phillips speaks of "White House implementation of domestic and international political agendas that seem to be driven by religious motivations and biblical worldviews."[18]

Toward the end of his sprawling jeremiad, Phillips insinuates that Bush crafts foreign policy in line with the fictional *Left Behind* books so beloved of evangelicals: "I cannot help but think that by the early 2000s—certainly by September 11—the *Left Behind* series provided an extraordinary context for a president with a religious mission. Its biblical framework already bundled together the terrorism of September 11, the oil politics of the Persian Gulf . . . and the invasion of Iraq-cum-Babylon."[19]

Such remarks reveal much about the image of evangelicals and fundamentalists in the secular, liberal, and radical left's mindset. Conservative Christians are said to have the same death wish when it comes to international relations that they do with regard to the environment (see chapter 2). They not only anticipate the apocalypse but wish to expedite its arrival. In accordance with what they see as prophecy, they are actually encouraged by Middle Eastern conflict—so much so that they seek to foment, through lobbying and political pressure, even greater chaos in Israel/Palestine.

This critique tends to equate mainstream and right-of-center Christianity with radical Islam.[20] An image of a "jihadized" evangelicalism emerges—a religion that so values the next world that it reck-lessly denigrates the present one. Confronted with the specter of com-plete global annihilation, these Christians respond, so goes the critique, with euphoric cries of "*Bring it on!*" Their weapons of choice are not suicide bombers or roadside explosives but the Amer-ican democratic process itself.

Premillennial Dispensationalism

Before deciding whether the beliefs discussed above are actually dri-ving U.S. foreign policy, we will need to define "premillennial dis-pensationalism." This is more difficult to do than its detractors (and proponents) often assume. Not helping matters are the "almost uni-formly unintelligible" writings of the school's leading light, John Nelson Darby.[21] Further, the dispensationalist movement has, like Protestantism itself, demonstrated a remarkable proclivity for inter-nal dissent and schism. In the absence of a Vatican of PD (and in the presence of many profitable books and movies on the subject) it is difficult to distinguish orthodox conceptions from heretical ones. What follows is a brief, common-denominator summary.

Premillennial dispensationalism was founded by John Nelson Darby (1800–1882) of Britain's Plymouth Brethren.[22] Darby visited the United States several times between 1862 and 1877, winning over audiences and becoming the Johnny Appleseed of his own theologi-cal handiwork.[23] His ideas established a foothold in North America at the Niagara Bible Conference (1883–1897).[24] Later they took root in major evangelical centers of higher learning such as the Dallas Theological Seminary, the Moody Bible Institute, and the Bible Insti-tute of Los Angeles.[25] Here generations of conservative Christian intellectuals were trained in PD's tenets and proceeded to disseminate them across the continent.

An even more formidable medium for propagating Darby's teach-ings has been the Scofield Reference Bible. It is replete with maps, lists, fun facts, trivia, and dispensational interpretations placed under-neath the text of the King James Version.[26] First published in 1909 and enormously successful ever since, Cyrus Scofield's work is, yes, the bible of premillennial dispensationalism.[27] Parenthetically, I would add that the recent 2002 edition is a masterpiece of industrial design. With its embossed leather and meaty but manageable heft, it is a pleasure to hold, or to thump on a lectern, or to raise in the air with one hand while clutching a microphone in the other.[28]

Surpassing even Scofield in its ability to popularize PD has been Hal Lindsey, the author of *The Late, Great Planet Earth* and a graduate of Dallas Theological Seminary. More recently, there is the *Left Behind* series of Tim LaHaye and Jerry Jenkins. This serialized Christian fiction has sold upwards of 62 million copies.[29] When asked about his intended readership, LaHaye replied, "I envisioned both Christians and unsaved souls as the primary audience. I was hoping to see Christians rededicate their lives to Christ in light of his coming and for the unsaved to receive him."[30]

The coming of Christ and the plight of the unsaved were very much on Darby's mind as well. In opposition to the popular postmillennialism of the early nineteenth century, Darby preached that Jesus' second coming would occur *before* the millennium, not after. The Scofield Bible describes the millennium as "that period of time during which Christ will reign upon the earth, a time of universal peace, prosperity, long life, and prevailing righteousness."[31]

Superimposed on this millennial schema was the idea of dispensations, or eras, in God's overarching redemptive plan. Scofield reasoned that the Bible divides history into seven dispensations. We are currently residing in the sixth dispensation. Otherwise known as the "Church Age," it has lasted two thousand years.[32] Standing between the present dispensation and the coming seventh dispensation is an event referred to by Darby as "the secret Rapture." This was one of his most peculiar inventions and a recurring bone of contention among Christians.[33] Also referred to as the doctrine of the "any-moment coming," it stipulates that Jesus could come to earth at any given instant.[34]

His arrival, however, will not be marked by noise and fanfare. It will only be discernible to the few lucky enough to be raptured.[35] When this happens, all right-professing Christians (living and dead) will be projected into the air with the Messiah. There Jesus and his saints will hover for seven years. Everyone else will be left behind.

PD is a philosophy of "dark foreboding," pessimism, and even fatalism.[36] It maintains that with each passing dispensation things deteriorate. As one scholar puts it, dispensationalists "thought that the world was going to hell or, more precisely, that the world was literally turning into hell."[37] If God-ordained social decline is inevitable, then it follows that human social action is useless. As D. G. Hart puts it, dispensationalists "looked to God's supernatural intervention into human affairs as the only hope to remedy evil."[38]

Accordingly, dispensational theory is skeptical about social change, skeptical about reform, skeptical about democracy, skeptical about any approach predicated on the ability of humans to improve their world.[39] What types of actions are useful? The saving of one's own soul is good. Also, the saving of other souls is highly recommended. In Paul Boyer's words, "Mankind's collective doom was certain, but *individuals* could escape."[40]

These considerations permit us to speculate on how the dispensationalist mentality may translate into political action. In one reading, those who believe in this theology can be seen as "passive fatalists." Given the Bible-scripted inevitability of Christ's return, the passive fatalist understands that little can be done. Life's itinerary is modest. Accept Jesus into your heart. Get saved. Live right. Convince the philanderer down the block to come to Christ. Monitor the news for "signs of the times." Wait patiently for the coming of the Lord. Here the possibilities of political action are stunted by the agent's dread realization that it's all in God's hands.

A very different orientation to politics might be referred to as "active fatalism." Here the dispensationalist is not content to wait around for the End. Rather, as one scholar humorously phrased it, he or she wants "to help move things along."[41] This person's agenda consists of *inducing* the apocalypse. A private citizen who undertakes this task is a local menace. An elected official who acts this way is a national, if not global, security threat.

Back to the theology itself. During the seven years that the church is floating up above with Jesus, Jews will endure awful calamities down below on earth. One of the most remarkable aspects of PD is the prominent role it assigns to both Jews and Israel.[42] In order for the rapture to occur, a variety of signs pertaining to the chosen people must come to pass. One of these signs is particularly relevant to modern times. As Bruce Waltke writes, "The restoration of the political state of Israel is universally regarded by dispensationalists as the first sign that God is about to return to this earthly program."[43] The return of the Jews to Israel in "unbelief" (i.e., not as converted Christians) is another stipulation of the scheme.

Once the rapture begins, the seventh and final dispensation will be set into motion. The Jews on earth will experience seven unpleasant years, referred to as "the Tribulation."[44] Scofield describes this as a period of "the unprecedented activity of demons."[45] Also known as the "time of Jacob's Trouble," it will begin when Jews sign a treaty with the antichrist and then rebuild the temple. In the three and a half (or seven, according to some) years of warfare, pestilence, and misery that follow, many Jews will repent and convert (some, however, will not).

In the end, as many as 144,000 ex-Jews (in some schemes) will fight the antichrist at the battle of Armageddon. Joining them in the final showdown will be Jesus, the saints, and the heavenly host. The antichrist will be vanquished, and *then* will come the one-thousand-year reign of Christ on earth.[46] Of less interest to us here (because it's too far off to think about) is a final cameo appearance made by Satan after ten centuries of Jesus' earthly rule.[47]

In PD, Jews and Christians are yoked together in ways that may be uncomfortable for both. It would seem to be a corollary of this theology that the Christian road to redemption is pocked with the speed-bumps of Jewish intransigence. If Jews don't return to Israel, if they don't rebuild the temple, and so forth, in some sense they are delaying or maybe even annulling Christian salvation. From the Jewish perspective, there is much to be concerned about as well. If all goes according to the dispensationalist plan, Jews and Judaism will cease to exist; they must either throw their lot in with the antichrist and perish, or get saved.

None of this, however, has prevented those who adhere to PD and some contemporary Jews from finding common cause. Premillennialists are inveterate observers of international affairs and staunch supporters of the modern state of Israel. Since the nineteenth century they have interpreted events in the Middle East as signs of the time.[48] Needless to say, the British capture of Jerusalem in 1917, the birth of Israel in 1948, and the Israeli army's reconquest of the entire city of

Jerusalem in 1967 stoked the imagination of many of the faithful.[49] Was this not a signal that the prophecy was on track?[50]

Foreign Policy, the Bible, and Bush

It seems highly unlikely that George W. Bush subscribes to dispensational theology. There is, of course, no way to know for sure. After all, this is not the type of personal conviction that an elected official discusses on *Meet the Press*.[51] With its talk of a "secret rapture" that results in billions of sad saps who are "left behind," PD is an election-year liability. Nor does PD hark back to America's finest traditions of ecumenism. Its tenets are not likely to be warmly embraced by Jews, or Muslims, or Catholics, or Mormons, or orthodox Christians, or mainline Protestants.

Or evangelicals and fundamentalists! Many in these groups vehemently reject Darby-style dispensationalism. With this we arrive at a point of considerable importance for assessing allegations that the conservative Christian base craves apocalypse. PD is by no means a definitive or authoritative teaching.[52] It is not central to the evangelical creed in the way that, say, the doctrine of biblical inerrancy has been. Truth be told, evangelicals themselves have often labeled PD as a heresy.[53] Even sympathetic scholars politely refer to the "genuine novelties" in the scheme and point out that the conception of a secret rapture "was unheard of" before Darby's intervention—a "distinctive development" as one commentator put it.[54]

When it comes to eschatology (as with many other things), the conservative Christian thought world is diverse. "Evangelicals do agree that the end will come," opines Martyn Percy, "it is just that they do not agree about how, why or when."[55] Thus, a politician fishing for votes solely among Bible-carrying Christians might think twice before delivering stump speeches about the secret rapture.[56]

Pursuing it from another direction, we might look to Bush's rhetoric for hints of his dispensationalist leanings. In his public comments he often sounds like an evangelical Christian. But he does not sound like a proponent of PD. The latter would accentuate the utter hopelessness of the human endeavor. He or she would oscillate between glum, get-saved-while-you-can banter and ecstatic can't-you-see-it-coming assertions. But such bleak musings are completely absent in Bush's oratory. Instead, his speeches are larded with booming proclamations about liberty, democracy, freedom, the expansion of markets, and the unique promise of America.

The same holds true for the administration's published foreign policy positions, such as the National Security Strategy (NSS). In accordance with the Goldwater-Nichols Act of 1986, each president is required to "submit an annual report to Congress setting forth America's grand strategy."[57] As Keir Lieber and Robert Lieber have observed, the typical NSS consists of "lofty rhetoric or uncontroversial restatements of foreign policy."[58] It would not be inaccurate to state that few analysts in Washington ever paid much attention to this report and its wonky platitudes.

For obvious reasons, however, the 2002 NSS and 2006 NSS have been scrutinized with especial interest. Anyone who reads through both statements would be hard pressed to find even the remotest connection to dispensational theology on their pages. In truth, not a word of evangelical rhetoric is to be found in either document. The texts make occasional pleas for freedom of worship, but for the most part they reflect the secular mindset of the foreign policy establishment discussed above.[59] What one does notice in NSS 2002 and 2006, incidentally, is not conservative Christian theology but a 100-proof, neoconservative worldview. Declarations on the importance of preemptive intervention, the creation of "a world of democratic, well-governed states," and the drawbacks of multilateralism abound.[60] The focus of these documents is not redemption through Christ but "human liberty protected by democratic institutions."[61]

Even if we were to find the complete thirty-six-volume set of John Darby's writings in the Oval Office, replete with Bush's handwritten annotations in the margins, there would still be reason to doubt that our geopolitical initiatives are set in accord with these teachings. This is because the nation's diplomatic priorities are not predicated on the views of one person, even those of a president. Elite policymaking is a lengthy and complex process. It involves many competing actors and no small share of behind-the-scenes bureaucratic knife fighting.[62] Legion are the stories of ideological clashes in the Bush administration. Legion are the tales of epic battles between the State Department, the Defense Department, and the Vice President's Office.[63] Any given policy prescription is the dividend of negotiations, power plays, compromises, pressure and interest groups, market considerations, and personality conflicts. Real and perceived threats to national security also have something to do with it.

To this point we have seen that Bush has never claimed to be a dispensationalist. His public comments give no indication that he professes this view. His foreign policy pronouncements point to no discernible connection to anything found in the *Left Behind* series, the *Scofield Study Bible*, or John Nelson Darby. This leaves the question of his conservative Christian base, depicted as passionately committed to premillennial views by the critics discussed earlier.

Let us linger on the idea of "passionate commitment." Secular and liberal critics tend to assume that *all* evangelicals hold *all* of their beliefs passionately. This stereotype reminds me of the not unentertaining movie *Team America* in which marionettes of turbaned Muslims flail their arms wildly and incessantly mutter, "*Jihad! Jihad! Jihad! Jihad!*" Similar images emerge when media elites depict conservative Christians. They portray the latter as people who emote "*Rap-CHA, Rap-CHA, Rap-CHA, honey!*" to themselves in a southern drawl. As far as many secularists and leftists are concerned, all evangelicals and fundamentalists are active fatalists.[64]

In both caricatures—one advanced by comedians, the other by political analysts—the faithful are seen as the mindless automatons of one religious precept. The comics, at least, can be forgiven for not appreciating an irony well known to scholars of religion. Believers of all stripes have an astonishing capacity to tune out, or overlook, or mute, or completely misunderstand seemingly salient components of their religion's dogma. They have always retained the ability to live with whopping contradictions, to create the most inexplicable ruptures between doctrine and practice. As Leo Ribuffo aptly phrases it, "Fundamentalists and evangelicals both read novels about Jesus' imminent return and sign up for thirty-year mortgages."[65]

James Kurth, a professor of political science at Swarthmore College and an evangelical, argues along similar lines in his review of Kevin Phillips's *American Theocracy*. Doubting whether Phillips had actually ever spoken "to an actual living, breathing evangelical," Kurth advances a more nuanced view of conservative Christians:

It is true that evangelicals will take the Book of Revelation to be inerrant, and that in the fullness of time there will be the end times described in the Book of Revelation . . . but in other books of the New Testament . . . it is made crystal clear that no man knows the time of the coming of Jesus, the Messiah . . . We are to live as if it could happen tomorrow. And we are also to live as if no one knows when it will come. Therefore, we must be simultaneously prepared for it to come tomorrow, or indeed in the next instant, or to not come for generations. And it is presumptuous for any person to claim it's coming any day now or in our own lifetime. That is another form of heresy, of false prophecy.[66]

We know that evangelicals have accepted Jesus into their hearts. But the degree to which they have accepted dispensationalist premises into their hearts has yet to be established.

Conclusion: Religion, not Bible

President Bush's rhetoric is laced with allusions to Scripture. His fondness for the Good Book is well known. His enthusiasm for daily Bible study is perhaps unsurpassed by any previous chief executive. One of his speechwriters, David Frum, tellingly (and distressingly) reports that the "first words he ever heard spoken in the Bush White House were, 'Missed you at the Bible study.'"[67]

Given what we know about the way Bush and his conservative Christian base esteem Scripture, it appears that the pundits on the left have posed the wrong question. What should be asked is not why there is so much, but *why there is so little* Bible in George W. Bush's Middle Eastern foreign policy. One obvious answer—albeit one inexplicably lost on many of those cited above—is that *rhetoric and policy are two very different things.*[68] Talking about one's personal faith in the public sphere is easy (though not without its hazards). Getting a psalm, or commandment, or parable to inform one's approach to international relations is hard.

It is hard because so many Americans—believers and nonbelievers alike—don't want a psalm, or commandment, or parable to be factored into governmental thinking. It is hard because so many Americans cling to rigid sectarian interpretations of these verses and will be outraged by any other rigid sectarian interpretation. It is also hard because the Bible is one of the poorest providers of coherent policy prescriptions imaginable.

Charles Krauthammer was certainly correct when he scoffed at the idea of using the Good Book in American statecraft. "I am sure," he exclaimed, "one can find any message one seeks in the Bible, depending on where one looks."[69] Krauthammer identifies a truth that has passed many scripturally literate conservative Christians by: the Bible seems to say everything about everything, and everything it says seems contradicted by something else it says.[70] PD confirms this truism. It is routinely assailed by other Christians as having no grounding in Scripture.[71]

Ornate biblical interpretations such as PD are not part of the Bush administration's foreign policy. As with all presidents, however, Bush has successfully incorporated very broad religious convictions into his statecraft. He seems, for example, to be obsessed with the idea of evil.[72] He has come to the conclusion that America's mission is synonymous with God's mission. Perhaps it is true, as Robert Bellah suggests, that his unilateralism is an expression of his radical Protestant individualism.[73]

Such convictions are too general to be called "biblical." They are too theologically inflected to be labeled as "neoconservative." We might call them broad religious values in the sense that they provide very general rules to live by and moral limitations. Religious values, unlike chapter-and-verse-based biblical ideas, are overarching conceptions that may motivate policymakers. It is simply wrong to say that our foreign policy is biblically based. Better to speak of certain religiously tinged worldviews that—for better or for worse—have guided the administration's thinking.[74]

None of the preceding should be seen as an endorsement or repudiation of the president's Middle Eastern foreign policies. What I do wish to repudiate is alarmist political analysis. The critique of Bush discussed here strikes me as unsubstantiated, overheated, and hyperbolic. This having been said, I want to say that the excesses of Bush's critics are understandable. Moreover, their protest is a "sign of the times"—one that shows that America is in for some tense and turbulent discussion about religion's proper place in politics.

The president, like so many others of this political generation, feels licensed to mention both biblical and religious themes in his rhetoric. This has been repeatedly hailed as a victory over a repressive secular ethos, one that rendered the public square "naked" and forced citizens to check their "religious beliefs at the public door."[75] I would suggest, however, that the outcry against Bush, in its pervasiveness and sheer nastiness, points to a signal drawback of dressing one's politics in priestly garments. Such confessions of faith tend to polarize the electorate and the punditry. They create premodern, generally un-American suspicions that something other than love of country impels our leaders to make the decisions that they make. Take the siren howls of secularists and religious leftists as a warning: the intersection of Bible, religion, and foreign policy is a very dangerous intersection indeed.

PART 2

Rhetoric and
Religious Imaging

Chapter 5

The Bible in Political Rhetoric

The Good, the Bad, and the Ugly

Right from the start of Campaign 2000 in that first phone conver-
sation, he [Bill Clinton] offered me valuable advice. He remem-
bered a speech I had given at the National Prayer Breakfast
earlier that year on the appropriate role of faith in our public life;
he urged me to circulate it widely. Stand strong against those who
might question your religious beliefs and behavior, he said. There
will be some people in the campaign who will try to keep you quiet
on this, but don't you hesitate to talk about your religion.
Joseph Lieberman, *An Amazing Adventure: Joe and*
Hadassah's Personal Notes on the 2000 Campaign

*I*t reflected somewhat poorly on Howard Dean—if not the Democratic Party as a whole—when, at the height of his 2004 presidential
run, he chimed in on matters scriptural. After helpfully informing
reporters that he knew "much about the Bible," Dean was asked to
name his favorite New Testament work. "The book of Job," he shot
back. Inspired by his source material, the governor of Vermont went
on to offer an impromptu and unsolicited homily on the text's compositional history and broader moral significance. Unless the present
chair of the Democratic National Committee knew something about
the canon that most exegetes do not, he was in error. The book of Job
is situated in the Old Testament.[1]

Scripture and politics, even in isolation from one another, are
highly combustible materials. Mix them together and the possibilities for an occasional "work accident" are considerable. Seekers and

holders of office please take note: when discussing the Bible in public, an element of volatility is always present. This is because its history is maddeningly complex. Just understanding what is in a given Bible (there are countless different translations and many different "originals") requires the type of "Introduction to Bible" class that Howard Dean apparently never signed up for.

Not everyone uses the same Bible, and this also requires rhetorical temperance. When trawling for votes among Catholics it would be prudent *not* to regale parishioners with the booming cadences of the Protestant King James Version. Don't cite the letter to the Hebrews in a synagogue even though all of those good people sitting in *shul* may strike you as descendants of biblical Hebrews (the letter to the Hebrews is not part of the Jewish canon). One should also be wary, as I have noted, of the tendency of the Bible's verses to make diametrically opposed claims. On Thursday you insist that the Good Book supports your policy on ethanol subsidies. On Friday your opponent cites a countertext suggesting that you are wrong and a blasphemer to boot!

When it comes to the Bible, however, politicians have shown themselves to be optimists, if not daredevils. None of the aforementioned hazards has dampened their enthusiasm to reference Scripture in their oratory. There is, however, a marked difference between those who make good political use of the sacred source and those who do not. This begs the question of how we define "the Good." By what criteria might we conclude that someone has done an exemplary job of bringing Scripture into his or her public pronouncements? One popular formula looks at the crispness of a speech's prose, "the incantatory elegance of the cadences," the seamless integration of sacred vocabularies with secular concerns.[2] Echoes of Lincoln's Second Inaugural ringing in their heads, some observers define good use of the Bible in politics in terms of oratorical aesthetics.[3]

My definition is somewhat different. I would like to define the Good as inextricably bound with the Victorious. Good use of the Bible is that use which in some way contributes to a politician's winning an election (or does not do any irreparable damage to his or her interests). Of late, the GOP has cornered the market on the Good. Some Democrats have recently approximated the Bad, the Un-Victorious. The woes of Howard Dean, Joseph Lieberman, and John

Kerry teach us a great deal about the scripts that succeed and fail with audiences in the American theater of politics.

The Ugly: Overthumping on the Fringe

Prior to discussing some of the differences between the Good and the Bad, a word must be said about a way of employing Scripture that has very little electoral appeal. The political marginality of those who use it in this manner, I believe, is indicative of a certain truth about religion's role in American public life. I am referring here to any type of speech in which the *entire* content of the address and/or argument is predicated on biblical verses.

Excessive reference to Scripture in political rhetoric is an incivility rarely associated with either Republicans or Democrats. It usually occurs outside of the two-party mainstream, on the political and cultural fringes. As with the chap holding the John 3:16 sign and wearing the rainbow wig at a football stadium, it is a form of faith-based expression that is not taken seriously. How many Americans would take seriously the following policy statement about homosexuality from the Westboro Baptist Church of Topeka, Kansas?

> In summary, sodomites are wicked and sinners before the Lord exceedingly (Gen. 13:13), are violent and doom nations (Gen. 19:1–25; Jgs. 19), are abominable to God (Lev. 18:22), are worthy of death for their vile, depraved, unnatural sex practices (Lev. 20:13; Rom. 1:32), are called dogs because they are filthy, impudent and libidinous (Deut. 23:17, 18; Mat. 7:6; Phil. 3:2), produce by their very presence in society a kind of mass intoxication from their wine made from grapes of gall from the vine of Sodom and the fields of Gomorrah which poisons society's mores with the poison of dragons and the cruel venom of asps (Deut. 32:32, 33), declare their sin and shame on their countenance (Isa. 3:9), are shameless and unable to blush (Jer. 6:15), are workers of iniquity and hated by God (Psa. 5:5), are liars and murderers (Jn. 8:44), are filthy and lawless (2 Pet. 2:7, 8), are natural brute beasts (2 Pet. 2:12), are dogs eating their own vomit and sows wallowing in their own feces (2 Pet. 2:22) . . .[4]

And on and on it goes. Scripture-soaked arguments of this sort can be found on thousands of Web sites. The following contestation of abortion from whatsaiththescripture.com is comparatively mild in its tone. Yet its tendency to correlate every single political position with a handy scriptural proof-text is of a kind with the quote seen above:

> Abortion is, first and foremost, a sin against God and His Perfect Law, "thou shalt not kill" (Exodus 20:13). The opposite of "giving" life is "taking" life, or in stronger words, "killing" life. The only One with the ability to "give" life is the LORD Creator of Heaven and Earth. "Jesus came and spake unto them, saying, ALL POWER IS GIVEN *unto ME* in Heaven and in Earth" (Matthew 28:18). The LORD Jesus Christ is the "Faithful Creator" (1 Peter 4:19). "All things were made by Him; and without Him was not any thing made that was made. In Him was Life; and the Life was the Light of men" (John 1:3–4). Therefore, He is the only deserving One to "take" life. Jesus said, "I lay down My Life, that I might take it again. No man taketh it from Me, but I lay it down of Myself. *I have power to lay it down, and I have power to take it again*" (John 10:17–18).[5]

While those who insist that we live in a theocratic state might disagree, it seems to me that this style of argument has very little mass appeal. Americans cannot—and do not—live by the Bible alone. Accordingly, they will not countenance a political argument wholly predicated on sacred words. This is because Americans are not bibliolaters; most recognize other documents and other forms of knowledge as legitimate and necessary when thinking about the common good.

With the exception of a few on the margins, evangelicals are no exception to this rule. Position statements found on the Web site of the centrist National Association of Evangelicals, or in the volume *Toward an Evangelical Public Policy*, are nowhere near as crammed with biblical citations or as myopically focused on given verses as the previous selections. One very perceptive commentator even suggested that groups such as Ralph Reed's Christian Coalition were much more likely to argue their public case "from shared human (i.e., middle class American) experience rather than by appeal to the transcendent authority of the Bible."[6]

This relatively restrained use of Scripture raises two fascinating possibilities about modern-day mainstream evangelicalism. Perhaps, like all social movements that come to political maturity, it has learned the strategic importance of not saying in public what it might say in private.

More provocatively, maybe evangelicals are far less influenced by the Bible than they imagine themselves to be. Parenthetically, I would mention that a good deal of centrist evangelical political literature contains an awful lot of nonbiblical influences. Doctrinally speaking, I await the moment when evangelical theologians confront the fact that so much of how they view the world does not flow from the fount of Scripture.

In any case, it is not unreasonable to assume that many conservative Christians—even those who oppose homosexuality and abortion—might concur with secularists who see statements such as those noted above as mean-spirited, if not bizarre. This leads me to state a handy rule of thumb: *the more a political actor or group makes rhetorical use of the Bible, the wackier and more electorally irrelevant they likely are.* The correlation between incessant Bible thumping and questionable mental health is understood by politicians, even very devout ones, who wish to achieve the Good.

The Good: The Citational Habits of Highly Effective Politicians

Having looked at biblically based political speech that is completely ignored, we can now draw inferences about biblically based political speech that has an accepted place in mainstream political life. What follows are some unwritten rules that characterize the way credible candidates and officeholders employ Scripture, as well as some examples from the oratory of national candidates who approximate the Good.

First, *citations must be sparse and measured.* Overdoing it lends a decidedly psychotic cast to the presenter's remarks. The successful orator, as we shall see, makes extremely restrained use of holy documents. Second, *be positive!* It is rare for today's politicians to call upon the Good Book for purposes of denigrating a particular individual or group as some of those above did. Biblical citations as employed by experienced politicians are almost always served up as a gesture of unity. The verses adduced are meant to laud broad, uncontroversial American values (e.g., love of freedom, concern for others). When bringing this document into political play one must be "dignified," not divisive.

The Bible, incidentally, is not uniformly "dignified" when addressing those with whom it disagrees. Incendiary and offensive language is routinely hurled at political opponents. Old Testament prophets are particularly adept at lobbing discursive grenades at adversaries. Amos exults in the physical violence that Yahweh will visit upon disobedient nations (Amos 1:1–2:3). Using a woman to symbolize Jerusalem, Ezekiel directs unmentionable taunts at her (Ezek. 16). Peter, as we saw, likens false teachers to dogs who sniff their own vomit (2 Pet. 2:17–22). So the "dignified" tone of nearly all contemporary biblically based political citation is not necessarily in keeping with all of the examples in the sacred text. It does, however, conform to American standards of acceptable public rhetoric.

Third, *vagueness is a virtue*. Few politicians would follow the lead of overthumpers and align a specific policy prescription with specific verses. This is because they fully understand that recourse to Scripture in political oratory is a symbolic move, and nothing else. The main objective of a Bible-citing operation is to signal to a huge chunk of the electorate that the candidate in question is, just like them, a decent, God-fearing person. It provides what one scholar has called "a character reference."[7] Accordingly, one must use the Bible in an ornamental, as opposed to a substantive, fashion. It should not (and cannot) provide the logical rationale for any political initiative. It can only furnish a moral veneer.

Fourth, I advise politicians to *avoid intellectual and theological depth*. Politics is not Proust; good rhetoric should not abound in complex metaphors and submerged symbols to be deciphered by the initiated. A good speechwriter does not want to cite a verse which upon deeper reflection unfolds into those vast Jupiter-sized expanses of meaning that exegetes have found in Scripture. Besides, no one except professors at theological seminaries and religious studies departments would be unwise enough to read a political speech in that manner anyhow. I repeat: a politician cites Scripture to establish credibility, not to plumb the hermeneutical depths of God's multivalent transmission.

My last recommendation for would-be speechwriters is to *conceal references*. In other words, never draw too much attention to the source one is quoting. Save special circumstances, citing chapter and verse is generally a no-no. The politician who opens with the words "As we read in 2 Chronicles 2:14 . . ." is running a variety of risks ranging from inducing tachycardia among church/state activists and the liberal media, to boring the audience to tears, to prompting Bible thumpers roll up their sleeves, crack open their Scofields, and scour the candidate's interpretation for evidence of doctrinal purity. Instead, the skilled orator inconspicuously integrates a scriptural quote, *or a piece of one*, into the body of an address.

George W. Bush and Bill Clinton: Masters of the Craft

To the would-be candidate who wishes to bring the Bible into his or her rhetoric, I have just counseled keeping it (1) sparse, (2) positive, (3) vague, (4) shallow, and (5) veiled. Earlier I correlated the Good in political oratory with the Victorious. By these somewhat unlofty metrics, let me raise my glass to two masters of the craft: George W. Bush and Bill Clinton. Both routinely salt their presidential rhetoric, *ever so lightly*, with scriptural allusions. Both have scored back-to-back national elections.

I do not claim, obviously, that they achieved electoral success solely because of the verses they cited (or didn't cite, as we are about to see). It is more prudent to say that their consistent, albeit understated, invocation of Scripture convincingly established their religious *bona fides* with an electorate for whom such things are important. In addition, their forays into the Bible did not endanger their campaigns by generating scads of negative publicity—and generating scads of negative publicity when playing the faith card is a peculiar forte of recent Democratic presidential hopefuls.

When reading through George W. Bush's seven State of the Union addresses and two inaugurals, it becomes apparent that he usually observes all of the aforementioned protocols. His yearly January orations contain precious few references to the Bible (in fact, even when Bush is outside of Washington addressing a Bible fellowship group he makes scant references to the Good Book).[8] No more than three or four allusions are made in each speech, if that many. In all, these comprise far less than one percent of the total number of words within each address. Still, this places him near the high end of the spectrum among mainstream politicians—a statistic that calls attention to the importance of keeping it sparse.

In the handful of cases when the Bible is called upon, the quotes are integrated seamlessly and stealthily into the flow of ideas. With one exception to be discussed momentarily, Bush rarely puts his adversaries on alert by citing chapter and verse. He never justifies a particular policy prescription by reference to a given text. His invocations are never set in acrimonious terms but offered as a means of celebrating the republic's finest virtues. And in terms of our criteria of shallowness he excels here as well; anyone searching for nuance and profundity in his use of scriptural citations would be disappointed.

Bush's speechwriters like to employ short phrases or clauses or snippets from the Bible, as opposed to entire verses. Thus, in his 2004 State of the Union address Bush exclaimed, "The same moral tradition that defines marriage also teaches us that each individual has dignity and value in God's sight."[9] The phrase "God's sight" appears a few times in standard English translations of the Old and New Testament.[10] Bush seems to be shadowing 1 Peter 3:4: "Instead, it should be that of your inner self, the unfading beauty of a gentle and quiet spirit, which is of great worth in God's sight" (NIV).[11] In his Second Inaugural he reached into the Psalms (without, of course, ever mentioning the Psalms) and paid homage to "the Maker of Heaven and earth."[12]

During one exceptional moment in American history, Bush did engage in explicit citation. On the evening of September 11, 2001, he spoke as follows: "Tonight I ask for your prayers for all those who grieve, for the children whose worlds have been shattered, for all whose sense of safety and security has been threatened. And I pray they will be comforted by a power greater than any of us, spoken through the ages in Psalm 23: 'Even though I walk through the valley of the shadow of death, I fear no evil, for You are with me.'"[13] Two days later, while proclaiming a National Day of Prayer and Remembrance, he cited Matthew 5:4: "Scripture says: 'Blessed are those who mourn, for they shall be comforted.'"[14]

On September 14, at the National Cathedral in Washington, DC, he intoned from Romans 8:38–39: "As we have been assured, neither death nor life, nor angels nor principalities, nor powers, nor things present nor things to come, nor height nor depth can separate us from God's love."[15] It is significant that Bush refrains from quoting all the way to the end of the verse. The complete text reads, "Neither height nor depth, nor anything else in all creation, will be able to separate us from the love of God that *is in Christ Jesus our Lord*." This telling omission teaches us another rule of good American political oratory: *Not too Christey!*

More in keeping with Bush's citational tendencies is his 2001 State of the Union address. It is virtually shorn of any biblical allusions save for the final words: "Together we can share in the credit of making our country more prosperous and generous and just, and earn from our conscience and from our fellow citizens the highest possible praise: Well done good and faithful servants."[16] The reference to the faithful servant (from Matt. 25:21) would not go unnoticed by any literate Christian. As such, the president did not need to cue his listeners with a remark on the order of "As Matthew's Gospel teaches us . . ."[17]

That Bush rarely acknowledges the biblical provenance of such remarks is an omission that drives his critics to distraction. Working under the mistaken presumption that a politician should be—or ever is—straightforward about anything in particular, commentators often lament the "hidden passages," "double coding," or "winks and nudges" in his public communications.[18] One exasperated commentator who tracked down covert biblical references in the Second Inaugural sighed, "Bush was cloaking our secular values of freedom and liberty and justice in distinctly Christian garb."[19]

No matter how much it may outrage pundits and scholars, this tactic is devastatingly effective. Bush's Christian supporters know Scripture like the backs of their hands. They do not require any reminder that they are hearing proclamations from on high. Accordingly, Bush can signal the base without raising the hackles of persnickety Establishment Clause purists. Indeed, nonbelievers in front of their television sets—who usually can't be bothered to think seriously about religion—continue munching away at their pretzels without having the faintest idea that the president has just communed with about a hundred million Americans. In so doing, Bush keeps the protestations of ACLU activists out of the next day's news cycle and often well beyond that.[20]

Bill Clinton is also quite skilled in smoothly working the Bible into his speeches. As one political scientist observes, "While he sometimes quotes directly from Scripture, he more often employs words and phrases that come from the Bible but have secular meanings as well. . . . Despite its special significance to Christian listeners, this language [does] not exclude people of other persuasions."[21] Thus, the reader of his First Inaugural encounters phrases with scriptural resonances such as "bring forth," "joyful mountaintop," "valley," and "trumpets."[22] In his 1993 State of the Union, Clinton addresses the fear of a cynical Congress thusly: "We must scale the wall of the people's skepticisms, not with our words but with our deeds."[23] This formulation is reminiscent of New Testament verses which insist that words are not enough.[24]

His important 1995 State of the Union was centered on his notion of the "New Covenant," defined as "a new set of understandings for how we can equip our people to meet the challenges of a new economy, how we can change the way our government works to fit a different time, and, above all, how we can repair the damaged bonds in our society and come together behind our common purpose. We must have dramatic change in our economy, our government and ourselves."[25] The relation between that particular set of marching orders and biblical notions of a "covenant" is anybody's guess. But why argue with electoral success?[26]

Chiding partisanship and interparty bickering in his Second Inaugural, Clinton paraphrases Isaiah 58:12, reminding his colleagues that the American people "call on us instead to be repairers of the breach, and to move on with America's mission."[27] The last few sentences of a State of the Union address usually comprise the Scripture-citing portion of a president's performance. True to form, Clinton closed his 1999 address by glossing the Psalms: "Let us lift our eyes as one nation and from the mountaintop of this American century, look ahead to the next one, asking God's blessing on our endeavors and on our beloved country."[28]

Even after his presidency Clinton continued doing what good politicians who connect with religious audiences always do. Aside from Barack Obama's speech (to be addressed in the next chapter), Clinton delivered the most memorable address of the 2004 Democratic National Convention. His use of a line from Isaiah 6:8, "Send me!" in reference to John Kerry's willingness to serve his nation was inspired political rhetoric.[29] It was an example of the kind of successful oratory that Democratic presidential candidates had the most difficult time emulating in 2000 and 2004.

The Bad: Lieberman and Kerry

Does Howard Dean's blunder in 2004 regarding the book of Job have any broader significance? Does it furnish the Democrats with lessons to be learned in 2008?

At first glance, the answer would seem to be no. After all, Dean simply made a factual error. He did so in the presence of a swarm of journalists hell-bent on filing stories about the hot topic of that year: the Democratic Party's "religion gap."[30] To top it off, the inimitable Dean made his mistake just a few moments after chest-thumpingly praising his own prodigious knowledge of the Bible.

So it was probably all just an unfortunate anomaly. A freak occurrence. Something that only the former governor of Vermont could get himself into. Then again, in recent years Democratic national candidates who have turned to Scripture in particular and religion in general have not achieved the Good. In truth, they have had the damndest time incorporating biblical and religious themes into their oratory. This raises the possibility that Dean's Joblike misfortunes may be indicative of more profound difficulties that the party has in navigating the nation's treacherous sacred/secular divide. Let's examine this possibility more carefully.

The decision by presidential nominee Al Gore to name Joseph Lieberman as his running mate was a bold and historic move. Never before had a Jew, let alone an Orthodox Jew, been selected to compete for national office on a major party ticket. Yet that milestone does not immediately spring to mind when we think of the 2000 campaign. Instead, we remember "hanging chads," a delightfully snippy exchange in the wee small hours of the morning between Bush and Gore, and the fateful number 537, whose deeper Kabbalistic significance I have yet to ponder.

We also remember the immense hullabaloo generated by Lieberman's frequent professions of faith. The endeavor by the senator from Connecticut to wear his religion on his sleeve amounted to one of the major distractions and strategic missteps of the Democrats' campaign. When Lieberman was initially selected it was widely feared that his candidacy would incite the nation's anti-Semitic fringe to emerge from its caves, bunkers, yurts, and remote mountain dwellings.[31] When all was said and done, however, it was America's liberal and Jewish-liberal establishment that was most visibly outraged by the candidacy of this "Bible-quoting moralist."[32] Antagonizing one's base is *never* a good idea. But antagonizing the base is precisely what the senator from Connecticut seems to have done. If his repeated disquisitions on faith and morality drove a scant 538 Floridian secularists into the arms of Ralph Nader, then the decision to have Lieberman let his religion hang out will haunt the party for decades.

For the Democratic contingent of hardcore church/state separatists—a contingent whose exact number and influence is a subject of some controversy (see chapter 6)—Joe Lieberman is a cause for concern.[33] This is a candidate who has a copy of the Ten Commandments in his office.[34] This is a candidate who draws inspiration for his thinking on the proper role of the government from the Babylonian Talmud.[35] This is a candidate who once predicated a Medicare provision on the decree in the Decalogue to honor one's mother and father.[36] This is a candidate who rebuked Bill Clinton on the Senate floor in ostentatiously moral terms over the Monica Lewinsky affair (though he did concede, "I know from the Bible that only God can judge people").[37]

Not surprisingly, faith was front and center in Lieberman's 2000 campaign rhetoric. "My religious beliefs," he later declaimed, "shape who I am and explain why I have dedicated myself to a life of public service."[38] In his oratory, Lieberman could thump Bible with the best of them. In a speech he gave at the National Prayer Breakfast a few months prior to being named Gore's running mate (this was the address that so enthralled President Clinton in the epigraph), Lieberman invoked the Good Book so conspicuously as to make George W. Bush look like a desk officer of Americans United for the Separation of Church and State.[39] He opened that speech as follows: "To each and every one of you I say, Blessed be they who come in the name of the Lord." Variants of this verse appear in all of the Gospels; it would be difficult for a Christian to miss that.[40] He closed this address this way:

So there is reason in this millennial year to go forward from this
48th National Prayer Breakfast with hope, ready to serve God with
gladness by transforming these good beginnings into America's
next Great Spiritual Awakening—one that will secure the moral
future of our nation and raise up the quality of life of our people.
"Let your light shine before others," Jesus said, "so that they may
see your good works and give glory to your Father in heaven"
[Matt. 5:16].[41]

Lieberman's rhetoric did not change much after he was selected as
Gore's vice president. In his August 27, 2000, communication at the
Fellowship Chapel in Detroit he reiterated that America needs "a new
spiritual awakening."[42] He reassured his listeners that that he would
help find "a place for faith in America's public life."[43] He lamented
the fact that religious values and institutions had been banished from
the public sphere.[44] Most famously he averred that "the Constitution
guarantees freedom *of* religion, not freedom *from* religion."[45]

Beholden to a rather dissimilar interpretation of the Constitution,
the Anti-Defamation League was now poised to make its entrance
into the fray. On August 28, Howard Berkowitz and Abraham Foxman, national chairman and national director of the ADL, respec-
tively, sent Lieberman a letter. "We believe," they wrote, "that there
is a point at which the emphasis on religion in a political campaign
becomes inappropriate and even unsettling in a religiously diverse
society such as ours."[46] "Appealing to voters along religious lines,"
said the ADL, was "contrary to the American ideal" and a tactic that
"risks alienating the American people."[47]

Why an organization devoted to combating anti-Semitism would
mix it up with a widely respected Orthodox Jewish candidate for vice
president is an episode that must abound in a delicious DC backstory.
Publicly, anyhow, Foxman's concerns were couched strictly in terms
of the wall of separation. He later commented that Lieberman's words
give those who want to base American morality on the teachings of
Jesus "the sense that 'if he [Lieberman] can do it, why can't we?
Because we talk about Jesus Christ? So he talks about Moses.'"[48]
Lieberman, performing damage control, responded that he was "a fervent believer in the First Amendment and the separation of church
and state."[49]

It is likely that the Gore-Lieberman campaign's imbroglio with the base weighed heavily on the thinking of John Kerry's handlers in 2004. They seem to have drawn the conclusion—and this was unequivocally the wrong conclusion to draw—that they should downplay or avoid questions pertaining to belief. In terms of connecting with religious constituencies, articulating their candidate's faith convictions, and finding ways to connect core Democratic issues with the concerns of believing Americans, the Kerry-Edwards campaign failed miserably.

The missteps are not hard to identify. Even though the "religion gap" was on everyone's minds in 2004, Kerry made his first prolonged attempt to discuss religion, the so-called faith and values speech, *nine days before the election.*[50] The person who coordinated the party's outreach to religious voters, Mara Vanderslice, was hired scarcely seven months before the election.[51] She was outfitted with a staff consisting of one unpaid intern (in comparison with a Republican volunteer network numbering in the tens of thousands).[52] When she was promptly (and predictably) identified as a dangerous leftist by conservative Christian and Republican operatives, no one bothered to defend her.[53] By all objective measures, the grassroots mechanisms of the party were abysmal in comparison to Karl Rove's multipistoned "Jesus machine."[54]

As for the candidate himself, he was notoriously uncomfortable discussing his faith in public. Commentators drew upon the English language's ample stock of words that describe lack of physical and psychological ease when describing his visits to places of worship. Terms such as "uncomfortable," "rigid," "emotionally cool and uninspiring," "insincere," "cold and distant," and "painful to watch" followed him around whenever he engaged in God-talk.[55] Unable, and apparently unwilling, to define his own religious worldview, Kerry allowed his eager opponents to do it for him.[56]

Even prior to the convention in July, there whirled about Kerry a theoretical discussion that would make any political handler cringe. All across America, bishops and parish priests (and journalists) were contemplating, discussing, and writing about the following hypothetical query: Would I, or would I not, deny Communion to this pro-choice, anti–gay marriage amendment presidential candidate if he came to my diocese or church? Not deft enough to outmaneuver a hierarchy that was freefalling from scandals, Kerry's team was left hoping for an even split among Catholic voters. This did not come to pass. A strange footnote to the 2004 election is that a Catholic presidential candidate somehow lost the Catholic vote to a Methodist.[57]

If Kerry's coreligionists were lukewarm on him, it should come as no surprise that white evangelicals were not his greatest fans. This would not be unexpected for any candidate whose NARAL rating was so high. As one journalist described it, Kerry was "more or less your average evangelical's worst nightmare."[58] Indeed, it was only among black mainliners, black evangelicals, and Spanish-speaking ones that Kerry seemed comfortable (and welcome).[59] As his handlers frog-marched him into African American churches, the irony of the situation was not lost upon pundits. Nor was it lost upon Barack Obama, who seems to be skewering Kerry in *The Audacity of Hope*: "Nothing is more transparent than inauthentic expressions of faith—such as the politician who shows up at a black church around election time and claps (off rhythm) to the gospel choir or sprinkles in a few biblical citations to spice up a thoroughly dry policy speech."[60]

In terms of the Bible, Kerry's scriptural sprinkles were conspicuous in the extreme. Every verse he cited seemed to spark a national referendum on his Scripture-citing technique. On March 28, 2004, Kerry appeared at an African American church in St. Louis and exclaimed, "The Scriptures say, 'What does it profit my brethren if some say he has faith but does not have works?' [Jas. 2:14]. When we look at what's happening in America today, where are the works of compassion? Because it's also written, 'Be doers of the word and not hearers only [Jas. 1:22].'" Verbatim quotes, I have suggested, are rarely a good idea. This citation also prompted a sharp rejoinder from a Bush spokesperson that these remarks were "beyond the bounds of acceptable discourse and a sad exploitation of scripture for political attack."[61]

Granted, the objection of the Bush operative sets new and impressive standards of hypocrisy. Yet it does accurately point to one discursive foul committed by Kerry: the Bible is not to be used in personal criticism on individuals or communities. Kerry, by making disparaging remarks about Bush being a "false prophet" and not resembling the "good Samaritan," deviated from the protocol of "dignity."[62]

That Kerry's use of Scripture was strained goes without saying. At his acceptance speech during the 2004 Democratic convention he proclaimed, "We believe in the family value expressed in one of the oldest Commandments: 'Honor thy father and thy mother.' As President, I will not privatize Social Security. I will not cut benefits."[63] As with all of Kerry's attempts to thump Bible, this one was awkward and forced. Even by a definition of the Good in public oratory that looks not at victory (which Kerry did not achieve) but at the quality of the prose, it failed.

Conclusion: The Democrats' Dilemma

Although it was undoubtedly offered in good faith, the advice that Bill Clinton gave Joe Lieberman was not exceedingly helpful. For starters, Clinton would probably not practice what Joe Lieberman preached. It is unlikely that the forty-first president would ever give a Scripture-drenched address the likes of which Lieberman did at that National Prayer Breakfast. Clinton simply did not need to signal so conspicuously to Christian America that he was a man of faith.

As a white, male Baptist from a region where the Good Book is enmeshed in everyday life, Bill Clinton had preapproved religious credibility in the American heartland. Although not an evangelical himself, the former governor from Arkansas certainly knew how to communicate with them. Contrary to what many blue-staters imagine, conservative Christians do not speak to one another in long strings of biblical citations. Accordingly, it never occurred to Clinton to make his political oratory resemble the sermons of a seventeenth-century Puritan divine.

If the misfortunes of Dean, Lieberman, and Kerry offer lessons to be learned for 2008, then one of them might be summarized as follows: it's hard to win if you are not, sociologically speaking, Bill Clinton or a reasonable facsimile thereof. Oh, how un-Bill-like they all were! All three were New Englanders. All three were northern liberal elites. All could claim Jewish ancestry (but let's leave that aside). All found themselves trying to do God-talk as a means of counteracting a criticism about Democrats—especially white Democrats from above the Mason-Dixon Line—namely, that their party was a bastion of godlessness. And all failed, I think, because God-talk in the United States is articulated in either a southern, Midwestern, or mountain region drawl. These candidates tried to speak a language of politics and religion that was not their own. Forced to express spiritual convictions in an unfamiliar idiom, they were vulnerable to the charge of shameless pandering. Not helping matters was their tendency to cite texts that were not plausibly part of their non–election year religious reading list. Was the book of Job really so central to Dean's religious worldview? Was the epistle of James really on the tip of Kerry's tongue? Was the New Testament a document that could conceivably shape the profoundest convictions of Joe Lieberman? This leads me to state another important rule of Scripture citation: *Unless you are a professionally trained actor, your confessions of faith had better be predicated on texts and doctrines that are really part of your religious thinking.*[64] Lieberman, Dean, and Kerry were all vulnerable to the charge of having the audacity —the utter audacity!—to use religion to garner votes.

But it wasn't only religious America that found their God-talk problematic. The notion of a Democratic "religion gap" is a tad simplistic. The party's challenge consists not only of bonding with religious constituencies *but in balancing religious constituencies and secular ones.* Every time that a Democrat cites a psalm, invokes a sura, or hums a few bars from a Negro spiritual, rest assured that an immense groan of dissatisfaction emerges from the collective abdomen of the party's secular wing. The Lieberman saga is an extended meditation, an instructional video, about what happens when nonbelievers and church/state separatists feel slighted. The successful Democratic presidential candidate, then, has a job to do. This thankless task consists of keeping both secular *and* religious America happy.

Keeping secularists happy, incidentally, is not a task that George W. Bush's handlers need to lose sleep over. Bush and candidates like him know that they will never carry the ACLU vote. And since at this point in American history this vote does not seem particularly lucrative, then *tant pis* for the ACLU. Soon I will wonder aloud if the Democrat Party itself may be asking whether it is time to say *tant pis* to part of its secular constituency and show this small slice of the base the door.

Do I mean to say that the only Democrat who can win a national election must be a non-northerner who either is an evangelical or knows how to dialogue with them? Not exactly, but a successful candidate had better know (or learn) the prevailing language in which American God-talk gets done. As we are about to see, this will certainly be the case in 2008.

Chapter 6

The Democrats, the Bible, and the Secularists

On the Trail of the God Vote

> *I think we make a mistake when we fail to acknowledge the power of faith in the lives of the American people, and so avoid joining a serious debate about how to reconcile faith with our modern, pluralistic democracy.*
>
> Barack Obama, *The Audacity of Hope: Thoughts on Reclaiming the American Dream*

*I*f the Democrats lose the upcoming presidential race it will set a standard of electoral futility unequalled in the twentieth century. It would mean that in the nearly four-and-a-half decades between the inauguration of Richard Nixon and the end of the next term (1969–2013) the party of Carter and Clinton will have occupied the White House for exactly twelve years.

Even though the law of averages suggests that something stands to change in 2008, party strategists are not leaving this to fate. Victory will be earned, according to many, through *faith*. Empirical support for this contention has been generously provided by Democratic triumphs in the midterm elections of 2006. A few examples come to mind. Vowing to be guided by "biblical principles," ordained Methodist minister Ted Strickland defeated a Scripture-toting evangelical conservative and became governor of Ohio.[1] Pro-life Catholic Robert Casey Jr. defeated pro-life Catholic Rick Santorum in Pennsylvania's Senate race.[2] Southern Baptist Heath Shuler, who won a congressional seat in North Carolina, never hesitated to talk about God and religion on the campaign trail. He even reminded America that "living consistently with the teachings of the Bible works in all aspects of life."[3]

These outcomes suggest that successful candidates must have a clear and compelling message about their personal beliefs. Viable aspirants must also be able to articulate a role for religion in American public life.[4] This year's Democratic frontrunners understand this well. Faith-based PR firms are being hired.[5] Policy positions are incorporating "recognizably biblical language."[6] High-profile prayer groups are being joined. Traditional party views on church/state separation and abortion are being tweaked and revamped.[7]

Former Clinton press secretary Mike McCurry described these developments in words so sincere that one feels instinctively compelled to read them ironically: "There is something of a Great Awakening happening among many Democratic political operatives."[8] But before these operatives start pitching the revival tent, so to speak, they need to think about the secularists.

Ah yes, the secularists! Is there a more beguiling constituency in our nation's politics? Do clouds of invective and confusion hang around any group more than they? What role do they play in the Democratic Party? How many of them are there? And what the heck is a secularist, anyway? Once these questions are answered we will better understand the unique challenges and opportunities that confront this year's crop of Democratic presidential hopefuls.

The Problem of the Secular

As befits a party experiencing a Great Awakening, the Democrats are eager to share the good news of their faith in God with their fellow Americans. Their fellow Americans, however, may not be receptive to the message. This is due to the widespread misconception that Democrats loathe religion, if not God Himself. "How is it," asked one former Clinton official, that Republicans have convinced America "that they are the party of the religious and the Democrats the party of the secular?"[9] How is it indeed?

Some of the wounds are self-inflicted. Michael Dukakis's referring to himself as a "card-carrying member of the ACLU," only to have George H. W. Bush concur with that assessment on a daily basis during the 1988 election, was ill advised.[10] Nor has the party's tendency to respond with NRA-like tenacity to any microbreach of the wall of separation been helpful. But for the most part, the association has emerged from a relentless campaign of misinformation. For years Republican operatives, conservative Christians, and right-wing shock pundits have tarred the Democrats as elitists, nihilists, and cultured despisers of religion.[11]

With less hyperbole, some scholars have noted this association as well. In a widely cited article entitled "Our Secularist Democratic Party," political scientists Louis Bolce and Gerald De Maio identify the McGovern presidential candidacy as marking a new fault line in American political culture. It was in 1972, they argue, that nonbelievers began infiltrating the party en masse.[12] When their "putsch" had been accomplished, the ranks of secularists had swelled greatly, so much so that their prominence among Democrats is now every bit as significant as that of conservative Christians among Republicans.[13]

The notion of a "secularist Democratic Party" is intriguing, though it needs to be carefully qualified. Bolce and De Maio, as do many pundits and pollsters, *equate secularism solely with nonbelief.* But if we tally up the number of atheists, agnostics, and the unchurched in the party, it becomes clear that the Democrats are *not* secularist in that particular sense. In other words, it is patently false that the majority of the party is composed of the godless.

A 2004 survey indicated that a mere 17 percent of those who identified themselves as Democrats professed no religious affiliation.[14] Bill Clinton's former pollster, Stanley Greenberg, set the number at roughly 15 percent.[15] Political scientist Geoffrey Layman studied data on delegates to Democratic National Conventions between the years 1972 and 1992. His findings demonstrate that the proportion of secularists spiked in 1972, comprising 21 percent of the delegates. The figure dipped to 14 percent in 1988 and rose to about 16 percent in 1996.[16]

Note to Republicans: by no conceivable statistical measure can the Democrats be described as a party of godlessness. Barack Obama's famous comment about worshiping "an awesome God in the Blue States" was not only a rhetorical masterstroke—it had the added advantage of being true.[17] As Amy Sullivan observed in 2004, "More than 60 percent of Democratic voters attend Church several times a month and 85 percent say that religion is an important part of their lives."[18] That so few in America are aware of this is a tribute to Republican spin techniques and Democratic incompetence.[19]

Bolce and De Maio, for their part, overestimate the prevalence of atheists and agnostics in the party. They may be on to something, however, when they point to the disproportional influence wielded by these nonbelievers. Democrats with secular worldviews, they argue, are entrenched in the elite newsrooms of America, such as those of the *New York Times* and the *Washington Post*.[20] To this I would add that the irreligious are overrepresented among America's artistic and intellectual elite. So although their numbers may be small, nonbelievers retain a significant ability to shape public opinion, if not party policies.

But to conceptualize secularism *exclusively* as nonbelief is to misunderstand the term itself. Secularism, as I noted in the introduction, can also refer to a view that opposes any sort of entanglement between government and religion. People who adhere to such a view need not be godless. So let us rethink our definitions. A secularist can be (1) a nonbeliever in favor of rigid church/state boundaries, or (2) a believer in favor of rigid church/state boundaries. (Another type, too idiosyncratic to dwell on but amusing to conjure up, would be a nonbeliever who prefers theocracy.)[21]

It is the second category that I want to focus on here. *Secular believers* comprise a significant, albeit rarely discussed, political constituency. Their ranks include, among others, liberal Catholics, Jews, and Muslims, most of whom adhere to Professor Berlinerblau's Law: *Religious groups with little or no chance of establishing their own religion as the religion of the state will strenuously oppose, on principle, all efforts to establish a religion of the state.*

Joining these "secularly religious," as I call them, are many mainline Protestants as well as some conservative Christian groups whose historical memories and/or creedal beliefs discourage them from descending into the profane world of politics. All of those just mentioned are "values voters" of a sort. But they will contest any attempt by the federal government to impose religious values on them. They thus share with that other secular constituency (i.e., nonbelievers) a disdain for trespasses on the wall of separation.

Of course, there are more than a few *nonsecularists* in the electorate as well. They want more, not less, religion in the schools, courts, and workplaces. This is not to claim that they are in favor of theocracy per se but that they feel religion has been unjustly purged from the nation's public life. While winning this group outright is probably impossible for Democrats, sluicing off a few votes here and there would seem within the realm of possibility. This can only occur if their candidates do not come across as hostile to religion. So the goal for the party in 2008 is to avoid a Kerry-like collapse among nonsecular evangelicals (Kerry lost 78 percent of their vote!) while scoring big among the secularly religious.[22] Atheists and agnostics, we shall see, are a small and unreliable constituency. There is then no use to pander to these highly unpopular nonbelievers in rhetoric or policy formation.

In the preceding remarks I have delineated three distinct groups: (1) nonreligious secularists (whose numbers are small), (2) religious secularists (whose numbers are large), and (3) nonsecularists (whose numbers are also large). So what does this all mean for the Democrats in 2008? It means that religious secularists, be they Democrats, undecideds, or Republicans, need to be wooed. It means that a viable presidential candidate will need to run on a platform that proclaims something to the effect of *"God? Yes! Theocracy? No!"* It means that he or she must try to pluck the low-hanging fruit of disaffected nonsecularists from the Republican vine. And for nonbelievers, it means that for the first time in thirty-six years it may no longer be safe to think of the Democratic Party as their home.

Hillary Clinton: A Lesson in Spiritual Humility

If the foregoing analysis is correct, then the Democratic Party has reason for some election-year optimism. This is because each of its three leading presidential candidates can riff competently—and in some cases masterfully—on the *"God? Yes! Theocracy? No!"* theme. Better yet, all of the frontrunners have crafted above-average to very-good narratives of personal faith. This could plausibly help siphon votes from "swing evangelicals" (i.e., nonsecularists) that are Democrat-curious.

How things have changed! Around Iowa Caucus time, the party always seems enthralled by candidates whose religious street credibility is dubious. Of the three frontrunners in January 2004 (John Kerry, Howard Dean, and John Edwards), two reeked of northeastern liberalism. In January 2000, the effortlessly pious Al Gore vied with Bill Bradley, whose faith commitments were always difficult to discern. In 1992, Southern Baptist Bill Clinton found himself comprising one smiling panel in the strange triptych that featured Paul Tsongas and Jerry Brown (whose campaign manager was rumored to be an ex-Maoist).

But unless something unexpected happens in 2008, the Democrats are assured of nominating a candidate who will be immune to charges of godlessness. Hillary Clinton, Barack Obama, and John Edwards each have credible biographies of belief. No one will need to beg and cajole them, a la John Kerry, to elaborate upon their personal religious convictions. As for appealing to religious secularists, each endorses a "commonsense" view of church/state separation, which differs markedly from the absolutist position that tends to characterize northeastern liberals. Indeed, this *rhetorical* shift to "lite" readings of the First Amendment is one of the major stories of this campaign. Whether it will actually affect the candidates' policy prescriptions is doubtful, but it remains to be seen.

Like her two Democratic competitors, Clinton combines a discourse of spirituality with one of spiritual humility. "Spiritual humility"—or as I prefer to call it, "false reluctance"—entails a refusal to aggressively import one's specific beliefs into the legislative arena. Why? Because God is so big, and I am so small. Clinton expressed this sentiment expertly in her book *It Takes a Village and Other Lessons Children Teach Us*:

> Religion is about God's truth, but none of us can grasp that truth absolutely, because of our own imperfections and limitations. We are only children of God, not God. Therefore, we must not attempt to fit God into little boxes, claiming that He supports this or that political position. This is not only bad theology; it marginalizes God.[23]

When they are at their worst, Christian conservatives make God look like something of an inerrant lobbyist, one whose legislative dictates they must obediently ram through the House and Senate. Similarly, religious Republicans rarely express doubts that their pro-life and antihomosexuality positions are consonant with the divine will. They display a confidence in their readings of God's writ that verges on arrogance.

Democratic religious rhetoric, in contrast, rarely claims acquaintance with the deity's inscrutable designs. Since they possess spiritual humility, Democrats are reluctant to equate their policy positions with those of God. And by a marvelous coincidence, their reluctance to do so meshes perfectly with the party's fundamental reading of the First Amendment! As Clinton puts it, "When public power is put behind specific religious views or expressions, it might infringe upon the companion freedom the First Amendment guarantees us to choose our own religious beliefs, including the right to choose to be non-religious."[24]

The difference between Hillary Clinton and John Kerry on this issue, incidentally, is nugatory. Both want to keep religion out of the business of state. Both say no to theocracy. Yet with his equivocations and his refusal to speak about faith, Kerry was perceived (or misperceived) as saying no to God as well. His objection to bringing religious ideas into government was predicated on a political conviction. Clinton, by contrast, has positioned herself to defend church/state separation by reference to a *religious* conviction. It is precisely because she holds God in such awe that she would never dare speak so confidently on His behalf.

A tensile position such as this only works when the candidate in question comes across as authentically religious. For more than a decade Clinton has tried to foreground her religious credentials. She has spoken about lifelong, unshakeable convictions grounded in the Methodist tradition. She has described her childhood family thusly: "We talked with God, walked with God, ate, studied, and argued with God."[25] She fondly recalls her membership in the First Methodist Church in Park Ridge, Illinois. Her experiences there "opened my eyes and heart to the needs of others and helped instill a sense of social responsibility rooted in my faith." It was here that Clinton attended Bible classes and her mother taught Sunday school.[26]

Part of a credible "faith narrative" for a presidential candidate consists of having a "spiritual mentor." At First Church Clinton met the man who would later play this role for her: the Reverend Don Jones.[27] Viable frontrunners also accentuate personal piety. To this end the senator from New York casually mentioned in 2005 that she has "always been a praying person."[28] In her 2003 memoir, *Living History*, she revealed that she and her husband prayed after George H. W. Bush conceded defeat in 1992.[29] During the Whitewater investigation, what

Clinton calls "the stresses of 1993 and 1994," she avidly read "my Bible and other books about religion and spirituality."[30] During the Monica Lewinsky affair, understandably, everyone from her mentor, to her prayer group, to the Dalai Lama tended to her spiritual well-being.[31]

Journalist Michael Tomasky, in an insightful study of the (first?) Clinton-Giuliani matchup in New York, suggests that she belongs to the tradition of "nineteenth century women's-movement reformer[s]" whose "impulses were rooted firmly in Scripture."[32] It seems clear that the Bible figures in both her cultural and personal history. She has let it be known, for instance, that she packs a Bible on the campaign trail and reads commentaries on the Scriptures.[33] Like all savvy candidates, Clinton has never been guilty of the error of overthumping. Her references to Scripture are uniformly sparse and "dignified."[34]

But on those rare occasions when she does invoke the Good Book, her citations are deployed with laser-guided precision. Her recent critique of President Bush's immigration bill is a good example: "It is certainly not in keeping with my understanding of the Scripture because this bill would literally criminalize the Good Samaritan and probably Jesus himself."[35] This remark has been discussed far and wide, but no one of yet has pointed to the preamble. Her reference to "my understanding" accentuates her modesty. It also indicates the aforementioned reluctance of the spiritually humble to extract *the* truth from Scripture.

As do many Democrats, Clinton argues that the Republicans have misunderstood the Bible's priorities. Speaking in 2003 at Tufts University, she intoned, "No one can read the New Testament of our Bible without recognizing that Jesus had a lot more to say about how we treat the poor than most of the issues that were talked about in this election."[36] That Jesus and Paul had little to say on the specific subjects of abortion or homosexuality is unequivocally true, and many Democrats have exploited this argument to good end.

She often recites James 2:26 to her staff: "Faith without deeds is dead."[37] These usages of Scripture are sensible and well orchestrated. What remains to be seen is if Clinton's hard work in depicting herself as a pious person will outweigh or neutralize the negative views about her that certain sections of the electorate hold. Her handlers must also understand that "she lacks the ability to discuss comfortably her faith and how it has informed her political persona."[38] In terms of reaching out to religious voters, be they secularists or nonsecularists, this is her greatest challenge, especially since her opponents in the primaries will ooze with considerably more religious vitality than she does.

Barack Obama: Master of Religious Imaging

Of all the presidential hopefuls, Democrat or Republican, none approaches the question of religion with as much intelligence and verve as Barack Obama.[39] When other frontrunners do God-talk their remarks typically parrot the sentiments of their pastors, handlers, or focus groups. The junior senator from Illinois, by contrast, has thought originally about the role of belief in his life and that of the nation. His willingness to tackle theological questions in a reasoned and even detached manner is rivaled among politicians only by Al Gore. The difference is that Obama is edgy. Al Gore is not.

His handlers probably wish he weren't so edgy. But first let's concentrate on the positives. A combination of unusual life experiences and a spry intellect has endowed Obama with the ability to connect with a lot of different people. Anyone who has read his *Dreams from My Father: A Story of Race and Inheritance* can only marvel at how many worlds he has glimpsed and how many religious (and irreligious) possibilities he has engaged.[40] This is a candidate who, on the basis of personal observation, can connect with Muslims, atheists, born-agains, substance abusers, senators, the working class, mainline Protestants, moms and dads, cigarette smokers, Hawaiians, African Americans, Middle Americans, lawyers, Kenyans, the Harvard set, Indonesians, and black evangelicals.

Not to be forgotten, of course, are white evangelicals. Obama has chided his own party—and chiding Democrats is something of a hobby for him—for not reaching out to them.[41] This raises the question of whether red-staters will vote for a candidate who is black and blue. It does not seem fair to automatically dismiss the possibility that conservative white Christians would support a qualified African American presidential nominee. In a head-to-head confrontation between, let's say, a Mormon such as Mitt Romney and a Protestant such as Obama, I would assume that religion would trump race. Perhaps a more significant impediment to white evangelical support is

Obama's membership in the United Church of Christ, one of the most politically liberal Protestant denominations.

Of course, the Democrats' rising star does not have to carry the evangelical vote. He just has to staunch the party's recent hemorrhaging. One conservative Christian pastor who was chagrined by Obama's positions on abortion conceded, "I wouldn't vote for him. . . . But if we had to have a Democrat, I'd like to have a Democrat like him."[42] This remark signals an opening. As we shall see in chapter 7, the Republicans may field a candidate who will be wholly unacceptable to many conservative Christians.

Obama *does* have to carry the religious secularists that compose the party's base. He also needs to appeal to constituencies that overlap with them: Catholics and mainline Protestants. To satisfy all customers, he must engage in a complex balancing act. The senator has to come off as a man of faith but not as a theocrat. He has to distance himself from extreme left-wing positions on church and state, without raising fears that he will lay a finger on the wall of separation. Judging from his rhetoric, he appears to have concluded that either nonbelieving secularists would never dare abandon him, or that they are simply not worth his time. His remarks are geared toward mollifying Americans of faith.

"The Democratic Party," he writes in *The Audacity of Hope*, "has become the party of reaction. . . . In reaction to religious overreach, we equate tolerance with secularism, and forfeit the moral language that would help infuse our policies with a larger meaning." Elsewhere he opines, "Not every mention of God in public is a breach in the wall of separation." And again: "secularists are wrong when they ask believers to leave their religion at the door before entering the public square."[43]

The Democratic script for 2008 demands that all presidential aspirants depict a character whose code name might be "Master of Church/State Equipoise." He or she must display religious exuberance (with an eye toward religious Americans in general and swing evangelicals in particular), *all the while* showing a principled willingness to tamp that exuberance down (with an eye toward religious secularists). Through a discourse of spiritual humility, Hillary Clinton assures the party's base that she will never slouch toward theocracy. Barack Obama makes the same point by dwelling on the concept of *doubt*. This, he suggests, is a quality of great American leaders, such as Abraham Lincoln, who was "wracked with self-doubt," and Martin Luther King Jr., who, similarly, "was a man frequently wracked with doubt."[44]

This self-questioning impulse, argues Obama, is grounded in the classical theology of the black church. This institution taught him that "faith doesn't mean that you don't have doubts, or that you relinquish your hold on this world."[45] Speaking of his religious conversion, he notes, "The questions I had didn't magically disappear. But kneeling beneath the cross on the South Side of Chicago, I felt God's spirit beckoning me."[46]

Why should religious secularists trust him with their votes? Because doubt is the braking mechanism, the internal check-and-balance ensuring that he will not trespass upon the sacred principle of separation (too, he taught constitutional law at the University of Chicago for a decade, and this may have endowed him with proper respect for the Wall's impregnability). Obama is a gifted innovator; he has fashioned a persona that permits him to wear his religion on his sleeve while simultaneously granting him the space to pull back and contest whatever aspect of faith suits his fancy under the pretext of doubt. This is state-of-the-art religious imaging.

But, in more concrete terms, how exactly does one go about balancing a desire to infuse public life with religion with a commitment to separation? This is no petty query. Traumatic memories of theocratic rule in Old Europe may just be one of the rawest wounds in the Western political psyche. The Democrats are bound by recent tradition to keep faith concerns out of the affairs of the state. Yet their oratory of late suggests that they are slacking off.

Like Clinton, Obama says little about how to bring public faith into American government without undermining the core beliefs of both his party and his nation. All he offers is the following pithy explanation: "What our deliberative, pluralistic democracy does demand is that the religiously motivated translate their concerns into universal, rather than religion-specific values. It requires that their proposals must be subject to argument and amenable to reason."[47] This sounds pleasant enough, but it is not excessively persuasive. When antiabortion candidates translate a reading of Psalm 139 into an argument regarding the sanctity of life, they have effectively made a religion-specific value into a universal one. They view their proposals about the rights of the unborn as eminently reasonable.

Few are the believers who doubt that their own parochial concerns aren't universal values. While some liberal groups (e.g., Unitarians, Reform Jews, progressive Catholics) may be able to question the applicability of their own faith concerns to society writ large, religious traditionalists tend not to lose sleep over such matters. The principle of separation has been upheld so rigidly, even maniacally, precisely because traditionalists often lack that self-critical impulse. In any case, bringing religion into American public life is a good deal more complicated than the senator suggests.

Of course, one need not overanalyze Obama's public invocations of the Bible and religion. They are strictly rhetorical. He has not grounded any policy position on a scriptural verse. His uses of the text are strictly symbolic. When announcing his candidacy, he lightly echoed Luke 11:17 in noting, "Divided, we are bound to fail," and he spoke of a "new birth of freedom on this earth."[48] After announcing his candidacy he "implicitly compar[ed] himself to Joshua."[49] At a commemoration for Martin Luther King Jr., he referred to the civil rights leader as "Moses" and cited Micah 6:8 as a prescription for righteous behavior.[50]

Obama is a champion of the hermeneutics of emphasis discussed in chapter 1. The Bible's stress on poverty indicates to him what our priorities should be. In reference to homosexuality, he writes that he is not "willing to accept a reading of the Bible that considers an obscure line in Romans [1:26–27] to be more defining of Christianity than the Sermon on the Mount."[51]

On one occasion, he has actually discussed his own hermeneutical approach to the sacred text: "When I read the Bible, I do so with the belief that it is not a static text, but the Living Word and that I must be continually open to new revelations—whether they come from a lesbian friend or a doctor opposed to abortion."[52] Though it will not endear him to many conservative Christians, this is about as shrewd an interpretive strategy as a politician could possibly advocate. Obama's hermeneutic of flexibility grants him miles of interpretive space. Once again, he has licensed himself to change his mind, to read the Bible in accordance with the demands of the day (and his polling figures).

But for all of his virtues, Obama does not lack for negatives. His spiritual mentor, unlike Hillary Clinton's, will certainly be of interest to the opposition research divisions of Republican (and Democratic?) opponents. The Reverend Jeremiah A. Wright is by all accounts a talented fulminator who is full of opinions on racial injustice in America.[53] He also is a proponent of liberation theology, and one could easily apply the tag "radical" to him, as anti-Obama operatives have undoubtedly already noted. Convincing the public that the junior senator from Illinois is not too far to the left will constitute one of his handlers' most complex tasks.

And then there is the book. By the middling standards of political memoir, *Dreams from My Father* establishes Obama as the genre's Nobel laureate. He is a decent stylist who can push a narrative along and even employ a symbol or two. The problem is that Republican attack dogs are not always kind to the prerogatives of artistic license. This autobiography provides them with targets of opportunity. First, the work seethes with a lingering anger at white privilege, both nationally and globally. One wonders how Obama's disquisitions on racial and economic injustice will play in white Middle America. Compounding the difficulties is a muted admission of using marijuana, alcohol, and "a little blow" during his college days.[54] Professor Berlinerblau's Second Law: *When a politician admits to having done something bad, rest assured that someone else will pop up and claim that he or she did something much worse.*

John Edwards: A Decency That Shapes Our Ends?

The Democratic Party's efforts to exorcise its godless image seem to be proceeding apace. But every now and then, the old spirits of nonbelief come back to haunt them. Consider the recent difficulties experienced by John Edwards.

In late January 2007 the Edwards campaign hired a few hip, young political bloggers to advocate for their candidate. On the surface, this would appear to have been a sound strategic decision. As demonstrated by Howard Dean in 2004 and by the success of outfits such as MoveOn.org, there are scads of Web-trawling American voters aged eighteen to thirty-five who tend to swing Democratic.[55] It also made perfect sense for Edwards to enlist individuals beholden to progressive political agendas. His positions on the war in Iraq, poverty, and the environment, among others, bear affinities to those held by various leftist coalitions. Enlisting youthful inhabitants of the blogosphere to help establish these connections seemed like a superlative idea.

In retrospect, it wasn't, and please allow me to reiterate a point just made in relation to Senator Obama's literary endeavors: the political repels the aesthetic. Ways of speaking (and thinking) that are edgy, hip, fashionable, and even creative must be avoided at all costs in national elections. The Edwards team failed to understand this. Nor did their vetting process perform optimally, for it quickly became apparent that two of the individuals whom they had hired had left behind a cyberflume of profanity-laced, antireligious postings.

The young women in question were both bloggers and nonbelievers—a flammable combination if there ever was one.[56] Atheist and agnostic culture has always reveled in antireligious ribaldry. The blogosphere, with its absence of restraints, accountability, peer review, and so forth, tends to encourage "frank expression." Accordingly, a nonbeliever let loose in cyberspace tends to say the damndest things—things like this: "What if Mary had taken Plan B after the Lord filled her with his hot, white, sticky Holy Spirit." And this: "What don't you lousy motherf—ers understand about keeping your noses out of our britches, our beds, and our families."[57]

These indiscreet musings did not escape the attention of conservative political watchdogs. The president of the Catholic League for Religious and Civil Rights issued a statement to the press on February 6, 2007, highlighting these remarks and others. He concluded as follows: "John Edwards is a decent man who has had his campaign tarnished by two anti-Catholic vulgar trash-talking bigots. He has no choice but to fire them immediately."[58]

All of these ructions gave Edwards's handlers a good opportunity to put their crisis management skills to the test.[59] After remaining silent for a few days, the candidate, who had never previously met the bloggers, announced that he was "personally offended" by "the tone and the sentiment" of their earlier writings. "Everyone is entitled to their opinion," he continued, "but that kind of intolerant language will not be permitted from anyone on my campaign, whether it's intended as satire, humor, or anything else." He did not dismiss the women because he believed "in giving everyone a fair shake."[60]

Although experienced under the combat conditions of national campaigns, the Edwards team obviously did a poor job in researching their new hires. Of course, the very thought of conscripting atheist bloggers to write for a modern political campaign is misguided. One perceptive writer who turned down an offer to work for Edwards recalls her astonishment that she would be permitted to continue posting on her own site while employed by the campaign: "A bunch of internet staffers with private blogs sounded like a disaster waiting to happen."[61]

An error was also made, I think, in the handling of the crisis. Given the electoral insignificance of snarky, youthful nonbelievers, the cruel Machiavellian logic of politics dictates that Edwards should have fired the bloggers immediately and, if at all possible, had their citizenship revoked. As it turns out, the two young women resigned quite gracefully and articulately made sense of their bizarre predicament.[62] In any case, their saga should serve as yet another indication of what the future holds for nonbelievers in the Democratic Party.[63]

In terms of religious imaging this was a misstep, and an uncharacteristic one at that. When it comes to connecting with large faith-constituencies, the former senator from North Carolina may have more going for him than any other presidential candidate. As the president of the Catholic League tacitly confirmed, Edwards exudes decency. He is far more emotive and at ease speaking about faith than is Hillary Clinton. True, he lacks the dash and headiness of Obama. But in a country that has shown itself to be impervious to the charms of complex theological speculation, that could be an advantage. Edwards comes across as a sincere, simple, down-to-earth Christian. His almost folksy charm will endear him to Middle Americans who can look beyond his vast personal wealth.

Edwards has an air-tight narrative of faith and will never be burdened with the suspicions that bedeviled his running mate in 2004. Raised "in a very Christian home and a Southern Baptist Church," his religious street credibility is impeccable (Edwards later joined the United Methodist Church). As with Barack Obama, he speaks of a moment when he reaffirmed the values that he now holds. The period after the death of his sixteen-year-old son in 1996 was one when his faith "came roaring back." Stressing that religion impacts him on a daily basis, he talks of "a personal relationship with the Lord so that I pray daily" and extols the value of "dominant day-to-day living faith."[64] The humility, the easygoing tributes to Christ, the themes of rebirth, prayer, and placing trust in God each and every day, will be very appealing to white evangelicals.[65]

An interesting hybrid, John Edwards is. As a Dixie Democrat he is fluent in the regional vernacular of the South and can also speak that related national faith dialect known as "red state." At the same time, he advocates a progressive agenda that will be popular with liberals. With his mea culpa on the war in Iraq and his stress on poverty, he could carry the traditional Democratic constituencies of mainline Protestants and liberal Catholics. By not firing the bloggers discussed above, his handlers may have concluded—correctly, for all I know—that nonbelievers will still vote for him.

If nonbelievers do vote for him, or for any of the Democrats discussed here, they will do so hesitantly. "I don't think," Edwards avers, "separation of church and state means you have to be free from your faith." Repeating Joseph Lieberman's line that "freedom of religion does not mean freedom from religion," Edwards assures his listeners that he would never impose his faith on others. In one of the few instances where he tries to illustrate, Edwards observes that he would not permit a public school teacher to lead a class prayer. He immediately finesses the point by adding that "allowing time for children to pray for themselves, to themselves" is acceptable.[66] As with Clinton and Obama, this is not a serious or carefully thought-out argument. Come to think of it, it makes no sense at all. It is a rhetorical ploy, a form of religious imaging that will most likely have little impact on his actual policies.[67]

When Edwards invokes the Bible he makes the standard argument that its central theme is poverty. This is one of his major concerns, what he refers to as the country's "great moral issue."[68] He will need to limn the ample resources provided by Scripture on this issue more industriously in the coming months. For now he makes general observations, such as this one: "If you took every reference to taking care of the least of these out of the Bible, there would be a pretty skinny Bible. And I think as a Christian, and we as a nation, have a moral responsibility to do something about this."[69]

In a rather curious citation, he seems to invoke a biblical passage only to reject its implications: "For you have the poor with you always, and whenever you wish you may do them good; but Me you do not have always"(Mark 14:7). Edwards reads this not as a prescription but a challenge: "We know that the Bible tells us that the poor will always be with us. Some people hear that as an excuse for inaction. I believe it is a call for us to act and a call for us to serve. My family and my faith didn't teach me to turn my back on a neighbor in need."[70]

When asked by an interviewer what aspects of American life would most outrage Jesus, Edwards responded, "I think that Jesus would be disappointed in our ignoring the plight of those around us who are suffering and our focus on our own selfish, short-term needs. I think he would be appalled, actually."[71] This use of the Bible exemplifies the Good as defined in the previous chapter. It is vague, vapid, and foolproof. After all, what type of Christian would demur and insist that Jesus is positively elated by the way America treats the poor? Yet, the idea of a Democrat measuring the nation's moral standing by reference to what a divine being would think indicates how much the party has changed.

Conclusion: Advice for Jilted Nonbelievers

In light of the preceding analysis, perhaps nonbelievers should consider experiencing a Great Awakening of their own. At best, the Democrats are trying to move atheists and agnostics backstage. At worst, the party is preparing to give them the old heave-ho. We have now familiarized ourselves with the relentless God-talk of Clinton, Obama, and Edwards. We have also noted an emerging oratorical fad: the candidates' tendency to blur church/state lines that were previously drawn quite sharply.

The good old days of McGovern and Dukakis are over. It is now high time that the godless reassess their relationship to the party without letting emotions and cheap nostalgia fog their analysis, for the sad truth is—to paraphrase the title of a recent self-help book for young women—that the Democrats just aren't that into them.

And why should they be? The party's lack of interest may be attributed to the emergence of a large, well-organized, and more electorally attractive evangelical movement. In addition, a general, nationwide upswing in religious fervor has forced the Democrats to rethink their policies and oratory. Politicians—can you blame them?—follow the votes, and the votes seem to be situated in that region of America that is under God. But the abandonment of nonbelievers can't be blamed entirely on the renascence of faith-based constituencies. The irreligious and areligious, to be perfectly honest, must incur some of the blame for their marginality as well.

It would be helpful, though, if they could at least acknowledge their marginality. Instead, many nonbelievers are convinced that their numbers are surging, that they are a political force to be reckoned with. The naturalist philosopher Daniel Dennett, for example, came to the conclusion that there were 27 million "Brights" in the United States.[72] Raising the ante, the Secular Coalition of America proclaimed that 63 million nontheists reside in this country (had they included my category of religious secularists, they surely would have identified one billion fellow travelers in the United States alone).[73] Some journalists speak of secularists as the fastest growing religious group in America.[74]

If these claims sound inaccurate and bloated—and they are—this has to do with the confusion that surrounds the term "secular."[75] The exaggerated figures arise from very dubious readings of survey data. To achieve these high tallies one must combine very different categories of secularists. Thus, those who tell a demographer they are atheists or agnostics are indiscriminately lumped together with those who claim no religious affiliation, or no religious preference.[76] The mistake lies in assuming that all of the aforementioned constitute a unified group, when in fact *they are better described as an aggregate*. That is, they share one broad characteristic in common: a lack of affiliation with any particular religion.[77] The aggregate I am describing is anything but a religious group. It has no center, no creed, no rituals, no organizing structure, no self-awareness, no unity. Nothing binds it together in any socially or politically meaningful way.[78]

If we strain out from this aggregate those who have made a deliberate, conscious, and informed decision to either question or not believe in the existence of God, then we can legitimately speak of two groups: atheists and agnostics. Some estimates place their numbers at around 3 percent of the population, or between 8 and 9 million citi-

zens; others have them at around 2 million.[79] Having disabused ourselves of the premise that nonbelievers are some sort of mass movement, we are now prepared to establish blame. For unlike other
statistically marginal groups, such as Jews, the godless somehow
manage to be politically marginal as well.

If atheists and agnostics are expendable to Democrats, then it is
because they are in a state of political disrepair. They are bereft of
effective and recognizable leaders. There is no atheist Jerry Falwell,
or agnostic Al Sharpton. When yet another televangelist lambastes
the godless, there is no secular anti-defamation league to fire off an
outraged press release. Aside from organizations such as the ACLU
and Americans United for Separation of Church and State (neither of
which, significantly, advocates nonbelief), the godless do not have
effective institutions to represent or defend their interests.

As for grassroots organizing, nonbelievers are Goofus to the evangelical Gallant. Insofar as they never congregate anywhere—like a
church—they are difficult to mobilize politically.[80] Lacking skilled
political leaders or political infrastructure or political clout, they tend
to express themselves through words, not political actions. When
nonbelievers get mad they roll up their sleeves and write a letter to
the editor, or a book, or a really hard-hitting post on a Web site
devoted to challenging the historicity of Jesus. Worst of all, evidence
indicates that come Election Day they underperform.[81] Is there any
mystery as to why Democrats are distancing themselves from a tiny,
atomized constituency whose fundamental beliefs about the cosmos
differ radically from those of nine out of ten Americans?

Of course, all's fair in politics, and the question needs to be raised
as to whether nonbelievers need to cling loyally to the Democratic
Party. In a strange twist of fate, they might find more ideologically
acceptable partners among the Republican candidates for the White
House.

Chapter 7

Republicans and Evangelicals

The Limits of Conservative Christian Power?

*Our form of government has no sense unless it is founded in a
deeply felt religious faith, and I don't care what it is.*

Dwight Eisenhower

*Thou fool, that shall say: A Bible, we have got a Bible, and we
need no more Bible. Have ye obtained a Bible save it were by
the Jews?*

The Book of Mormon, 2 Nephi 29:6

*H*ow did this happen? After hundreds—no, thousands—of articles
about the "God gap," about "values voters" being in the pocket of the
GOP, about Karl Rove's preternatural genius for mobilizing conservative Christians, a circumstance prevails that no pundit could have
imagined possible four years ago: not one of the leading Republican
presidential hopefuls in 2008 is particularly attractive to evangelical
leaders. Of course, this presupposes another curious fact: not one of
the leading Republican presidential hopefuls *is* an evangelical.

Somehow the conservative Christian movement has not been able
to convert its demographic and organizational assets into the ability
to promote a viable, homegrown contender for high office. Maybe
this is merely a question of time. It takes time for a new social formation to identify, cultivate, and position its rising stars. It takes time
to steer these aspirants through the countless stations of the presidential cross. Rest assured, by 2012, the latest 2016, the Republican
primaries will abound in God-fearing evangelical candidates, each
more determined than the next to overturn *Roe v. Wade* and provide
us with a Federal Marriage Amendment.

Then again, maybe the movement has peaked. Or it could be that we are hearing the voice of the electorate. Perhaps that other 75 percent of the voting public, the non–conservative Christian majority, is not that keen on evangelical politicians and their biblical worldviews. Ah, America's religious diversity—the secularist's best friend. But the most puzzling thing of all is the current crop of first-tier Republican candidates. Not only are they not evangelicals, but each has neon-light-blinking negatives. For Mitt Romney it is his religion. For John McCain it is past altercations with movement higher-ups. And for Rudy Giuliani it is just about everything.

Yet in spite of what their leaders think, Republican evangelicals tell pollsters that they prefer "America's Mayor" for the party's nomination.[1] Their popularity forces us to engage possibilities not often discussed in the thousands of articles mentioned above. This support for Giuliani and to a lesser extent McCain may reveal the existence of "daylight" between evangelical demagogues (who are suspicious of both men) and much of their rank and file (who seem ready to grace them with their votes). It also challenges a standard assumption of the faith-and-politics pundits. It just may be that many religious voters do not require that their candidates possess impeccable religious credentials.

Rudolph Giuliani: The Perfect Imperfect Catholic

The Bible does not figure prominently in Rudy Giuliani's oratory or policy formation. No major surprise there. Giuliani is a Catholic, and Catholics by intellectual and theological disposition are not given to paroxysms of scriptural citation. As noted earlier, when seeking illumination they are no more likely to consult the Gospels than they are to peruse Augustine, or the latest papal encyclical, or something Father Tonelli mentioned at mass last week.

Geography also explains Giuliani's infrequent invocation of the Good Book. The former United States attorney is a child of New York City and Long Island. In those colorful five boroughs and on the shore, white, Bible-carrying Protestants are rare and exotic birds. His upbringing, therefore, afforded him few opportunities to study their habits. Nor did he get too many more chances during his eight years as mayor of New York City. Dropping Scripture bombs *might* go over well with black Protestants in Harlem and parts of Brooklyn and Queens. But it is best avoided in gay Chelsea, or the Jewish and liberal Upper West Side, or the Latino Sunset Park, or the Caribbean-American and Orthodox-Jewish Crown Heights, or in the hipster-saturated Williamsburg, or the Italian and Irish Staten Island, or the ex-Soviet Brighton Beach, or the Muslim enclaves of the city, not to mention Chinatown.

New York, for all of its cosmopolitanism, is still very much a city of tribes, be they based on religion, ethnicity, ideology, lifestyle, sexual orientation, and so forth. Few of these tribes have the King James as their totem. Since the Bible is far too parochial to function as the spiritual charter of a city as heterogeneous as this one, its mayor cannot overplay the scriptural themes. Aware of this, Giuliani cast himself as a champion of religious pluralism and a defender of standards of public decency. As he noted in 1994, "The condition of diversity—the condition most obvious to any one looking at New York—mandates that we live in respectful disagreement."[2]

All those years serving as chief of tribal New York taught him how to chant in an ecumenical, as opposed to sectarian, dialect. It is safe to say that no other current presidential candidate has had as much hands-on experience governing religious diversity. His performance was generally good, the exception being his dismal relations with African Americans. Giuliani was estranged from this community from almost the moment he took office.

There are perfectly good reasons to expect that he will fail with white evangelicals as well. But canny politician that he is, Giuliani has carefully cultivated an image that may minimize the damage. To begin with, he plays only to his strengths. Riffing on the moral message of Thessalonians is not one of them. But casting himself as a man of strong, lifelong religious convictions certainly is. He will also show voters that he has defended religious sensitivities (including those of the very sensitive evangelicals). Last, his willingness to keep overzealous secularists in their cages will be emphasized.

Good religious imaging, I have suggested, begins with a credible narrative of faith. Giuliani's identification with Catholicism is total—he cannot be comprehended without it. Observers have often noted Giuliani's "monkish intensity" or his "priestlike" demeanor.[3] Having attended a Catholic elementary school, high school, and college, it is no coincidence that he seriously contemplated joining the priesthood as a young man. Unlike John Kerry (who once flirted with a similar career path) Giuliani did not wait until his presidential run to flaunt his spiritual roots. "The church," he declared in 1994, "has built the road that allows my intellect to traverse the outer reaches of what is comprehensible and, at that point, the church offers a leap of faith to carry me where my intellect cannot go. For me, being a Catholic is not limiting but liberating."[4] His dream of becoming the first Italian-Catholic president also testifies to the centrality of faith and ethnicity to his sense of identity.[5]

Although not a perfect, or even exemplary, Catholic, Giuliani has shown himself to be extraordinarily attuned to the feelings of the Catholic Church. This empathy extends to religious traditionalists of all stripes. During his years of public service he performed acts of religious demagoguery that would have made many a televangelist blush. Most memorably, there was the mixed martial arts combat he engaged in with the Brooklyn Museum over its *Sensation* exhibit in 1999. As he told the press, "It offends me. The idea of, in the name of art, having a city-subsidized building have so-called works of art in which people are throwing elephant dung at the Virgin Mary is sick."[6]

It is likely that Giuliani *was* personally offended by an installation not lacking in anti-Catholic provocations. It did not hurt, of course, to share his pain as publicly as possible prior to his Senate run against Hillary Clinton. As one commentator dryly noted, the whole imbroglio gave Giuliani "his chance to score campaign points with conservative Catholics without the drudgery of a conventional campaign."[7]

The mayor's gift for meshing personal conviction with copper-bar-to-the-teeth New York politicking also came to the fore in a 1998 controversy. This one involved a Latina evangelical substitute teacher who was dismissed for leading sixth-graders in prayer. Coming to her defense, the mayor argued that she should not have been fired. A simple warning, he thought, would have been more appropriate. With his characteristic scathing wit he declared, "Sure, you should not pray in public school. I guess I was a little bit confounded by the fact that we have teachers who have been accused of sex crimes, pedophilia and larceny, who remain hanging around for two, three and four years with very, very vigorous representation."[8]

A few years later, he once again strafed the board of education and unions. In a fundraising letter, he maintained that teachers should be permitted to post the Ten Commandments in their classrooms. The Decalogue, he insisted, is "part of Western civilization. . . . If teachers want to emphasize what is in it and talk about it, there shouldn't be some kind of inquisition that they can't do that."[9]

It is, then, not beyond the realm of the possibility that Giuliani could make inroads among traditional Catholics and Protestants. But in order to do so, he will need to overcome rather conspicuous personal and professional negatives. As for the former, there are marriages gone sour, murky divorces, and well-documented "other women" in his life.[10] Conservative religious voters are not wont to overlook this.[11] Evangelical leader Richard Land—who appears to be mounting an anti-Giuliani crusade—has averred that he would never vote for a man who lied to his wife. Asked about this remark in an interview, Giuliani couched his response in Gospel terms:

> I would suggest that maybe you sort of take a look at the teaching from the Gospel about he without sin not case [*sic*] the first stone [John 8:7]. And the reality is that we're all imperfect. We're all striving as best we can to improve ourselves and to be better. I've made mistakes in my life. I've prayed about them. I've asked for help about them. I try very, very hard to improve myself.[12]

Protestant and Catholic traditionalists will surely be concerned by his close friendships with gay people. The fact that he's been caught at least twice cross-dressing for a party will surely not tickle their puritanical funny bones. But it ensures that Giuliani will supply opponents with more visual materials for negative campaign ads than any presidential contender in American history.[13]

As for the issues, a comment of Herman Badillo's comes leaping to mind: "I don't see how he makes friends with the Christian right wing of the Republican Party."[14] His support of gun control (obligatory for a mayor of New York City) won't make him too many friends in the red states. His refusal to pursue a Federal Marriage Amendment (ditto) is another strike against him. This brings us to the Issue. Like evangelicals, Giuliani is personally and passionately opposed to abortion. But whereas many conservative Protestant politicians believe that their personal religious beliefs must inform, even dictate, their public policy decisions, Giuliani the Catholic has theological resources at his disposal that permit him to separate the two spheres. He thus speaks about enforcing the existing laws of the land and not demonizing those with differing opinions.

Giuliani recently rehearsed these themes at, of all places, Houston Baptist College. Not only did he live to tell about it, but he seemed to have charmed a few in the audience.[15] This was an audacious move on his part, akin to lecturing the NRA about the merits of the Brady Bill, or passing out palm cards at a Gay Pride Parade advertising therapeutic cures for homosexuality. The strategy of "honesty" is risky but not without a certain logic. Knowing that conservative Christians have been promised the repeal of *Roe* many times before, he may be trying to minimize his losses by showing himself to be a "straight talker." On issues of reproductive rights, Giuliani is built to appeal to the American center, as opposed to the Republican base. His objective may not be to win evangelicals but to avoid losing them completely.

In short, we have a candidate who is not an easy sell for conservative Christians. Polls indicate, however, that the rank and file appears receptive to him. Why is this so? For starters, Giuliani is the mayor who slew the beast of liberalism in New York (or, in the opinion of others, he is the mayor who happened to be around as the beast expired from a protracted, self-inflicted malignancy). Some may be optimistically reasoning that if he can nationalize this accomplishment, liberalism as we know it will cease to exist in the United States. Another selling point to evangelicals is his hard line on Islamic terrorism and the leadership he demonstrated in the fall of 2001.

The former mayor also has a reputation of not suffering fools, no matter how powerful they might be. One wonders if conservative Christians—and other citizens—who are exasperated by a nightly parade of anti-American invective on the news, might relish having a president who will defend national honor. How might President Giuliani respond to the latest taunts of Mahmoud Ahmadinejad? What might he say (or do?) were Hugo Chávez of Venezuela to taunt a secretary of state with sexist innuendo on his watch? The mind races.

There may, however, be another explanation for his popularity. It could be that there is something about Giuliani's *flawed* Catholicism that speaks to evangelicals and other religious Americans. He is a shining example of a group I elsewhere labeled the "secularly religious."[16]

This refers to those who are unequivocally devoted and loyal to their religious traditions but do not abide by all of its beliefs and practices. Their church/synagogue/mosque attendance may be shoddy or nonexistent. They may ignore dogmas and practices with which they do not agree. They do not hesitate to question or even criticize their own religious leaders. This is rarely done, however, in an aggressive or confrontational manner. There is no need to. The secularly religious feel very "at home" in their religions, and *they couldn't imagine themselves living anyplace else.* And since the old orthodoxies retain limited power to evict them anyway, histrionics are not necessary. Such are the perks of being a believer in the modern West.

Twice divorced but devoted to his faith, refusing to outlaw abortion but personally in accord with the church's view on the issue, maintaining close friendships with gay people who according to official church teachings are living in sin—Giuliani is a poster-child for the type of person I am describing. My guess is that, with his unshakeable, albeit imperfect relation to his faith, *he resembles most religious Americans.* This may include a sizeable chunk of rank-and-file evangelicals who may not share exactly the same worldview of their national leaders.

John McCain: A History with Evangelicals

I have just proven that it takes much more effort to explain why evangelicals would vote for Rudy Giuliani than why they would not. With John McCain, the reverse would appear to hold true. On paper, in theory, and in a computer-enhanced 3D simulation, the senator from Arizona should do just fine among them. Above all, this is because he seems willing to deliver the goods on the Issue. Save for a few extenuating circumstances, McCain now says that he favors overturning *Roe v. Wade.*[17]

While some mild flip-floppery has been evident in his antiabortion policy (especially during his 2000 run for the presidency), he has been firmly within the pro-life camp for the entire breadth of his political career.[18] The same cannot be said about either Giuliani or Mitt Romney. Driving this point home for an evangelical audience in 2007, the senator helpfully invoked a biblical metaphor: "I certainly think I have done my labor in the vineyards for 24 years. I have a 24-year solid, consistent pro-life voting record."[19]

But there is so much more. The former prisoner of war has voted to retain the reference to God in the Pledge of Allegiance. He has kept an open mind about intelligent design, going so far as to suggest that it might be taught in public schools alongside evolutionary theory.[20] He supports faith-based initiatives and the death penalty. He voted against permitting gay marriage in Arizona, although he is not inclined to take this to the federal level.[21] Regarding human embryonic stem cell research, here too he could do better by evangelicals. He would permit federal funding for research on the so-called spare embryos, though he opposes the creation of embryos for scientific purposes.[22]

But his support for the Issue should make all of that pretty irrelevant. Besides, McCain is far more familiar to evangelicals than either Giuliani or Romney. He is not a Catholic or Mormon but a Protestant, a lifelong Episcopalian. Although he belongs to a mainline denomination, by some remarkable coincidence he worships at a Southern Baptist megachurch in Phoenix.[23] This congregational affiliation offers McCain a symbolic portal to the evangelical community.

This being said, McCain is far less publicly effusive about his faith than his more conservative coreligionists. When it comes to religious oratory, he is the strong and silent type. This has left some evangelicals confused about where he stands.[24] This reluctance to emote about faith in public might be expected from an Episcopalian and a war hero descended from two generations of four-star admirals. It is also to be expected from someone who is not an evangelical and does not share their unique style of testifying to the glory of God.

Yet McCain is a Protestant after all, and if any document plays a spiritual role in his life, it is the Bible. The importance of Scripture becomes evident in his autobiography, *Faith of My Fathers*. There the senator recounts the story of the time he asked one of his Vietnamese captors to procure a Bible for him. Allowed to glance at the Good Book for a few minutes, McCain writes, "I leafed through its tattered pages until I found an account of the Nativity." From there, the future senator copied the passage and delivered remarks on the birth of Jesus on Christmas night for his fellow prisoners.[25] He recollects another experience from his confinement where "I gave a little talk, not a sermon, but a little talk, about the parable of Christ when he was asked should they pay taxes." He has been known to say that his favorite prayer is Psalm 23.[26] Indeed, he reports that he prayed fervently during the half decade he spent in prison. He likens the experience of captivity to that of biblical Job, gallantly acknowledging that other Americans POWs suffered far worse than he did.[27]

A pastor at McCain's Southern Baptist church volunteered that the Senator "is not a biblically versed, mature Christian. He's a novice scripturally." Nevertheless, the cleric adds that he "was convinced he [McCain] had that personal faith."[28] In short, Senator McCain appears to possess the qualities that conservative Christians are looking for. He is a pro-life Republican. He is a war hero. He is an author who lauds (and exudes) courage and character. He is a true patriot and a man of deep, if somewhat muted, faith in God. If you are an evangelical, what's there not to like?

Plenty, apparently. The reasons for his difficulties with religious Republicans are not always transparent. One popular explanation is that the McCain-Feingold Act of 1999 did much to curtail the power of Christian broadcasters to endorse certain candidates. Perhaps this accounts for the nastiness that characterized the senator's campaign swing through South Carolina in 2000. Fresh off an upset victory in New Hampshire, the McCain-for-President team encountered staunch opposition from pro-Bush forces in the Palmetto State. Incensed by a string of attack ads and aspersions on his character (and a drubbing in the primary), McCain went to Virginia Beach and lashed out, referring to Pat Robertson and Jerry Falwell as "agents of intolerance."[29]

The throw-down-the-gauntlet candor of the speech was striking; it almost reads like a declaration of war. Having taken a day to cool off, the notoriously hotheaded McCain calmed himself down, took a deep breath, and then, inexplicably, *proceeded to excoriate them again.* On a bus trip he referred to the duo as "forces of evil."[30] He quickly apologized, but as the *Washington Post*, put it, he had now "set fire to his own campaign."[31] When recently asked about that episode, McCain responded:

> I'll give you some straight talk. I was angry after what happened. Many of them [rumors and smear tactics] were traced directly to many in the Evangelical movement. Not overall, but there was a professor at Bob Jones University who told CNN that John McCain

had to prove that he didn't father illegitimate children. That's not the way. So of course I was angry. And sometimes you say things in anger that you don't mean. But I have put that behind me. It's over. And it's something that happened, it's finished and I move forward not back.[32]

There may have been a little history in that conflagration of 2000. A decade earlier McCain had tangled with a prominent conservative Christian. This occurred during the nomination hearings for John Tower, a close friend of McCain's. Selected by George H. W. Bush to be secretary of defense, Tower endured a drawn out and controversial hearing process. Tales of his carousing and womanizing tantalized Washington. Senate Democrats were the most tantalized of all. What was supposed to be a perfunctory confirmation hearing stretched on endlessly, bringing new, fresh, and salacious accusations daily. As a member of the hearing committee, McCain had the opportunity to watch his friend subjected to the Washington equivalent of waterboarding.

Testifying against Tower's character and morals was one Paul Weyrich, an architect and mainstay of the Christian right. In his 2002 book *Worth the Fighting For*, McCain renders this description:

Weyrich possesses the attributes of a Dickensian villain. Corpulent and dyspeptic, his mouth set in a perpetual sneer as if life in general were an unpleasant experience, he is the embodiment of the caricature often used to unfairly malign all religious conservatives. He is the joyless preacher who for the sake of God and country sorrowfully consents to participate in the profane business of politics, and whose sour disposition is a natural reaction to the distasteful duty of consorting with the morally inferior beings who populate the profession. . . . I like to think I know a pompous, self-serving son of a bitch when I see one, a facility that God, who loves His sinners as well as His saints, has seen fit to bless me with.[33]

Gaining the Republican nomination won't come easy if McCain continues to indulge his talent for sharing blunt, stylistically rendered portraits of conservative Christian power brokers with the American people. As a gesture of reconciliation, he delivered the 2006 commencement address at Jerry Falwell's Liberty University. His rehabilitation among conservative Christians seems to be proceeding apace, but there are stumbling blocks. James Dobson, who is to McCain what Richard Land is to Rudy Giuliani (and who is allied with Weyrich), has opined, "I pray that we will not get stuck with him" and "I will not vote for John McCain under any circumstances."[34]

A week after his address at Liberty, McCain headed off to the New School for Social Research in New York to deliver another graduation speech. These two institutions are about as ideologically opposed to one another as can be imagined. The one exception is that both occasionally engage in the ritualistic devouring of some unsuspecting liberal who happens to stumble into their maws. The ultraprogressive New School has always retained a contingent of hard-core radical left students and faculty. By sending McCain into the lion's den, one presumes that his handlers wanted to show off their candidate's prodigious range, the Maverick's ability to connect with the left and right alike.

They miscalculated. During, before, and after his remarks, McCain was taunted by the audience. One senior speaker went off on him for his support of the war, and signs in the audience indicated an awareness that McCain had labored in pro-life vineyards for twenty-four years. Pundits who wanted to probe everything from the incivility of "kids these days" to the indomitable spirit of our nation's youngsters were provided with enough material to keep the item alive in the news cycle for days.

I mention this incident because it underscores that the seemingly independent McCain abounds in negatives among liberals and those to their left. Blue-staters have their litmus tests too. Many will not even consider voting for a pro-life candidate who supports the war, no matter how much of a straight talker or good guy he appears to be. Come Election Day, many liberals won't give a hoot about McCain's principled stances on soft money and his quixotic bid to revoke congressional parking privileges at Reagan National Airport.[35]

This means that McCain *must carry conservative Christians en masse or perish.* By taking such an unambiguous pro-life stance, the senator from Arizona puts himself at great risk. In return for his position he must be rewarded by massive—as opposed to moderate—evangelical support. By this I mean the type of support that George W. Bush received in 2004—replete with endorsements, volunteers, photo-ops in the pews with smiling Christian babies, access to the "lists" and phone banks, and the full complement of the grassroots organizations that constitute the "Jesus Machine."[36] This seems a long way off. Evangelical leaders clearly have reservations about him. Yet they too are incurring risk. For them to shun a viable pro-life candidate on the basis of the McCain-Feingold Act raises questions about the degree to which their political agenda overrides their religious one. Had they vilified McCain because of his monumental lapses of judgment with Charles Keating in the eighties, then one could understand how, as persons of moral scruple, they were dissatisfied. But it seems awfully strange for servants of Christ to work themselves into a tizzy over campaign finance reform.

The refusal to embrace McCain is also strategically dubious. Put simply, he has the best record on the Issue of any first-tier Republican candidate in the race. In terms of overturning *Roe v. Wade,* only a few options remain if McCain flounders. One is the eleventh-hour championing of a B-list candidate such as Mike Huckabee of Arkansas. Another is Fred Thompson, who at the time of the writing of this book remains unannounced and saddled by accusations that he once worked for pro-choice groups. The third is Mitt Romney.

Mitt Romney: Man of Faith

W. Mitt Romney, a credible, talented, and well-funded presidential aspirant, is a Mormon. This former governor of Massachusetts, who accepts no compensation for his public service and speaks of possessing "an overdeveloped community service gene," is a member of the Church of Jesus Christ of Latter-day Saints.[37] Mitt Romney is a Mormon, and no faith-and-politics pundit can let go of this fact.

And they are not alone. His private religious belief is an irrelevant attribute, one that should have no bearing on his fitness for office. But in an America whose politicians willingly entangle religion and politics, this is not the case. Romney's religion appears to be singularly disconcerting for many Americans, among them fundamentalists and evangelicals.

But there is a twist. As if the gods of compelling fictional narrative had become engrossed with the 2008 election, it turns out that Romney's policy platform meshes almost seamlessly with that of conservative Christians. It could be plausibly argued that on the Issue and the Federal Marriage Amendment he has more energy and more eagerness to please than McCain (Giuliani, as we saw, is a lost cause here). This raises the question of whether conservative Christians can put aside serious theological and moral objections to a politician's faith in the hopes of achieving long-cherished legislative gains.

In order to do so they will need to disabuse themselves of extremely pervasive and longstanding prejudices. The same holds true for many other Americans whose attitudes toward Mormons do not seem to reflect enlightened tolerance. In a 2007 survey, 46 percent of respondents had an unfavorable opinion of the LDS faith.[38] Other surveys show that between 37 percent and 66 percent of the populace have reservations about a Mormon president.[39] The Reverend Al Sharpton made national headlines expressing just such a prejudice. In a conversation with the antitheist Christopher Hitchens—who, ironically, was hawking a book which argues that the endpoint of all religious belief is bigotry and intolerance—Sharpton reasoned, "As for the one Mormon running for office, those that really believe in God will defeat him anyway, so don't worry about that."[40]

The difficulties may be even more pronounced among those constituencies Romney is courting. Amy Sullivan observes, "Evangelicals don't have the same vague anti-LDS prejudice that some Americans do. . . . To Evangelicals, Mormonism isn't just another religion. It's a cult."[41] This claim has a certain truth, but it needs to be qualified a bit more carefully. One evangelical confessed to a journalist, "I don't believe he would be guided by God."[42] Similar opinions have been aired in South Carolina, the scene of the January 29 Republican primary and a place where members of the GOP tend to dispense with the intraparty niceties. A McCain supporter who is also a state representative declared, "This is South Carolina. We're very mainstream, evangelical, Christian, conservative. It will come up. In this of all states, it will come up."[43] Another put it like this: "As an Evangelical Christian it is a big thing for me. . . . His faith is inconsistent with my faith. His faith is consistent with the Book of Mormon. My faith is consistent with God's word, the Bible, and they're not compatible."[44]

Such sentiments also find expression in shelf upon shelf of anti-Mormon literature written by conservative Christians. The sheer volume and intensity of these tomes leaves little doubt that in some quarters there is a deep animus toward the LDS faith. Mormon theological beliefs can clash fairly thunderously with evangelical doctrine, so much so that it is not unusual for evangelicals to deny that Mormons are actually Christians. Historically, the violent, traumatic history of Mormon persecution in the nineteenth century has not helped foster mutual respect. There is even a global competition being waged between the faiths. Both evangelicals and Mormons are tireless, relentless missionaries who conduct their outreach efforts all over the world. In a very real sense, they are competing for souls.

But as we have seen again and again in this study, conservative Christians are nowhere near as monolithic as their critics imagine them to be. In May 2007 Pat Robertson invited Mitt Romney to lecture the graduating class at his Regent University.[45] The late Jerry Falwell remarked, "If he's pro-life, pro-family, I don't think he'll have any problem getting the support of Evangelical Christians."[46] "I have a deep disagreement with Romney's theology," said Southern Baptist leader Frank Page, "but I won't rule him out. . . . He's the closest to the Southern Baptists in his social and moral beliefs."[47] Although it is difficult to speak with certainty, we seem to have a reversal of a trend noted earlier with Giuliani and McCain. It is the evangelical rank and file, not their leaders, who have the greatest misgivings about Romney.

The actual proclivities of conservative Christians will only be known when the data from the primaries is sifted and analyzed. Still, on the issues alone, Romney will be appealing to them. True, there has been some "elasticity" in his policy positions (during his failed 1994 bid to unseat Senator Kennedy the latter ingeniously quipped that Romney was "multiple choice" on the abortion question).[48] On abortion, stem cell research, gay marriage, and gun control, Romney has shifted his opinion hard to the right in the past few years. Dubbing himself an "evangelical Mormon," his views on the issues have become more evangelical than Mormon.[49]

But if they can look past the radical changes of heart, the 2008 version of Romney is one that could be quite enticing to conservative Christians. When asked point blank if he would overturn *Roe*, he responded, "Yes. . . . I would like to see each state be able to make its own decision regarding abortion rather than have a one-size-fits-all blanket pronouncement by the Supreme Court."[50] As opposed to

McCain, who has demonstrated little willingness to support a Federal Marriage Amendment, Romney seems enthusiastic. Emphasizing that he is not homophobic and would never countenance discrimination, he nevertheless concludes that he believes marriage is between a man and a woman.[51]

In an interview with *60 Minutes*, Romney tied this argument to a scriptural proof-text: "We're people that are designed to live together as male and female and we're gonna have families. . . . There's a great line in the Bible that children are an inheritance of the Lord and happy is he who has or hath his quiver full of them" (Ps. 127:5).[52] The Bible figures prominently and, as I am about to argue, conspicuously in Romney's rhetoric. When asked what his favorite book was, he responded "the Bible." (In the same breath he also cited Scientology founder L. Ron Hubbard's *Battlefield Earth* as one of his other preferred texts. His handlers will make sure that such a literary assessment is never, ever expressed again.)[53]

Romney is fond of showing reporters the Bible that both he and his father (the former governor of Michigan) were sworn in with.[54] He has commented, "I'm not perfect, but I'm one aspiring to be a good person as defined by the biblical Judeo-Christian standards that our society would recognize."[55] At one of the Republican debates he intoned: "I believe in God, believe in the Bible, believe Jesus Christ is my savior. I believe God created man in his image."[56] After the Virginia Tech shootings, the governor told a crowd that his first response "was to pick up my Bible and reread the account of the murder of Abel by his brother and reflect on the nature of evil."[57]

In terms of the frequency of his scriptural thumping, Romney scores on the higher end of the spectrum, near someone like the master, George W. Bush. Most of the time, however, he makes generic references to "the Bible." Every now and then he executes the cite-and-run technique. Yet a slightly deeper analysis reveals something a bit odd. Let us recall that a Mormon does not live by the Bible alone. As the scholar Kent Jackson describes it, "Latter-day Saints hold a view of canon that is not restricted to the revelations of the past. . . . The canon is not closed, nor will it ever be. To them, revelation from God has not ceased; it continues in the church." Among what Mormons call their "Standard Works" are the Bible (in the King James translation), the Book of Mormon, the Doctrine and Covenants, and the Pearl of Great Price.[58]

Romney's invocations, I feel compelled to point out, center on the Bible, *not* the Pearl of Great Price. Nor do his policy positions stem from the revelations given to Joseph Smith by the angel Moroni. The reasons for his narrowing of the LDS literature to include just canonical Christian Scripture are obvious. The texts just mentioned are sectarian documents which only 5–6 million Mormon Americans would recognize as authoritative. Thumping the Book of Mormon would most likely chime the theological fight-or-flight bells of conservative Christians and many others. As such, appealing solely to canonical Old and New Testament texts makes perfect tactical sense.

It also explains why Romney is often heard trumpeting the virtues not of *his* faith, but faith in general. His religious rhetoric is ecumenical through and through. In an interview with George Stephanopoulos he remarked, "I think the principles of all faiths have, as their foundation, the idea that there is a supreme being, that this supreme being is a heavenly father, and that all of the people in our country and in all countries are sons and daughters of the same separate being."[59]

At points, Romney embraces an Eisenhowerian conception of how religion informs politics. (Romney's appreciation for the thirty-fourth president is so great that he has tried, unsuccessfully, to have his grandchildren address him by "Ike" and his wife by "Mamie.") Echoes of Eisenhower's well-known quip in the epigraph are seen in Romney's remark: "I think the American people want a person of faith to lead the country. I don't think Americans care what brand of faith someone has."[60]

When reporters get too pushy about the particular tenets of Mormonism and their influence on his thought, Romney refuses to indulge them. "I am not here to run for cardinal," he told a prying journalist, "and I am not going to get into discussions about how I feel about all my church's beliefs and my church's doctrines. . . . All that does, in my view, is play into religious bigotry."[61] A reasonable riposte—but somewhat specious coming from a politician who drags faith into his every pronouncement.

The media's obsession with Romney the Mormon and Romney's strategic counterobsession with Romney the Man of Faith has led them all to spend too little time on Romney the Executive. And Romney the Executive, fascinatingly, seems to be secular in the extreme. Religious passions do not infuse his day-to-day leadership style. The

Standard Works are not consulted as he oversees budgets. On the contrary, he is a rationalist, enthralled to statistics, research, science, the bottom line—whatever it takes to turn a profit or solve a problem.[62] A reading of his book *Turnaround: Crisis, Leadership, and the Olympic Games* underscores his preoccupation with "strategic audits" and his love of managerial human interest stories. Had George W. Bush written a similar book, he would have paused on a dozen occasions to reflect on how members of the scandal-ridden IOC needed to get right with God, or how he felt "a Presence" at the opening ceremonies, or how he huddled in prayer with coreligionists who were to compete in the two-man luge event. Not Mitt Romney. His is a story of the Winter Olympics told from the (not entirely gripping) perspective of a chief executive officer. Why talk about God when you can offer a detailed treatment of negotiations with a purveyor of office supplies? (I, for one, would have appreciated a little more attention to the curling competition.)

The media downplay these "secular" qualities, all the while harping on Romney's religious beliefs. Romney, of course, must shoulder some of the blame for this. Yet this puts him at a disadvantage; it draws attention away from his substantive accomplishments as a businessman and politician.

When all is said and done, Mitt Romney's candidacy for the presidency will tell us a lot about conservative Christianity. It will give us a good sense of whether the movement's values tilt toward the "politics" or the "faith" side of the scale. Put differently, it might reveal if conservative Christians care more about making their issues the law of the land than they care about the religious "imperfections" of the president who will shepherd them into being. Romney's run will also shed light on the question of their commitment to religious tolerance. It will help us discern whether its members' zeal to bring faith into the public square is, as many critics allege, really a ruse to bring *their* own particular faith into the public square.

Conclusion: A Few Polite Suggestions

In chapter 5 I noted that it is difficult for northern, liberal Democrats to excel in the God-talk competition. Now let me pick up this line of analysis and note that similar obstacles confront an overlapping, but not identical, cohort: those who are not conservative Protestants.

My examination of the religious imaging strategies of half a dozen presidential candidates leads me to conclude that the faith and values playing field is anything but level. The sport in question is governed by rules that unequivocally favor traditional Protestant candidates, especially those of the conservative variety. The document that one is supposed to invoke when running for high office is the Bible, not the Talmud, not the *Confessions* of Augustine, not the Qur'an, and not the Pearl of Great Price.

The preferred manner of citing Scripture is the classic one-verse invocation. This is a form of textual proofing that comes quite naturally to Protestants. Cite-and-run operations or generic invocation, however, are practices fairly alien to Jews and Catholics. Ascribing a less central role to the Bible, they have more copious theological resources at their disposal. Put differently, they are reluctant to break God's will down into one pithy scriptural sentence.

Nor are Jews and Catholics particularly at home wearing their faith on their sleeves. Emoting publicly does not come naturally to them. They have been historically conditioned to keep their spiritual sentiments to themselves in a nation where they are minorities. It follows that they rarely exult in proclaiming God's glory to the throngs. They don't have much experience talking up their conversion experiences, or pointing to that one incandescent moment when it all came together, when they saw the light.

That God-talk in a historically Protestant nation is done in a manner that reflects the cultural and theological peculiarities of the majority is neither unusual nor necessarily unfair. Yet it is often forgotten how much strain this places on non-Protestant candidates. Although I have criticized John Kerry's religious imaging strategies, it must be acknowledged that he was saddled with a severe handicap.

Testifying publicly, King James in hand, is not something a Catholic can do with ease. The second a Catholic does it—as Kerry learned—charges of pandering and hypocrisy will rain down from the turbulent punditry skies. As Mike McCurry, a Clinton stalwart who advised Kerry on religious outreach, put it, "When you're in an outwardly professing faith tradition like the Baptists, your ability to communicate from a religious perspective comes almost naturally. It's much harder for buttoned-up mainline Democrats to do that. I think that's where we've gotten in trouble."[63]

One surmises that Giuliani will learn from the errors of his coreligionist. If he is smart, which he is, he will keep his thumping activities to a minimum. Instead, he will focus on the issues, national security in particular. Throughout it all he will emphasize his track record of defending the civil liberties of the religious.

As for Mitt Romney, the rules of the game are even more tilted against him. In order to pander effectively, he must essentially suppress three-quarters of his scriptural canon. Imagine what would happen if he based his appeals for an ecumenical faith not by citing Genesis but 1 Nephi 17:35: "Behold, the Lord esteemeth all flesh in one; he that is righteous is favored of God." Scriptural off-roading of this type is risky. Of course, if he refrains from doing so, some pundit will predictably tar him as insincere—which he most likely is, but no more so than any other candidate profiled in this book.

Romney alone is expected by the press to explain the "objectionable" aspects of his faith. Jewish, Catholic, and Protestant candidates are not asked to defend the massacres of the book of Joshua or the misogyny of Paul. But the Mormon candidate is badgered constantly about polygamy in his church (which outlawed the practice in 1890), a history of racism among Latter-day Saints, and—this actually happened—whether he wears highly specialized Mormon undergarments.[64]

A non-Protestant presidential aspirant entering a contest whose rules were created by (and for) conservative Protestants is walking uphill, lugging 50-pound ankle weights. It is astonishing that even with such advantages the latter have yet to field a viable organic candidate. I am beginning to wonder if the viability of Giuliani, McCain, and Romney points to the fact the media have not overplayed the religion card themselves. If this is indeed the case, then the storyline of 2008 will not be about values voters but the secularly religious.

Conclusion

The Symbol and the Separation

The evil: treating the Bible simply as a storehouse of emotive phrases to be exploited for partisanship. The good: reminding . . . hearers of Scripture's intrinsic power.

Mark Noll, "The Politicians' Bible"

Evangelicals

The Bible *is* back. And it's as somewhat relevant as ever. True, there is more Bible thumping in politics today than there was in the days of, let's say, the Nixon administration. True, Bible-carrying Christians lead the nation in the categories of grassroots political organizations, well-funded special interest groups, and manifestos posted on the Web. True, *undeniably true*, secular elites have run out of ideas, qualified personnel, and steam.

But it is simply not the case that America is turning into "Bible country," or that the Constitution has become subservient to the book of Revelation. There are, as we have seen, a number of formidable constraints on Scripture's ability to directly influence domestic and foreign policy. The first is that pesky First Amendment. The second is the hard labor, past and present, of civil liberties groups in the judicial trenches. The third is a large stock of moderately religious Americans (i.e., the secularly religious) who will simply never tolerate an established religion. And should all these lines of defense somehow collapse, *nonsecular conservative Christians themselves would, ultimately, stave off theocracy with their own bare, New-International-Version-clutching hands.*[1]

Glancing at American history in chapter 1, we saw that the Scriptures consistently fail to illuminate policy debates. That is because the Bible is to clear and coherent political deliberation as sleet, fog, hail, and flash floods are to highway safety. Groups who live by the Bible have rarely shown any sustained ability to tame this scriptural chaos. In other words, achieving consensus on the proper interpretation of the unruly Holy Writ has been more the exception than the rule.

As is well known, Protestantism, with all of its sects, has shown a predilection toward schism. In this regard the Bible is its "enabler." All evidence suggests that disagreement, division, and more than occasionally, strife, are tantamount to "the natural cause of death" among communities bound by this text. Of course, the history of Protestantism has shown that before the mourning begins, breakaway groups are immediately formed afresh; the Good Book's multivalence is at once a cause of communal destruction and communal creation.

"Evangelicals," writes Martyn Percy, "have shown themselves to be prone to persistent and damaging schisms."[2] Nothing in this work gainsays that observation. Evangelicals and their literalist precursors have failed to reach accord about what the Bible mandates regarding the divine right of kings, sabbath laws, slavery, political action (chapter 1), the environment (chapter 2), whether poverty or abortion is Jesus' priority (chapter 3), and what the end time will look like (chapter 4).

Were secularism to disappear, were all the secularists to be raptured into the air, the conservative Christian voting bloc would rapidly relearn an old lesson: it is nearly impossible to get one Protestant denomination to agree on what the Bible says, let alone dozens of them. My surmise, then, is that *the more the Good Book would become capable of actually influencing the judicial and legislative activities of our government, the more the coalition of Bible-carrying Christians would unravel.* The irony is that secularists serve as the unwitting glue that holds all the divergent parts of the Christian right together. Only common fear and hatred of state-sponsored godlessness could send so many diverse Christians, with such freighted historical relations, running into one another's arms.

This is not to say that proponents of the wall of separation should relax and pay no attention to First Amendment adjudication. I do wish to suggest that maybe a more subtle strategy may be in order. It would consist of giving potentially antagonistic religious groups fewer opportunities to unite against the common enemy of "secular humanism." At the same time, a more Machiavellian approach might craftily maneuver different denominations and religions to explore their own inevitable differences of opinion. This strategy of decentering secularism so that faith communities concentrate on eviscerating one another, however, presupposes political leadership—and this is nowhere to be found in the camp of nonbelief.

This raises an important question: do the majority of Bible-carrying Christians actually want the theocracy that secularists accuse them of so coveting? I confess to being baffled by this. Citing survey data, Christian Smith notes, "Evangelicals are much more likely than any other group to believe that Christian morality should be the law of the land."[3] Many associated with the more right-leaning factions, observes another scholar, "have little desire to maintain the separation of church and state."[4] Some groups on the fringe (e.g., Christian Reconstructionists) appear to bear out this claim.[5]

Mainstream evangelicals, however, usually swear that this is not the case. The very sober sociologist Alan Wolfe, who has studied them extensively, assures us that they "accept the separation of church and state" and America's "culture of toleration."[6] I am generally inclined to agree with Wolfe's assessment. Still, the rhetoric and political initiatives that I encountered while researching this book—emanating from both the evangelical right and left—occasionally gave me reason for pause. If evangelicals, good and decent citizens that they are, want to gain the trust of other Americans, a clear disavowal of any theocratic designs (in the form of an Internet statement with fifty million signatories) would be ideal.

What would also be ideal is a more sophisticated doctrinal take on the Bible—at least with regard to its intersection with politics. I am troubled by the tendency among evangelicals to characterize interpretations that challenge their own as based on foolishness or malice, as opposed to honest differences of opinion. Call this the "hermeneutic scandal" of conservative Protestantism. They have a difficult time acknowledging that their readings are just readings. But who, after all, can ground an interpretation of Scripture in fact? Who can legitimately claim that his or her take is, according to all objective criteria, the right take?

Evangelicals explicitly acknowledge the infallibility and inerrancy of Scripture. But implicitly they ascribe infallibility and inerrancy to their own interpretive endeavors. The oft-heard evangelical exhortation *"It's in the Bible!"* tacitly arrogates uncanny powers of accuracy to its exhorter. The statement of the theologian Alister McGrath, "Scripture when rightly interpreted, leads to Christ," illustrates the scandal.[7] Who defines "rightful" interpretation? Who gets to decide if Christ-proximity has been achieved?

Nonbelievers and the Secularly Religious

This brings us to the second constituency whose story we have looked at through the prism of the Bible's role in the nation's public life. Contemporary American secularism, I have argued, is composed of two unequal parts. The very large part consists of church/state separatists who are believers. The very small part is made up of nonbelievers (who are also church/state separatists). The very small part, however, is so raucous that in the popular imagination the relative sizes of the two constituencies have been inverted. Secularism itself has come to be associated with brash, boisterous godlessness. Yet card-carrying, politically mobilized atheists and agnostics, as best I could tell in chapter 6, number only a scant few million—chump change, as far as electoral coalitions go.

The symbolic return of the Bible to the public square is itself a symbol of the crisis that American secularism is currently undergoing. The most visible manifestation of the crisis is apparent on the legislative and judicial levels. In terms of the former, religious special interest groups are sweeping scads of faith-based politicians into office. As for the Supreme Court, the recent appointments of Justices Alito and Roberts suggest that a somewhat less than high-Jeffersonian conception of church-state separation will prevail over the coming decades. Let us not exaggerate: Mr. Jefferson's wall will not become a picket fence or a patch of forlorn pansies anytime soon. But it is clear that changes are afoot. The Golden Age of Secularism is over.

Randall Balmer, a progressive and independent-minded evangelical scholar, has asked with justifiable astonishment how the Democrats can head into election after election holding a position on abortion which virtually guarantees that half the electorate will not vote for them.[8] In a similar vein, I wonder: How could the Democrats associate themselves with a constituency of nonbelievers who are not only wildly unpopular in every red state in America but deliver little in terms of ballot-box payoff?

All the evidence encountered earlier indicates that the party is now asking itself the same questions. Escorting nonbelievers politely, but firmly, to the wings of the stage (if not the door) appears to be their strategy. With regard to those other secularists, the believing church-state separatists, the Democrats are willing to take the following risk. They will *significantly modify their rhetoric* and thus deemphasize their traditional, uncompromising reading of the First Amendment (and here their speechwriters have understood that the Bible's winged words are useful in de-secularizing the party's image). At the same time, they will *slightly modify their policies* in a more religion-friendly direction (some mild faith-based initiatives here, some give and take on reproductive freedoms there). If they know how far to go without going too far, the Democrats will keep religious secularists under their big tent. After all, where else are they are going to go?

Nonbelieving secularists, by contrast, are free to go wherever they please. Aside from Mayor Michael Bloomberg of New York City, I cannot think of one credible potential candidate for the presidency who might have the least bit of interest in, or affinity with, this constituency. The present election year, then, provides as good a time as any for some soul-searching and introspection. Permit me to suggest a helpful analogy. One positive development (depending on how you look at it) that emerged from the retreat of the fundamentalists after Scopes nearly ninety ago was the eventual rise of the mellower, less bellicose evangelicals (sometimes called neo-evangelicals) in the forties and fifties. If atheists and agnostics were to undertake a similar hiatus from public affairs, it could give them an opportunity to regroup, rethink, calm down, and reemerge as a more politically savvy version of themselves.

In truth, atheists and agnostics could learn a lot from evangelicals. They lack what these Bible-carrying Christians possess in abundant supply: dynamism.[9] Nonbelievers are short of political leaders, a state of affairs not unrelated to their complete lack of a grassroots political infrastructure. Their writers and rank and file have become excessively entangled with the Democratic Party and liberalism. Here again they could learn from evangelicals. In the past decade the latter have, finally, diversified their membership across the political spectrum. They are no longer perfectly synonymous with the religious right. The emergence of a group of godless Republicans would be good for secularists (and Republicans). Successful campaigning for the presidency is about, among other things, building coalitions. It is extremely difficult to do this with a partner who insists on referring to all others in the coalition as mentally deficient. An unyielding critique of religion has emerged in recent years in the works of Christopher Hitchens, Sam Harris, and Richard Dawkins, to name a few.[10] Two things strike me about these antireligious screeds. The first is that even though they have sold briskly, they have not translated into any sort of political movement or momentum. No significant grassroots initiative has emerged in the wake of these best sellers. The second is that these books are so relentless in their denunciation of *all* forms of religious belief that one wonders how long the secularly religious will be able to tolerate their snarling, underperforming, political bedfellow.

As for the "secularly religious," what makes them so interesting is the fact that, in theory, they can be found in all denominations and all religions. There are even secularly religious evangelicals and Orthodox Jews. Who knows, there may be secularly religious Amish too! Granted, it is much easier to find them milling about in a Unitarian church or kibbitzing in a Reform synagogue. Still, no religion in America is immune to the presence of those who are moderate, self-critical, and open to accommodating the modern world. My hunch is that some intelligent Democratic strategist out there has understood that the secularly religious fear *both* the religious right and the secular left. The trick lies in crafting rhetoric and policies that appeal to them.

While conservative Christians have shrewdly made a scapegoat of godless secularism for decades (and profited handsomely for doing so), they have perhaps misunderstood the identity of their most daunting adversary. In terms of competition for hearts and minds, in terms of the competition for political influence, it is religious moderates and religious defenders of the Establishment Clause, not village atheists, who will give them a run for their money in the coming decades. An alignment of mainline Protestants, liberal Catholics, Jews, Muslims, and members of non-Abrahamic faiths *along with* stray secularly religious conservative Christians would pose the biggest challenge to nonsecular Bible-carrying Protestants.

Abuse and Use: A Disclaimer

In the introduction to this work I pointed to an essential tension that characterizes the Bible's position in American public life. The Bible is held in great esteem by politicians and voters alike, yet its ability to directly influence the processes of government is severely limited. As far as secularists are concerned, the text should be neither a national symbol of what "we as Americans hold dear," nor a shaper of policy. For conservative Christians the reverse holds true. They want it to be not only a symbol but a primary resource that profoundly informs the thinking of public servants, be they legislators, judges, teachers, and so forth.

Little that we have seen in *Thumpin' It* indicates that the Bible has actually made the jump from "national icon" to "major influence on governmental policy." The doomsday scenarios of the secular left have yet to come true. The dream of the evangelicals remains unfulfilled. As for the latter, the sheer inertia of the Golden Age checks them at every turn. This, however, should not obscure the fact that conservative Christians have achieved much and are poised, perhaps, for even greater attainments in the years ahead. They have, after all, succeeded in restoring the public prominence of the Bible after its descent into oblivion at midcentury. The resurgence of the Scriptures marks a milestone in the ongoing struggle to desecularize the public square. Its increased salience in national discourse reflects profound electoral, demographic, and cultural shifts that may irrevocably alter the future of the country.

On the other hand, the Bible's boundless energy flows awkwardly, unevenly, into a political grid powered by rational modes of thought and Enlightenment principles. To wit, the ancient Scriptures don't always speak very clearly, and modern democracies are not often structured or inclined to listen to them anyway. Highly visible and much revered, yet constrained in its ability to directly and profoundly influence the nation's public life—that is the fate of the Good Book in modern America.

What would the presidential aspirants whom I surveyed make of this situation in the innermost recesses of their hearts? Would they confess to wanting the Bible to assume the function of an irrelevant artifact, icon, or policy maker? This is impossible to know. What is clear is that all want to get elected and none of them can ignore the immense popular appeal of the Scriptures. Invoking the Bible is something like a "confidence-building measure," a presenting of one's moral credentials, to the American electorate. One finding of this work is that a viable presidential contender *must* have a Scripture game and a narrative of faith. This game, I suggest, is played by rules that put all those who are not conservative Protestants at a significant disadvantage. This is a problematic state of affairs, one that dooms the candidacies of many qualified politicians who are either areligious or who loathe open display of their beliefs.

The tense, unstable, and perhaps temporary equilibrium that I am describing—in which Christians get their symbol and secularists get their separation—is not without its dangers. In chapter 4 I looked at the hullabaloo surrounding the influence of premillennial theology on the Bush administration's Middle East policy. The charge struck me as unwarranted. But the president's incessant harping on his faith, and his adoption of biblical and religious symbolism, both overt and covert, invites the mistrust and rancor that we witnessed in that discussion. The raw power of the Bible is so great (and so incompatible with the wiring of democracy) that it risks short-circuiting the American political system itself. Even the "mere" symbolic use of Scripture creates a substantive risk of polarizing the electorate.

Let me not mince words. It is an abuse of the Bible to claim that the answer to highly nuanced and complex modern problems simply sits on its pages. Ronald Reagan's remark "It is an incontrovertible fact that all the complex and horrendous questions confronting us at home and worldwide have their answer in that single book" is demagogic and ill-advised.[11] Moreover, such statements have the most pernicious effect on the trust of citizens who do not live by that "single book." But insofar as Reagan, like nearly all American presidents, did not show much desire to let the answers in that single book inform his questions about domestic and foreign policy, then he did not make the unconscionable leap from symbol to substance. With all respect to the estimable Mark Noll cited in the epigraph, letting the Bible be used solely as a symbol, solely as "a storehouse of emotive phrases to be exploited for partisanship," is the lesser of all evils.[12]

It is also an abuse to fail to call attention to arguments within Scripture that contradict one's own reading. On this count, conservative Protestant leaders, who know the Scriptures backward and forward, are particularly vulnerable to criticism. Indeed, a question I asked myself repeatedly was how they could fail to even *address* biblical passages that so blatantly undermine their own scripturally based policy prescriptions. Evangelicals or fundamentalists can't very well claim to be unaware of verses that challenge their positions.

Because I am generous of spirit, I will say that this inability to see how the Bible actually contradicts their preferred opinions is usually an unconscious oversight. Political passions tend to obscure our more critical faculties of judgment. That being said, the Christian who does *consciously and knowingly* ignore some words of the Bible in order to advance a political agenda is, I would surmise, committing a grievous sin. Once again, as a means of gaining the trust of fellow citizens, conservative Christians might consider drawing attention to such misuses of the Bible in their midst as a means of preventing abuse of their sacred Scriptures. Maybe they could form an internal oversight committee, their own Department of Scriptural Affairs. Like the motion pictures rating board, it would be paid for and staffed by evangelicals in the "industry." Its mission would be to ensure the quality and integrity of the industry's spiritual product.

In deference to the title of this book, the reader may be justifiably wondering if I see anything other than "abuse" of the Bible in politics. I can think of at least one instance that strikes me as nonabusive. Readers of congressional proceedings have become grimly familiar with eulogies delivered for American soldiers who have died serving in Iraq. Typically a congressperson offers a few words of consolation and then a line from Scripture. These invocations are so melancholy, so shorn of any palpable gain or lucrative target audience, that it would be absurd to cast suspicion on them. They are what they are: expressions of remorse offered by public servants in good faith.[13]

There are certainly other nonabuses of the Bible in public life, and for this reason there is no need to outlaw scriptural citation or to draft a constitutional amendment banning the invocation of the Good Book. There is a need, however, to be wary of letting the text and its raw power remain unchecked. There is also a need to recognize, as my intoxicated colleague pointed out at the beginning of this book, that the Bible says so many things as to almost neutralize itself. May we make a communal vow (followed by a national fast) to avoid the protracted, indecisive, proof-text warfare that has drained the energy of American politics time and time again?

Politicians are certainly free to use the Scriptures in their oratory, though they should exercise restraint and Jeffersonian common sense. They are also free to be inspired by certain "great ideas" in the Good Book. But it is incumbent upon them to understand that for other citizens those ideas may mean something entirely different or not be so great. Perhaps all presidential candidates who insist on thumping Bible should preface their cite-and-run operations with the following disclaimer:

My fellow Americans, I am about to cite one verse from the Bible. It's kind of ironic, actually, for were I elected president it would be my sworn duty to preserve, protect, and defend the Constitution (so help me God)—a circumstance that would make it impossible (and impeachable) to establish my interpretation of the aforesaid verse as the law of the land. Moreover, I cannot be certain that the line I am about to quote actually means what either I, or my junior staffer with the MA from that divinity school who brought it to my attention, think it says. From what I hear, even folks down at my own church disagree about its meaning. And I won't even start with all those theologians and biblical scholars.

In any case, I assure you that I sincerely respect that your reading may differ from mine. But for justice to go out, I also assure you that neither your reading nor mine shall ever impact upon the governance of our republic. If that were to come to pass, the religious tranquility we share in this great country, the religious tranquility that makes us an envy of the world and a light to the nations, would turn to tumult. Thank you, and may God, who gave us this forthcoming Scripture—most likely to beguile us, but hopefully not to divide us—bless America.

Notes

INTRODUCTION: "THE BIBLE IS RAW POWER"

1. The reference to "anachronistic ding dongs" is found in David Kuo's *Tempting Faith: An Inside Story of Political Seduction* (New York: Free Press, 2006), 60.

2. Network of Spiritual Progressives, "An Ethical Way to End the War in Iraq," *New York Times*, May 17, 2007, A13.

3. See William King, "The Biblical Basis of the Social Gospel," in *The Bible and Social Reform*, ed. Ernest Sandeen (Philadelphia: Fortress, 1985), 59–84.

4. Jeffrey Siker, "President Bush, Biblical Faith, and the Politics of Religion," SBL Forum, June 2006, http://www.sbl-site.org/Article.aspx?ArticleId=151.

5. Quoted in Dana Stevens, "Oh God," *Slate*, April 29, 2004, http://www.slate.com/id/2099698/.

6. Quoted in "Bush on God," *St. Petersburg Times*, January 16, 2005, 5a.

7. The examples cited in this paragraph will be discussed at length throughout this work.

8. Barack Obama, "'Call to Renewal' Keynote Address," June 28, 2006, http://obama.senate.gov/speech/060628-call_to_renewal/.

9. David Kirkpatrick, "Consultant Helps Democrats Embrace Faith, and Some in Party Are Not Pleased," *New York Times*, December 26, 2006, A10. The consultant is Mara Vanderslice.

10. Mike McCurry, "Mike McCurry on Faith and Politics," SBL Forum, April 2007, http://www.sbl-site.org/article.aspx?ArticleId=658.

11. Quoted in Tony Carnes, "Swing Evangelicals," *Christianity Today*, February 4, 2004, http://www.christianitytoday.com/ct/2004/002/11.15.html.

12. Nina Bernstein, "Mrs. Clinton Says GOP's Immigration Plan Is at Odds with the Bible," *New York Times*, March 23, 2006, http://www.nytimes.com/2006/03/23/nyregion/23hillary.html?ex=1185249600&en=39bf971a3bd2750a&ei=5070.

13. David Klinghoffer, "Where Religious Left Meets Right," *National Review Online*, June 2, 2006, http://article.nationalreview.com/?q=NmIyYmNjZjc0MzY4MGM4YTMwN2QzYTIlOWE1YTdhMzA=.

14. Joseph Gaer and Ben Siegel, *The Puritan Heritage: America's Roots in the Bible* (New York: Mentor, 1964), 20.

15. Ibid., 19, 26.

16. On antimonarchism in the Bible and the ancient Near East, see Jacques Berlinerblau, *Official Religion and Popular Religion in Pre-Exilic Ancient Israel* (Cincinnati: Department of Judaic Studies, 2000). This is a published edition of the Twenty-Third Annual Rabbi Louis Feinberg Memorial Lecture in Judaic Studies, May 11, 2000.

17. Abraham Katsh, *The Biblical Heritage of American Democracy* (New York: KTAV Publishing House, 1977), 133; Gaer and Siegel, *Puritan Heritage,* 55.

18. This is reported without substantiation in Katsh, *Biblical Heritage,* 70.

19. Mark Noll, Nathan Hatch, and George Marsden, *The Search for Christian America* (Colorado Springs, CO: Helmers & Howard, 1989), 76.

20. Ibid., 72.

21. Quoted in F. Forrester Church, "Thomas Jefferson's Bible," in *The Bible and Bibles in America*, ed. Ernest Frerichs (Atlanta: Scholars Press, 1988), 153.

22. Martin Marty, "America's Iconic Book," in *Humanizing America's Iconic Book: Society of Biblical Literature Centennial Addresses 1980*, ed. Gene Tucker and Douglas Knight (Chico, CA: Scholars Press, 1982), 3.

23. On Washington's kiss, see Jon Meacham, *American Gospel: God, the Founding Fathers, and the Making of a Nation* (New York: Random House, 2006). Marty, "America's Iconic Book," 7, notes that Washington left behind very few allusions to the Bible in his writing.

24. Quoted in Noll et al., *Search for Christian America*, 75.

25. Ibid., 81.

26. Garry Wills, *Under God: Religion and American Politics* (New York: Simon & Schuster, 1990), 383.

27. Cited in Ronald Reagan, "Proclamation 5018—Year of the Bible, 1983," February 3, 1983, http://www.reagan.utexas.edu/archives/speeches/1983/20383b.htm.

28. See D. G. Hart, *That Old-Time Religion in Modern America: Evangelical Protestantism in the Twentieth Century* (Chicago: Ivan R. Dee, 2000), 27.

29. Louis Weeks, "God's Judgment, Christ's Command: Use of the Bible in Nineteenth-Century American Political Life," in *The Bible in American Law, Politics, and Political Rhetoric*, ed. James Turner Johnson (Philadelphia: Fortress, 1985), 63.

30. For a review of this period and these issues see my *The Secular Bible: Why Nonbelievers Must Take Religion Seriously* (New York: Cambridge University Press, 2005), and "'Poor Bird Not Knowing Which Way to Fly': Biblical Scholarship's Marginality, Secular Humanism, and the Laudable Occident," *Biblical Interpretation* 10 (2002): 267–304.

31. Douglas Sweeney, *The American Evangelical Story* (Grand Rapids: Baker, 2005), 169.

32. John Green, "Seeking a Place: Evangelical Protestants and Public Engagement in the Twentieth Century," in *Toward an Evangelical Public Policy: Political Strategies for the Health of the Nation*, ed. Ronald Sider and Diane Knippers (Grand Rapids: Baker, 2005), 17.

33. On the importance of groups in this period such as the American Civil Liberties Union, the American Jewish Congress, and Protestants and Other Americans United for Separation of Church and State, see James Hitchcock, *The Supreme Court and Religion in American Life*, vol. 1, *The Odyssey of the Religion Clauses* (Princeton, NJ: Princeton University Press, 2004), 90–121. On the Jehovah's Witnesses, see pp. 43–59.

34. Quoted in ibid., 90. The decision in *Everson v. Board of Education* was actually a minor setback for secular interests.

35. Ed Dobson, "The Bible, Politics, and Democracy," in *The Bible, Politics, and Democracy*, ed. Richard John Neuhaus (Grand Rapids: Eerdmans, 1987), 3.

36. On the tremors that this decision set off for the religious right, see, for example, Dobson, "Bible, Politics, and Democracy."

37. Blackmun's decision can be found in Robert Baird and Stuart Rosenbaum, eds., *The Ethics of Abortion* (Buffalo: Prometheus, 1981), 13–22.

38. I am persuaded by Randall Balmer's argument that in the immediate aftermath of *Roe v. Wade*, "the vast majority of evangelical leaders said virtually nothing about it" (Balmer, *Thy Kingdom Come: How the Religious Right Distorts the Faith and Threatens America: An Evangelical's Lament* [New York: Perseus, 2006], 12). Balmer makes the provocative claim, on the basis of firsthand dealings with many evangelical opinion makers of that time, that the issue that actually galvanized them was, in fact, the 1972 *Green v. Connally* decision, which prohibited segregation and threatened the tax-exempt status of Bob Jones University. Also see Ernest Ohlhoff, "Meeting People 'Where They Are At' Essential to Winning Battle for Life," n.d., National Right to Life Committee, http://www.nrlc.org/news/2000/NRL01/ernie .html. I thank my colleague Tom Banchoff for making me aware of this article.

39. Andrew Flint and Joy Porter, "Jimmy Carter: The Re-emergence of Faith-Based Politics and the Abortion Rights Issue," *Presidential Studies Quarterly* 35 (2005): 48.

40. On Reagan as evangelical, see Erling Jorstad, *Evangelicals in the White House: The Cultural Maturation of Born-Again Christianity, 1960–1981* (New York: Edwin Mellen, 1981), 144–47.

41. Reagan, "Proclamation 5018—Year of the Bible, 1983," http://www.reagan .utexas.edu/archives/speeches/1983/20383b.htm.

42. Susan Harding, *The Book of Jerry Falwell: Fundamentalist Language and Politics* (Princeton, NJ: Princeton University Press, 2001), 23.

43. See Jeffrey Bell, "What Falwell Wrought: Just the Biggest Voter Realignment in Modern History," *Weekly Standard*, May 28, 2007, 13–14.

44. On religion and the 1988 election, see James Guth and John Green, eds., *The Bible and the Ballot Box: Religion and Politics in the 1988 Election* (Boulder, CO: Westview, 1991).

45. Steven Waldman and John Green, "Freestyle Evangelicals: The Surprise Swing Vote," September 22, 2003, http://www.beliefnet.com/story/129/story_12995 .html. An interesting discussion of the use of and butchering of Scripture in 1992 can be found in Mark Noll, "The Politician's Bible," *Christianity Today* 36 (1992): 16–17.

46. On the question of whether Bush himself is an evangelical, see Adelle Banks, "Is Bush an Evangelical?" *Religion News Service*, April 13, 2005, http://www.beliefnet.com/story/165/story_16508_1.html.

47. Robert Denton Jr., "Religion and the 2004 Presidential Campaign," *American Behavioral Scientist* 49 (2005): 23. Also see the important analysis of James Guth, Lyman Kellstedt, Corwin Smidt, and John Green, "Religious Influences in the 2004 Presidential Election," *Presidential Studies Quarterly* 36 (2006): 223–43, from which the comment about the "religious mainstay" comes.

48. The principle of co-belligerency is associated with Francis Schaeffer and discussed in relation to the Moral Majority by Dobson, "Bible, Politics, and Democracy," 3.

49. Richard Kyle, *Evangelicalism: An Americanized Christianity* (New Brunswick, NJ: Transaction, 2006), 2. Kyle also writes, "At the beginning of the twenty-first century, evangelicalism must be regarded as a big tent or large extended family" (13).

50. Carnegie Council, "Evangelical Reflections on the U.S. Role in the World," September 15, 2005, http://www.cceia.org/resources/transcripts/5230.html/:pf_printable.

51. Evangelicalism is not a religion per se but a *mode* of being religious. It unites born-again, bibliocentric Protestants from across sundry denominations. This is why a Methodist can be an evangelical, as can a Southern Baptist. There are also self-professed Catholic evangelicals, and, as we shall see in chapter 7, Mitt Romney refers to himself as a Mormon evangelical. For a discussion of some of these issues, see Frank Newport, "Who Are the Evangelicals?" Gallup Poll News Service, June 24, 2005, http://www.freerepublic.com/focus/f-news/1532746/posts.

52. "Evangelical Protestantism," according to two political scientists, "remains the major religious tradition whose very identity is tied to positive affirmations about the Bible. In a church context in which reading the Bible is widespread, Bible studies are everywhere, and biblical exegesis is standard fare in Sunday worship services, it is not surprising that attitudes towards the scripture are related to political attitudes and behavior." Lyman Kellstedt and Corwin Smidt, "Doctrinal Beliefs and Political Behavior: Views of the Bible," in *Rediscovering the Religious Factor in American Politics*, ed. David Leege and Lyman Kellstedt (Armonk, NY: M. E. Sharpe, 1993), 194.

53. Martyn Percy, "Whose Time Is It, Anyway? Evangelicals, the Millennium, and Millenarianism," in *Christian Millenarianism: From Early Church to Waco*, ed. Stephen Hunt (Bloomington: Indiana University Press, 2001), 33.

54. Roger Olson, *The Westminster Handbook to Evangelical Theology* (Louisville, KY: Westminster John Knox, 2004), 154.

55. Gary Bauer, "The Conservatory of Virtue," in *One Electorate Under God? A Dialogue on Religion and American Politics*, ed. E. J. Dionne Jr., Jean Bethke Elshtain, and Kayla M. Drogosz (Washington, DC: Brookings Institution Press, 2004), 55.

56. National Association of Evangelicals, "For the Health of the Nation: An Evangelical Call to Civic Responsibility," October 8, 2004, http://www.nae.net/images/

civic_responsibility2.pdf. It continues: "Evangelical Christians seek in every area of life to submit to the authority of Scripture (2 Tim. 3:16–17; Rom. 15:4; 1 Cor. 10:11)."

57. Evangelical Climate Initiative, "Climate Change: An Evangelical Call to Action," October 8, 2004, http://www.christiansandclimate.org/statement.

58. He finally voted for the first time at the age of 62.

CHAPTER 1: THE BIBLE IN AMERICAN POLITICS

1. Quoted in Rob Boston, "Weekend Warriors," Americans United for Separation of Church and State, June 2002, http://www.au.org/site/News2?page=News Article&id=5572&abbr=cs_.

2. The initial articles in the *Houston Chronicle* were Ron Nissimov, "DeLay's College Advice: Don't Send Your Kids to Baylor or A&M," *Houston Chronicle*, April 18, 2002, 23; and Nissimov, "Comment about Baylor, A&M Misunderstood, DeLay Says," *Houston Chronicle*, April 19, 2002, 31. Also see the editorial, "Fanatic," *Houston Chronicle,* April 19, 2002, 38. For a review of the event and the remarks made by DeLay, read Alan Cooperman, "DeLay Criticized for 'Only Christianity' Remarks," *Washington Post*, April 20, 2002, A05.

3. "Senator Edward M. Kennedy Discusses America's Future in Iraq at the Johns Hopkins School of International Studies," January 27, 2005, http://kennedy.senate.gov/newsroom/speech.cfm?id=f92a453a-5f2f-4139–8ff9–16c1a4d250e1.

4. Barack Obama, "'Call to Renewal' Keynote Address," June 28, 2006, http://obama.senate.gov/speech/060628-call_to_renewal/index.php.

5. Ronald Sider and Diane Knippers, introduction to *Toward an Evangelical Public Policy: Political Strategies for the Health of the Nation*, ed. Ronald Sider and Diane Knippers (Grand Rapids: Baker, 2005), 10.

6. I address the question of the Bible's views on homosexuality in chapter 7 of *The Secular Bible: Why Nonbelievers Must Take Religion Seriously* (New York: Cambridge University Press, 2005).

7. Quoted in Tim Grieve, "Life of the Party," Salon.com, May 2, 2005, http://dir.salon.com/story/news/lotp/2005/05/02/jim_wallis/index.html.

8. See the interesting discussion of this point in Peter Gomes, *The Good Book: Reading the Bible with Heart and Mind* (San Francisco: HarperSanFrancisco, 1996), 285–311.

9. For a discussion of this, see Abraham Katsh, *The Biblical Heritage of American Democracy* (New York: KTAV Publishing House, 1977), 128–38.

10. Louis Weeks, "God's Judgment, Christ's Command: Use of the Bible in Nineteenth-Century American Political Life," in *The Bible in American Law, Politics, and Political Rhetoric*, ed. James Turner Johnson (Philadelphia: Fortress, 1985), 74.

11. Walter Wink, "EcoBible: The Bible and EcoJustice," *Theology Today* 49 (1993): 466.

12. James Brewer Stewart, "Abolitionists, the Bible, and the Challenge of Slavery," in *The Bible and Social Reform*, ed. Ernest Sandeen (Philadelphia: Fortress, 1982), 51.

13. For an interesting discussion of how the exact same dispute played itself out among American Jews of the period, see Rifat Sonsino, "The Bible and Politics," *Judaism* 125 (1983): 77–83.

14. Mark Noll, "Battle for the Bible," *Christian Century*, May 2, 2006, 25.

15. Sider and Knippers, introduction to *Toward an Evangelical Public Policy*, 10.

16. I explore these themes at length in *The Secular Bible*.

17. On the diversity of evangelicalism, see Richard Kyle, *Evangelicalism: An Americanized Christianity* (New Brunswick, NJ: Transaction, 2006), 2.

18. In their practice, as opposed to their doctrine, conservative Christians sometimes tend to decenter the text ever so slightly and ever so pragmatically.

19. National Association of Evangelicals, "For the Health of the Nation: An Evangelical Call to Civic Responsibility," http://www.nae.net/images/civic_responsibility2.pdf.

20. Bruce Waltke, "An Evangelical Christian View of the Hebrew Scriptures," in *Evangelicals and Jews in an Age of Pluralism*, ed. Marc Tanenbaum, Marvin Wilson, and A. James Rudin (Lanham, MD: University Press of America, 1984), 111.

21. We should recall that many evangelical claims about inerrancy and infallibility relate to the original autographs, or original texts of the Bible. We do not possess these autographs so this raises the theological question of the relative inerrancy of the modern versions we use and the witnesses they were based on. A clear discussion of this problem can be found in John Brogan, "Can I Have Your Autograph? Uses and Abuses of Textual Criticism in Formulating an Evangelical Doctrine of Scripture," in *Evangelicals and Scripture: Tradition, Authority and Hermeneutics*, ed. Vincent Bacote et al. (Downers Grove, IL: InterVarsity Press, 2004), 94–111.

22. Quoted in Dan Gilgoff, *The Jesus Machine: How James Dobson, Focus on the Family, and Evangelical America Are Winning the Culture War* (New York: St. Martin's Press, 2007), 193.

23. "Evangelical Christians seek in every area of life to submit to the authority of Scripture (2 Tim. 3:16–17; Rom. 15:4; 1 Cor. 10:11). Nevertheless, many contemporary political decisions—whether about environmental science, HIV/AIDS, or international trade—deal with complex sociological or technological issues not discussed explicitly in the Bible. As Christians engaged in public policy, we must do detailed social, economic, historical, jurisprudential, and political analysis if we are to understand our society and wisely apply our normative vision to political questions. Only if we deepen our Christian vision and also study our contemporary world can we engage in politics faithfully and wisely." National Association of Evangelicals, "For the Health of the Nation."

24. Norman Allen, "Walking on Water? How Liberal Christians Interpret the Bible," *Baltimore Sun*, June 4, 2006, 19A.

25. L. William Countryman, "The Bible, Heterosexism, and the American Public Discussion of Sexual Orientation," in *God Forbid: Religion and Sex in American Public Life* (New York: Oxford University Press, 2006), 172.

26. Ibid., 174.

27. Ibid., 179.

28. J. Leslie Hoppe, "Don't Bully People with the Bible," *US Catholic*, September 1993, 16.

29. Michael Luo, "For Clinton, Faith Intertwines with Political Life," *New York Times*, July 7, 2007, A1, A8.

30. John Green, "Seeking a Place: Evangelical Protestants and Public Engagement in the Twentieth Century," in Sider and Knippers, *Toward an Evangelical Public Policy*, 17.

31. Jerry Falwell, *Strength for the Journey: An Autobiography* (New York: Simon & Schuster, 1987), 290.

32. In the same sermon mentioned in the previous footnote he cited Philippians 3:20 ("our commonwealth is in heaven").

33. Jerry Falwell, *Listen, America!* (Garden City, NY: Doubleday, 1980), 262.

34. A similar initiative was actually undertaken by the Continental Congress. Katsh, *Biblical Heritage of American Democracy*, 133.

35. Randall Balmer makes a similar argument as he wonders why Baptists, with their unique history, seem so seduced by the lure of state power. Balmer, *Thy Kingdom Come: How the Religious Right Distorts the Faith and Threatens America: An Evangelical's Lament* (New York: Perseus, 2006), 35–69.

CHAPTER 2: THE BIBLE AND THE ENVIRONMENT

1. On the Kerry campaign's belated recognition that "values" issues would be important in the election, see Robert Denton Jr., "Religion and the 2004 Presidential Campaign," *American Behavioral Scientist* 49 (2005): 11–31. On discussions about the role of religion within the party in the run-up to the election, see Amy Sullivan, "The Religion Gap," *Commonweal* 131 (2004): 10–11.

2. Or, to use the words of the demographers, "Evangelicals have become the religious mainstay of the GOP." James Guth et al., "Religious Influences in the 2004 Presidential Election," *Presidential Studies Quarterly* 36 (2006): 223–43.

3. It was estimated that these freestyle evangelicals comprised perhaps between 30 and 40 percent of the evangelical base. See Ayelish McGarvey, "Reaching to the Choir," *American Prospect* Online, March 23, 2004, http://www.prospect.org/ cs/articles?article-reaching_to_the_choir. The term "freestyle evangelicals" was coined by Steven Waldman and John Green, "Freestyle Evangelicals: The Surprise Swing Vote," Beliefnet, September 22, 2003, http://www.beliefnet.com/story/ 129/story_12995.html. Also see Tony Carnes, "'Swing Evangelicals,'" *Christianity Today*, February 2004, http://www.christianitytoday.com/ct/2004/002/11.15.html.

4. On Clinton's appeal to evangelicals as an "Arkansas 'good old boy,'" see Waldman and Green, "Freestyle Evangelicals."

5. Carnes, "'Swing Evangelicals.'"

6. Quoted in Tim Grieve, "Life of the Party," Salon.com, May 2, 2005, http://dir.salon.com/story/news/lotp/2005/05/02/jim_wallis/index.html. This piece also touches on some of Kerry's and Dean's difficulties in appearing authentic to religious voters. A profile of Wallis is offered by David Paul Kuhn, "The Gospel according to Jim Wallis," *Washington Post*, November 26, 2006, W20. For a critique of Wallis

from the secular left, see Katha Pollitt, "Jesus to the Rescue?" *Nation* 280, no. 5 (February 7, 2005): 10.

7. Franklin Foer, "Beyond Belief," *New Republic* 229, no. 26–28 (December 29, 2003): 22–25.

8. Ruth Marcus, "The New Temptation of the Democrats," *Washington Post*, May 23, 2006, A17.

9. Quoted in David Espo, "Sen. Obama Urges Democrats to Court Evangelicals," Associated Press, June 28, 2006. Bill Clinton made a similar call a few months earlier. See Beth Fouhy, "Clinton Calls on Democrats to Find Common Ground with Evangelical Voters," Associated Press Worldstream, April 11, 2006, http://www.high beam.com/doc/1P1–121675496.html.

10. Evangelical Climate Initiative, "Climate Change: An Evangelical Call to Action," http://www.christiansandclimate.org/statement. For a strident critique of the statement, see Iain Murray, "Beware False Profits," *National Review* Online, February 9, 2006, http://www.nationalreview.com/comment/murray200602090813.asp.

11. On the charge that most of the signers of the ECI were academics from evangelical colleges, see Mark Tooley, "Religious Climate Change?" *Daily Standard*, May 3, 2006, http://www.weeklystandard.com/Content/Public/Articles/000/000/012/177wfzau.asp.

12. Jimmy Carter has made a remark that leads one to speculate that such issues have long been of interest to some evangelicals: "At least one Sunday each year was devoted to the protection of the environment, or stewardship of the earth. My father and the other farmers in the congregation would pay close attention to the pastors' sermons, based on such texts as 'The earth is the Lord's, and the fullness thereof.'" Carter, *Our Endangered Values: America's Moral Crisis* (New York: Simon & Schuster, 2005), 19.

13. See http://www.creationcare.org.

14. See http://www.whatwouldjesusdrive.org.

15. "On the Care of Creation: An Evangelical Declaration on the Care of Creation" can be found on EEN's Web site, http://www.creationcare.org/resources/scripture.php. The ecological problems in question were land degradation, deforestation, species extinction, water degradation, global toxification, alteration of the atmosphere, and human and cultural degradation. Who is to be blamed for these calamities? One of the dogmatic tics of evangelical theology is an all-pervading sense of moral guilt. True to creedal form, EEN looked inward: "We have sinned, we have failed in our stewardship of creation. Therefore we repent of the way we have polluted, distorted, or destroyed so much of the Creator's work." On the Web site five hundred signatories to this document are listed and the date of 1994 is given. It is very difficult to ascertain when this statement was first posted on the Web, and media accounts are often inaccurate, confusing it with the "Climate Change" document of the ECI.

16. National Association of Evangelicals, "For the Health of the Nation: An Evangelical Call to Civic Responsibility," http://www.nae.net/images/civic_responsibility2.pdf.

17. Lani Perlman, "Evangelicals Embrace 'Creation Care' of God's Green Earth," *Dallas Morning News*, March 12, 2006, http://www.dallasnews.com/shared content/dws/dn/religion/stories/031106dnrelenvirochurch.b80a3d5.html.

18. Bill Berkowitz, "The Evangelical Climate Initiative: A Small Crack in the Conservative Movement," Media Transparency, February 22, 2006, http://www .mediatransparency.org/storyprinterfriendly.php?storyID=112. Also see Associated Press, "Baptists Warn Environmental Politics Could Divide Evangelicals," *Dallas Morning News,* July 15, 2006, http://www.dallasnews.com/sharedcontent/dws/dn/ religion/stories/071506dnrelgreenbaps.46a6f93.html. And see the response of the NAE to the ECI discussed below. On signs that the Republicans in general are losing ground among white evangelicals, see Laurie Goodstein, "In Poll, Republican Party Slips as a Friend of Religion," *New York Times,* August 25, 2006, A12.

19. Also see Jim Wallis. *The Soul of Politics: Beyond Religious Right and Secular Left* (San Diego: Harvest, 1995), 213.

20. How many secular liberals would feel comfortable partnering with the ECI? The latter is, after all, a group whose first solution to the global warming crisis is to "pray—seek guidance and encouragement from the Lord" (http://www.christians andclimate.org/action). On the danger presented to core Democratic values by cozying up to evangelicals, see Ruth Marcus, "The New Temptation of Democrats," *Washington Post,* May 23, 2006, A17.

21. Quoted in Amanda Griscom Little, "Cizik Matters," *Grist,* October 5, 2005, http://www.grist.org/news/maindish/2005/10/05/cizik/. Cizik was a signatory of the "The Sandy Cove Covenant and Invitation" of June 2004, which can be found on the NAE's Web site.

22. As another example of evangelicals in support of environmental issues, see R. Scott Rodin, who writes, "As evangelical leaders we need to step up to our responsibilities to be leaders in the fight for clean air and water, to stop the burning of the rain forests, cruelty to animals, overuse of pesticides, and the countless other issues that result from our consumer-oriented lifestyles." Rodin, "Stewardship," in *Toward an Evangelical Public Policy: Political Strategies for the Health of the Nation,* ed. Ronald Sider and Diane Knippers (Grand Rapids: Baker, 2005), 280.

23. Quoted in Mark Tooley, "Religious Climate Change?" *Daily Standard,* May 3, 2006. For more on the debates between ECI and ISA with the NAE caught in the middle, see Mark Bixler, "Faithful Split on Global Warming," *Atlanta Journal-Constitution,* February 8, 2006, B1; Josh Rutledge, "Evangelicals Spar over Climate," *Washington Times,* July 31, 2006, A4; and Adelle Banks, "Evangelicals Split on Global Warming," *Christian Century,* March 7, 2006, 10. A useful view from the camp of James Dobson is offered in Dan Gilgoff, *The Jesus Machine: How James Dobson, Focus on the Family, and Evangelical America Are Winning the Culture War* (New York: St. Martin's, 2007), 272.

24. Gilgoff, *The Jesus Machine,* 272. For more on the split within the NAE, see Katharine Mieszkowski, "Christians' Burning Issue," Salon.com, February 9, 2006, http://www.salon.com/news/feature/2006/02/09/evangelicals/index_np.html; and Jim Wallis, "An Evangelical Climate Change," *Sojourners,* May 2006, 5–6. Also see

Laurie Goodstein, "Evangelical's Focus on Climate Draws Fire of Christian Right," *New York Times*, March 3, 2007, A9.

25. In a previous incarnation the group was known as the Interfaith Council for Environmental Stewardship.

26. This would seem to be a legacy of the loquacious Puritans. See the excellent article of Sacvan Bercovitch where their love of words is discussed, "The Biblical Basis of the American Myth," in *The Bible and American Arts and Letters*, ed. G. Gunn (Philadelphia: Fortress, 1983), 219–29.

27. Calvin Beisner et al., *A Call to Truth, Prudence, and Protection of the Poor: An Evangelical Response to Global Warming* (Interfaith Stewardship Alliance, 2006), 13. The document is available at the ISA's Web site: http://www.interfaith stewardship.org.

28. Ibid., 17.

29. Ibid., 16.

30. Ibid., 18. Not very subtly arguing that environmentalists are Western elites, they ask if environmentalists (and members of the ECI) would like to live in the world engendered by the Kyoto Protocols: "What climate activist . . . would willingly, for even a month, live in a mud hut in malaria-infested rural Africa under the indigenous conditions their policy prescription would perpetuate? Who among them would be glad to drink the locals' contaminated water, eat their paltry, mold-infested food?" (20). In 1999, an earlier incarnation of the ISA issued the "Cornwall Declaration on Environmental Stewardship." Less an evangelical than an ecumenical statement, the "Cornwall Declaration" presages all of the themes seen here. It can be found at http://www.interfaithstewardship.org/pages/cornwall.php.

31. This is evident in the aforementioned "Cornwall Declaration." More criticisms of this type can be found on the linked Web page of the Acton Institute for the Study of Religion and Liberty: http://www.acton.org/ppolicy/environment/cornwall .php. That site provides more developed theological arguments. Of particular interest is the unsigned piece "A Biblical Perspective on Environmental Stewardship." The institute, of which Calvin Beisner—who coauthored *A Call to Truth*—is affiliated with, is partly funded by ExxonMobil. See Alexander Lane, "Evangelicals Fight Global Warming: Their Stance Has Some Church Leaders Upset," *Times-Picayune* (New Orleans), February 25, 2006, 6. Making the explicit charge that Beisner and his group are beholden to business interests is Balmer, *Thy Kingdom Come*, 152–53.

32. Though see the previous note.

33. "Acceptance Remarks by Bill Moyers for the Global Environmental Citizen Award," Harvard University, Center for Health and the Global Environment, New York, December 1, 2004, http://www.chge.med.harvard.edu/events/documents/ Moyerstranscript.pdf, 3.

34. James Watt, "The Religious Left's Lies," *Washington Post*, May 21, 2005, A19.

35. According to Watt in the article cited in the previous footnote, Moyers "made a personal apology."

36. Corrections and an apology to James Watt were appended to the online article itself. The original article that contained the erroneous quote was Glenn Scherer,

"The Godly Must Be Crazy," *Grist*, October 27, 2004. It can be accessed online at http://www.grist.org/news/maindish/2004/10/27/scherer-christian. The retractions were added by *Grist* on February 4 and February 11, 2005.

37. Paul Chesser, "Bible Bending Propaganda," *American Spectator* Online, February 23, 2006, http://www.spectator.org/dsp_article.asp?art_id=9446. On the situation in which some evangelicals subscribe to the types of beliefs Watt finds erroneous, see Rodin, "Stewardship," 279.

38. Moyers, "Acceptance Remarks," 4.

39. Glenn Scherer, author of the offending article in *Grist*, comments, "Why care about the earth when the droughts, floods, and pestilence brought by ecological collapse are signs of the Apocalypse foretold in the Bible? Why care about global climate change when you and yours will be rescued in the rapture?" ("Godly Must Be Crazy)." Another variant of this view is offered by Joseph Martos: "If evangelicals believe that the rapture is coming soon, why would they be concerned with ecology?" (Martos, *May God Bless America: George W. Bush and Biblical Morality* (Tucson, AZ: Fenestra Books, 2004), 36. For the opinion that this is a fringe belief in Christianity, see the remarks of John Green in Blaine Harden, "The Greening of Evangelicals," *Washington Post*, February 6, 2005, A1.

40. H. H. Schmid, "Earth, Land," *Theological Lexicon of the Old Testament*, vol. 1, ed. Ernst Jenni and Claus Westermann, trans. Mark Biddle (Peabody, MA: Hendrickson, 1997), 177.

41. Isa. 13:13; 41:5; Joel 2:10; Jer. 10:10; 51:29; Pss. 18:8; 99:1.

42. Job 9:5; Mic. 1:3–4; Pss. 74:15; 107:33–34.

43. Isa. 13:9–10; also see 24:23.

44. He renders Israelite land a waste (Lev. 26:32). He pulverizes Babylon (Jer. 51:42–43), lays Egypt desolate (Ezek. 32:15), and does the same to Israel throughout Ezekiel.

45. Isa. 51:6; also see Ps. 102:25–26. The sun and the moon will be rendered obsolete (Isa. 60:19).

46. Peter Craigie, *Psalms 1–50*, Word Biblical Commentary 19 (Waco, TX: Word, 1983), 246, 249. In Josh. 10:12–14 we learn of an instance where the God of Israel seemingly empowers a mortal to halt the trajectory of the sun (this lends a new meaning to the idea of human stewardship over God's creation). Other commentators have pointed to more un-eco-friendly themes in Scripture. Gene Tucker notes that "throughout the Hebrew Scriptures, the desert is dreadful and dangerous, a wasteland" (Tucker, "Rain on a Land Where No One Lives: The Hebrew Bible on the Environment" *Journal of Biblical Literature* 116 [1997]: 10). Walter Wink also seems aware of the less pro-environment attitude of Scripture. See his discussion of Gen. 1:26 in "EcoBible: The Bible and EcoJustice," *Theology Today* 49 (1993): 472.

47. Al Gore, *Earth in the Balance: Ecology and the Human Spirit* (Boston: Houghton Mifflin, 1992), 1.

48. Ibid., 245.

49. Ibid., 263; also see 62.

50. Ibid., 263.

CHAPTER 3: THE BLASTOCYST AND THE BIBLE

1. The editorial by Kennedy, "Bush's Wrong Choice on Stem-Cell Research," *Hill*, July 26, 2006, 28, closely resembles remarks made by Kennedy on the Senate floor on July, 17, 2006. In both places Kennedy cites the verse from Proverbs.

2. As Bill Frist, Republican senator from Tennessee, put it, H.R. 810 "restricts funding to blastocysts left over after IVF that would otherwise be discarded." "Frist Floor Statement on Stem Cell Research," *Congressional Quarterly*, July 17, 2006, http://docs.newsbank.com/openurl?ctx_ver=z39.88–2004&rft_id=info:sid/iw.news bank.com:AWNB:&rft_val_format=info:ofi/fmt:kev:mtx:ctx&rft_dat=112F3102C C6E76F0&svc_dat=InfoWeb:aggregated4&req_dat=0D0CB4F83B341AB5.

3. Edward Kennedy, speech, United States Senate Floor, Washington, DC, July 17, 2006, http://kennedy.senate.gov/newsroom/statement.cfm.

4. This was not the first time Kennedy had used the Bible. See, for example, his 1983 "Truth and Tolerance in America" address at Liberty College, http://www.americanrhetoric.com/speeches/tedkennedytruth&tolerance.htm.

5. Orrin Hatch, "Hatch: Senate Backs Expanding Stem Cell Research," July 18, 2006, http://hatch.senate.gov/index.cfm?FuseAction=pressreleases.View&Pressre lease_id=1620.

6. "Falwell Decries Stem Cell Research," *Christian Post*, August 23, 2006, http://www.christianpost.com/pages/print.htm?aid=24223.

7. They must also be pondering the intriguing fact that H.R. 810 passed through the Republican-controlled House. A highly informative account of the back room dealing and machinations among Republicans to have the bill cross the floor is found in Wes Allison, "Republican v. Republican: A Cellular Division," *St. Petersburg Times*, August 13, 2006, 1A.

8. The official Web site for Hatch's music is http://www.hatchmusic.com/index.html.

9. The Pew Forum on Religion and Public Life reported in 2005 that 57 percent of Americans viewed stem cell research and its attendant advantages as more important than the possible destruction of embryos (http://pewforum.org/news/display.php?NewsID=5238). A July 21–23, 2006, USA Today/CNN Gallup Poll found that 58 percent disapproved of President Bush's veto of H.R. 810 (http://www.usatoday.com/news/polls/tables/live/2006–07-24-poll.htm#stemcell). This would seem consistent with a June 20–24, 2001, finding that 60 percent favored federal funding (Gary Langer, "Public Backs Stem Cell Research: Most Say Government Should Fund Use of Embryos," June 26, 2001, http://www.abcnews.go.com/sections/politics/DailyNews/poll010626.html).

10. That human embryonic stem cell research could be a winning issue for Democrats was discussed in August 2004. See Morton Kondracke, "Democrats Have a Wedge Issue: Stem-Cell Research," *Tulsa World*, August 18, 2004, A15.

11. Thomas Okarma, "Human Embryonic Stem Cells: A Primer on the Technology and Its Medical Applications," in *The Human Embryonic Stem Cell Debate: Science, Ethics, and Public Policy*, ed. Suzanne Holland, Karen Lebacqz, and Laurie Zoloth (Cambridge, MA: MIT Press, 2001), 5.

12. Norman Ford and Michael Herbert, *Stem Cells: Science, Medicine, Law, Ethics* (Strathfield, Australia: St. Paul's Publications, 2003), 10; David Prentice, *Stem Cells and Cloning* (San Francisco: Benjamin Cummings, 2003), 3.

13. James Thomson et al., "Embryonic Stem Cell Lines Derived from Human Blastocysts," *Science* 282 (1998): 1145–47.

14. James Thomson, "Human Embryonic Stem Cells," in Holland et al., *Human Embryonic Stem Cell Debate*, 17.

15. Ibid., 16, 17.

16. Okarma, "Human Embryonic Stem Cells," 3.

17. On some of the potential treatments, see ibid., 2.

18. On the figure of 100 million see ibid., 11. Ford and Herbert place it at 128 million (*Stem Cells*, 65), though they ultimately reject the practice.

19. For discussions of the limitations, unknowns, and dangers of the science, see Prentice, *Stem Cells and Cloning*, 9–11.

20. Maureen Condic writes, "With few exceptions, adult stem cell research has demonstrated equal or greater promise than embryonic stem cell research at a comparable stage of investigation." Maureen Condic, "The Basics about Stem Cells," in *The Stem Cell Controversy: Debating the Issues*, ed. Michael Ruse and Christopher Pynes (Amherst, NY: Prometheus, 2003), 263.

21. "In a nation with forty-four million medically uninsured persons, the society of beneficiaries is not going to be inclusive. In a world in which millions of people live on less than a dollar a day and die from lack of clean drinking water, nutrition, basic health care, and diseases like malaria, tuberculosis, and AIDS, the regeneration of tissue by stem cell techniques is as exotic as it is expensive." Lisa Sowle Cahill, "Stem Cells and Social Ethics: Some Catholic Contributions," in *Stem Cell Research: New Frontiers in Science and Ethics*, ed. Nancy Snow (Notre Dame, IN: University of Notre Dame Press, 2003), 135.

22. This is much to the chagrin of David Prentice: "The debate regarding the early embryo is not the abortion debate. A women's choice of whether to allow her body to gestate the embryo is not in question. The debate centers around an embryo in a petri dish or freezer and the question of creating embryos for various purposes." Prentice, *Stem Cells and Cloning*, 34.

23. Karen Lebacqz, "Stem Cell Ethics: Lessons from the Context," in Snow, *Stem Cell Research*, 93.

24. George W. Bush, "President Discusses Stem Cell Research Policy," July 19, 2006, http://www.whitehouse.gov/news/releases/2006/07/print/20060719-3.html. In 2001 Bush opined, "I also believe human life is a sacred gift from our creator. I worry about a culture that devalues life, and believe as your president I have an important obligation to foster and encourage respect for life in America and throughout the world." "Bush Announces Position on Stem Cell Research," Washingtonpost.com, August 9, 2001, http://www.washingtonpost.com/wp-srv/onpolitics/transcripts/bushtext_080901.htm.

25. Ford and Herbert remark, "The embryo at the zygote stage is *already* a human individual and a person." *Stem Cells*, 77. I am not claiming, though, that these researchers are evangelicals.

26. For a sharp challenge to the view that the blastocyst should be accorded the same dignity as a human, see Michael Brannigan, "Fixations on the Moral Status of the Embryo," in *Stem Cell Research*, ed. James Humber and Robert Almeder (Totawa, NJ: Humana Press, 2004), 43–57.

27. This statistic is cited in Sondra Wheeler, "Christians and Jews in the Embryonic Stem Cell Debate," in *God and the Embryo: Religious Voices on Stem Cells and Cloning*, ed. Brent Walters and Ronald Cole-Turner (Washington, DC: Georgetown University Press, 2003), 156.

28. Prentice, *Stem Cells and Cloning*, 29.

29. On the legality of the procedure and the importance of the private sector in providing funding (James Thomson's research was privately funded), see Ann Kiessling and Scott Anderson, *Human Embryonic Stem Cells: An Introduction to the Science and Therapeutic Potential* (Boston: Jones & Bartlett, 2004), 189.

30. "US Senator Tom Harkin (D-IA) and Governor Jim Doyle (D-WI) Deliver Remarks at the Center for American Progress on Stem Cell Research," *Congressional Quarterly*, August 4, 2006, http://docs.newsbank.com/openurl?ctx_ver=z39 .88–2004&rft_id=info:sid/iw.newsbank.com:AWNB:&rft_val_format=info:ofi/fmt: kev:mtx:ctx&rft_dat=11351FC3EF63DDD0&svc_dat=InfoWeb:aggregated4&req _dat=0D0CB4F8.

31. In a recent article, D. Gareth Jones has looked at how the Good Book figures in the human embryonic stem cell debate. He identifies four ways in which political actors think about its ability to shed light on this problem. One of his categories is described as follows: "The Bible alone provides a complete guide to ways in which blastocysts should be treated, *making scientific input irrelevant.*" Jones, "Responses to the Human Embryo and Embryonic Stem Cells: Scientific and Theological Assessments," *Science and Christian Belief* 17 (2005): 214; my emphasis.

32. Roger Olson, "Infallibility/Inerrancy," in *The Westminster Handbook to Evangelical Theology* (Louisville, KY: Westminster John Knox, 2004), 213.

33. Jews and Muslims, for their part, generally favor this research.

34. As the liberal Protestant biblical scholar John Rogerson observes, "The Bible does not directly mention abortion anywhere. However, this does not prevent the misuse of passages that are thought to indicate a pro-life stance in the Bible, and there is a danger that overzealous advocates of pro-life viewpoint may damage their cause by using the Bible in ways likely to be repugnant to people who are not hard-line fundamentalists." (Rogerson, "Using the Bible in the Debate about Abortion," in *Theory and Practice in Old Testament Ethics* [London: T & T Clark, 2004], 88). On the lack of references to abortion in the Hebrew Bible, see Daniel Schiff, *Abortion in Judaism* (Cambridge: Cambridge University Press, 2002), 2.

35. See, for example, Scott McConnaha, "Blessed Are the Pluripotent: New Testament Guidance for the Embryonic Stem Cell Debate," *National Catholic Bioethics Quarterly* 5 (2005): 708.

36. The term "evangelical bioethics" is used by Nigel M. de S. Cameron, who also emphasizes the importance of *imago Dei* imagery. Cameron, "The Sanctity of Life in the Twenty-First Century: An Agenda for *Homo Sapiens* in the Image of God,"

in *Toward an Evangelical Public Policy: Political Strategies for the Health of the Nation*, ed. Ronald Sider and Diane Knippers (Grand Rapids: Baker, 2005), 215.

37. Southern Baptist Convention, "Resolution: On Human Embryonic and Stem-Cell Research," in Waters and Cole-Turner, *God and the Embryo*, 179–80.

38. John Rogerson writes, "Even if we assume that the 'image' is asserting something ontological about mankind, what we do not know is whether the 'image' (whatever it is) is present from the moment of conception, or whether, on Old Testament terms, it is there only after the 'unformed substance' has reached its definite form." Rogerson, "Using the Bible," 93–94.

39. That *'adam* is a collective term and does not refer to individual human beings is clear. See on this issue Nahum Sarna, *Genesis*, JPS Torah Commentary (Philadelphia: Jewish Publication Society, 1989), 12; and Gerhard von Rad, *Genesis: A Commentary*, rev. ed., trans. John Marks, Old Testament Library (Philadelphia: Westminster, 1972), 57.

40. For a comprehensive discussion of the structure of this passage, see Jan Holman, "The Structure of Psalm CXXXIX," *Vetus Testamentum* 21, no. 3 (1971): 298–310. JPS translates, "It was you who created my conscience" (*JPS Hebrew-English Tanakh*, ed. Rabbi David E. Sulomm Stein [Philadelphia: The Jewish Publication Society, 1999], 1586), thus reading the Hebrew term *kelāyot*, "kidneys," symbolically. In the Hebrew Bible, classic rabbinic exegesis, and patristic interpretation, kidneys receive a variety of symbolic interpretations. These range from emotional interiority, to reproduction, to moral instruction, to sexual desire.

41. The verb in question, *s-k-k* most likely, is highly problematic, with connotations of "weaving," "shaping," and, alternately, "shutting off" or "protecting." See T. Kronholm, "*s-k-k*," in *Theological Dictionary of the Old Testament*, vol. 10, ed. G. Botterweck, H. Ringgren, and H. J. Fabry (Grand Rapids: Eerdmans, 1995), 236–54.

42. Verses 14–16 are highly problematic for a variety of reasons. See the discussion of M. Mannati, "Psaume 139:14–16," *Zeitschrift für die alttestamentliche Wissenschaft* 83 (1971): 257–61, and his somewhat predictable efforts to defend the text from any charge of corruption. Others translate "bone structure" in lieu of my rendering, "bones" (see Leslie Allen, *Psalms 101–150*, Word Biblical Commentary [Waco, TX: Word, 1983], 249). Such an interpretation gives off a more visual sense of a fetus.

43. This verse seems to imply that creation of human beings takes place in the earth. Perhaps earth is a metaphor for womb, but as Briggs notes (*Psalms*, 497), the idea of life being created in the underworld or in the earth is highly unusual in and of itself.

44. The complex Hebrew term *golem*, which appears only once in the Hebrew Bible, is the crux of this passage. Many Christian commentators are eager to translate it as "embryo." They come to this reading by working with parallels from the Mishnah and the Septuagint. Parallels with Aramaic would seem to suggest "a formless mass" or "an incomplete vessel." Ludwig Koehler and Walter Baumgartner, *The Hebrew and Aramaic Lexicon of the Old Testament*, vol. 1 (New York: E. J. Brill, 1994), 194.

45. J. Kerby Anderson, "Cloning, Stem-Cell Research, and the Bible," *Bibliotheca Sacra* 159 (2002): 468.

46. John Jefferson Davis, "The Moral Status of the Embryonic Human: Religious Perspectives," *Ethics and Medicine* 22 (2006): 9–23.

47. See note 44.

48. Paul Simmons identifies parallels to Plato's *Republic* in his "Personhood, the Bible, and Abortion," in *The Ethics of Abortion: Pro-Life vs. Pro-Choice*, ed. Robert Baird and Stuart Rosenbaum (Buffalo: Prometheus, 2001), 175. The one Old Testament text rarely discussed by conservative Christians is Exodus 21:22–25. The verse speaks of two men who are fighting and accidentally push a pregnant woman. If she miscarries but is not injured, a fine is to be paid. If she is injured the principle of an eye for an eye sets in. What is very clear from this verse in Hebrew is that the health of the woman is a primary concern and that of the fetus something of an afterthought. A detailed discussion of this verse, its translation into Greek, and its interpretation by rabbinic scholars is found in Schiff, *Abortion in Judaism*, 1–26.

49. The question arises as to when the prophet Jeremiah was commissioned. This particular call narrative, like those before it, is somewhat vague on this. As Jack Lundbom writes, "The point is that Yahweh's call of Jeremiah to prophetic office took place long before the present moment when Jeremiah is informed of the decision. The time is intentionally left unspecified. Only Yahweh knows when the decision was made. It did not occur when Jeremiah was in the womb, much less at his time of birth." Lundbom, *Jeremiah 1–20*, Anchor Bible (New York: Doubleday, 1999), 231.

50. T. K. Cheyne translated, "Jehovah hath called me from the womb, from my mother's lap." (*The Prophecies of Isaiah*, vol. 2 [London: Kegan Paul, Trench & Co., 1882], 11). Franz Delitzsch offered the pretty "from my mother's bosom hath he thought of my name" (*Biblical Commentary on the Prophecies of Isaiah*, trans. S. R. Driver, 4th ed. (Edinburgh: T & T Clark, 1892), 235. Others see the verse as referring to Yahweh "naming" the prophet; see Brevard Childs, *Isaiah* (Louisville, KY: Westminster John Knox, 2001), 379.

51. Lonsdale Ragg, *St. Luke: With Introduction and Notes* (London: Methuen, 1922), 18.

52. Jones, "Responses to the Human Embryo," 215.

53. Mark Noll, *The Scandal of the Evangelical Mind* (Grand Rapids: Eerdmans, 1994), 160.

54. Ronald Sider and Diane Knippers, introduction to *Toward an Evangelical Public Policy*, 9.

55. Scott McConnaha, "Blessed Are the Pluripotent," 708. As Margaret Farley notes, "The Catholic community has no uncomplex, single voice on such questions." Farley, "Roman Catholic Views on Research Involving Human Embryonic Stem Cells," in Holland et al., *Human Embryonic Stem Cell Debate*, 113.

56. McConnaha, "Blessed Are the Pluripotent," 710.

57. Ted Peters and Gaymon Bennett note that the arguments of evangelical Protestants are beholden to traditions that "may not have traveled the same arduous

course of ethical deliberation" as Roman Catholics. Peters and Bennett, "A Plea for Beneficence: Reframing the Embryo Debate," in *God and the Embryo: Religious Voices on Stem Cells and Cloning*, ed. Brent Walters and Ronald Cole-Turner (Washington, DC: Georgetown University Press, 2003), 114.

58. Joseph Donceel, "A Liberal Catholic's View," in *Abortion in a Changing World*, vol. 1, ed. R. Hall (New York: Columbia University Press, 1970), 38–45.

59. See Daniel Harrington's excellent discussion of the 1993 document of the Pontifical Biblical Commission, "The Interpretation of the Bible in the Church." Harrington, *How Do Catholics Read the Bible?* (Lanham, MD: Rowman & Littlefield, 2005), 12.

60. John Paul II, "Address of Pope John Paul II to the President of the United States of America, H. E. George Walker Bush," July 23, 2001, http://www.vatican .va/holy_father/john_paul_ii/speeches/2001/documents/hf_jp-ii_spe_20010723_ president-bush_en.html.

61. Farley, "Roman Catholic Views," 115–16.

62. Edward Furton, "Levels of Moral Complicity in the Act of Human Embryo Destruction," in Snow, *Stem Cell Research*, 102.

63. Ibid., 101.

64. John Langan, "Stem Cell Research and Religious Freedom," in Snow, *Stem Cell Research*, 43.

65. Stevan Davies, *Jesus the Healer: Possession, Trance, and the Origins of Christianity* (New York: Continuum, 1995), 66.

66. For a few other examples see Matt. 4:23; 9:35; Luke 6:17–18; Acts 10:38.

67. United Church of Christ, "Support for Federally Funded Research on Embryonic Stem Cells," in Waters and Cole-Turner, *God and the Embryo*, 182.

68. Lebacqz, "Stem Cell Ethics," 96.

CHAPTER 4: THE BIBLE AND INTERNATIONAL RELATIONS

1. Surveying the history of U.S. foreign policy, Leo Ribuffo concludes, "No major diplomatic decision has turned on religious issues alone. . . . Religious ideas have had at most an indirect impact on policy makers." Ribuffo, "Religion in the History of U.S. Foreign Policy," in *The Influence of Faith: Religious Groups and U.S. Foreign Policy*, ed. Elliot Abrams (Lanham, MD: Rowman & Littlefield, 2001), 21.

2. Madeleine Albright, *The Mighty and the Almighty: Reflections on America, God, and World Affairs* (New York: HarperCollins, 2006), 8. Also see Albright's discussion of the importance of religion in foreign policy on pp. 66, 73.

3. James Lindsay, "Morality Is Really Hard," in *Liberty and Power: A Dialogue on Religion and U.S. Foreign Policy in an Unjust World*, ed. E. J. Dionne Jr., Jean Bethke Elshtain, and Kayla Drogosz (Washington, DC: Brookings Institution Press, 2004), 100.

4. In a major article Daniel Philpott remarks that "international relations scholars have long assumed the absence of religion among the factors that influence states." Philpott, "The Challenge of September 11 to Secularism in International Relations," *World Politics* 55 (2002): 67.

5. "In the World of Good and Evil," *Economist*, September 16, 2006, 37–38.

6. "Evangelical Reflections on the U.S. Role in the World," Carnegie Council, September 15, 2005, http://www.cceia.org/resources/transcripts/5230.html/:pf_printable.

7. Walter Russell Mead, "God's Country?" *Foreign Affairs* 85, no. 5 (September–October 2006): 24.

8. See Mark Amstutz, "Faith-Based NGOs and U.S. Foreign Policy," in Abrams, *Influence of Faith*, 175–87.

9. Mead, "God's Country?" 7.

10. Mead even goes as far as to suggest that a "Muslim-evangelical dialogue may be one of the best ways to forestall the threat of civilizational warfare" ("God's Country?" 10). Offering an endorsement of Mead's assessment is Jonathan Aitken, "Faith in Foreign Affairs," *American Spectator*, November 2006, 58–59.

11. Nicholas Kristof, "Following God Abroad," *New York Times*, May 21, 2002, A1.

12. Tony Campolo, "The Ideological Roots of Christian Zionism," *Tikkun* 20 (2005): 20.

13. Rick Perlstein, "The Jesus Landing Pad," *Village Voice*, May 18, 2004, http://www.villagevoice.com/news/0420,perlstein,53582,6.html. An editorial version of this critique can be read in Olof Scott, "How Do You See Israel? Prophecy or Political Convenience: The Answer Says a Lot about You, and the World," *Charleston Gazette*, September 17, 2006, 1C.

14. Tony Judt, "America and the World," *New York Review of Books*, April 10, 2003, http://www.nybooks.com/articles/16176.

15. Michael Ortiz Hill, "The Looking Glass War," *Counterpunch*, October 19, 2002, http://www.counterpunch.org/hill1019.html.

16. Lawrence Davidson, "Christian Zionism and American Foreign Policy: Paving the Road to Hell in Palestine," *Logos*, winter 2005, http://www.logosjournal.com/issue_4.1/davidson_printable.htm.

17. Ibid. Davidson continues: "They support the ethnic cleansing of Palestine in the name of Christ."

18. Kevin Phillips, *American Theocracy: The Peril and Politics of Radical Religion, Oil, and Borrowed Money in the 21st Century* (New York: Viking, 2006), vii, ix.

19. Ibid., 261.

20. The equation of evangelicalism and Islam as twin extremisms can be seen in Bob Chodos, "The PD Factor: Christian Fundamentalists and U.S. Policy in the Middle East," *Inroads* 16 (2005): 63. See also Phillips, *American Theocracy*, vii; and Hill, "Looking Glass War."

21. Ernest Sandeen, *The Roots of Fundamentalism: British and American Millenarianism 1800–1930* (Chicago: University of Chicago Press, 1970), 31. Others refer to Darby's "poor and convoluted" writing style (Mark Patterson and Andrew Walker, "'Our Unspeakable Comfort': Irving, Albury, and Origins of the Pre-Tribulation Rapture," in *Christian Millenarianism: From the Early Church to Waco*, ed. Stephen Hunt [Bloomington: Indiana University Press, 2001], 101). As Roger Olson notes, "The precise meaning, contours, and boundaries of

the theological perspective known as dispensationalism are strongly disputed even by scholars who have studied it for decades." *Westminster Handbook to Evangelical Theology*, 73.

22. For the argument that Edward Irving, not John Darby, is the founder of dispensationalism, see Patterson and Walker, "Our Unspeakable Comfort." On Darby, see Olson, *Westminster Handbook to Evangelical Theology*, 111–13.

23. Sandeen, *Roots of Fundamentalism*, 71. Dispensationalism became a part of the American landscape toward the end of the nineteenth century. See T. P. Weber, "Dispensationalism," in *Dictionary of Christianity in America*, ed. Daniel Reid (Downers Grove, IL: InterVarsity Press, 1990), 358.

24. See Sandeen, *Roots of Fundamentalism*, 132–61.

25. See ibid., 182–83; and Irvine Anderson, *Biblical Interpretation and Middle East Policy: The Promised Land, America, and Israel, 1917–2002* (Gainesville: University Press of Florida, 2005), 41–43.

26. The more recent versions use the text of the New King James Version.

27. Olson comments that the notes in the Scofield Bible "came to be considered second in authority only to Scripture itself by many conservative lay evangelicals." *Westminister Handbook to Evangelical Theology*, 74.

28. J. Michael Utzinger writes that this Bible "had the psychological effect of virtually making Scofield's notes part of the Holy Writ." *Yet Saints Their Watch Are Keeping: Fundamentalists, Modernists, and the Development of Evangelical Ecclesiology, 1887–1937* (Macon, GA: Mercer University Press, 2006), 121.

29. Tim LaHaye, Jerry Jenkins, and Sandi Swanson, *The Authorized Left Behind Handbook* (Wheaton, IL: Tyndale House, 2005), 3.

30. Ibid., 8. For a critique of the *Left Behind* series, see Carl Olson, "No End in Sight," *First Things* 127 (2002): 12–14.

31. *The Scofield Study Bible: New King James Version*, ed. C. I. Scofield, D.D., and Doris W. Rikkers (New York: Oxford University Press, 2002), 1743.

32. On the varying number of dispensations in the varying schemes, see Randall Balmer, "Dispensationalism," in *Encyclopedia of Evangelicalism* (Waco, TX: Baylor University Press, 2004), 211–12; also see Olson, *Westminster Handbook to Evangelical Theology*, 74.

33. Sandeen, *Roots of Fundamentalism*, 38. Olson writes, "Nondispensationalist biblical scholars do not find any reference to a 'secret rapture' in Scripture" (*Westminster Handbook to Evangelical Theology*, 112). Barbara Rossing effectively undermines claims that this approach reads the Bible literally (*The Rapture Exposed: The Message of Hope in the Book of Revelation* [New York: Basic Books, 2005]).

34. Sandeen, *Roots of Fundamentalism*, 63.

35. Ibid.

36. The claim that PD is pessimistic and fatalistic is widespread. See Timothy Weber, "How Evangelicals Became Israel's Best Friend," *Christianity Today*, October 5, 1998, 49; and D. G. Hart, *That Old-Time Religion in Modern America: Evangelical Protestantism in the Twentieth Century* (Chicago: Ivan R. Dee, 2002), 39.

37. Douglas Sweeney, *The American Evangelical Story: A History of the Movement* (Grand Rapids: Baker Academic, 2005), 163.

38. Hart, *That Old-Time Religion*, 39.

39. These themes are explored cogently in Paul Boyer, *When Time Shall be No More: Prophecy Belief in Modern American Culture* (Cambridge: Harvard University Press, 1992), 80–112.

40. Ibid., 97.

41. Weber, "How Evangelicals Became Israel's Best Friend," 41. Weber notes that this has always been a small minority of dispensationalists. Sandeen, *Roots of Fundamentalism*, xvii, notes the paradox of dispensationalists who were at once active and passive fatalists.

42. As Olson observes, Gentiles, for Darby, are something of "an afterthought within God's redemptive plan." *Westminster Handbook to Evangelical Theology*, 112.

43. Bruce Waltke, "An Evangelical Christian View of the Hebrew Scriptures," in *Evangelicals and Jews in an Age of Pluralism*, ed. Marc Tanenbaum et al. (Lanham, MD: University Press of America, 1984), 127. Also see Rossing, *Rapture Exposed*, 49.

44. The seven-year period is typically referred to as "the Tribulation" and the final three and a half years as "the Great Tribulation." *Scofield Reference Bible*, 1728. Also see Matt. 24:21.

45. *Scofield Reference Bible*, 1728. On the complex accounting that leads dispensationalists to read Daniel 9:24's references to "seventy weeks" as meaning a seven-year period of tribulation, see George Marsden, *Fundamentalism and American Culture: The Shaping of Twentieth-Century Evangelicalism, 1870–1925* (New York: Oxford University Press, 1980), 52.

46. This means that in the second coming, Jesus will actually come twice—first, to rapture his church, and then to defeat the antichrist and establish the kingdom. Sandeen, *Roots of Fundamentalism*, 63.

47. Satan's ultimate defeat will be followed by the last judgment, the end of the earth and heaven, and the creation of "the new heavens and the new earth." *Scofield Reference Bible*, 1742.

48. Yaakov Ariel, "Where the End Times Begin: Jerusalem and the Millennial Vision of Evangelical Christians," in *Studies in Jewish Civilization*, vol. 12, *Millennialism from the Hebrew Bible to the Present*, ed. Leonard Greenspoon and Ronald Simkins (Omaha, NE: Creighton University Press, 2002), 40.

49. Ariel, "Where the End Times Begin," 38; Hart, *That Old-Time Religion*, 101; Weber, "How Evangelicals Became Israel's Best Friend," 42, 45.

50. There is no doubt that in these circles, political advocacy for Israel is the norm. In the wider evangelical world, a pro-Israel tilt is also undeniable. Evangelicals may favor Israel for reasons of prophecy, but their affinity may also be predicated on a more generalized American fondness for Israel based on its role as a strategic ally, and as a familiar Western-style democracy. Sensing that Israel has few allies (and scores of enemies), many Jews in the United States and Israel have welcomed the support of conservative Christians, all the while managing to overlook the implications of the second coming.

51. Leo Ribuffo speculates, reasonably, that Bush's handlers intentionally steer him away from addressing these sorts of issues. ("George W. Bush and the Latest Evangelical Menace," *Dissent* 53 (2006): 48.

52. Olson points out that even those evangelicals who believe in premillennialism "do not consider it an essential of the gospel or necessary to sound Christian theology." Even so, he continues, it is included in the doctrinal statements of many evangelical denominations. Olson, *Westminster Handbook to Evangelical Theology*, 244.

53. There is reason to believe that dispensationalists, in the words of Tim Weber, "have always made up a minority of the entire evangelical family." Weber, "How Evangelicals Became Israel's Best Friend," 49.

54. Stephen Spencer, "Dispensationalism," in *The Encyclopedia of Christianity*, vol. 1, *A–D*, ed. Erwin Fahlbusch et al. (Grand Rapids: Eerdmans, 1999), 854–55; Olson, *Westminster Handbook to Evangelical Theology*, 308; Sandeen, *Roots of Fundamentalism*, 64.

55. Martyn Percy, "Whose Time Is It, Anyway? Evangelicals, The Millennium and Millenarianism," in *Christian Millenarianism: From Early Church to Waco*, ed. Stephen Hunt (Bloomington: Indiana University Press, 2001), 33. An evangelical or a fundamentalist can be a postmillennialist, an amillennialist, a progressive dispensationalist, a historical dispensationalist, none of the above, and so on. On differences of opinion among premillennialists, see John Walvoord, *The Blessed Hope and the Tribulation: A Historical and Biblical Study of Posttribulationism* (Grand Rapids: Zondervan, 1976), 7.

56. F. L. Arrington points to the curiosity that while many Pentecostals accept the broad outlines of dispensationalist theology, dispensationalist theology can be quite hostile to fundamental tenets of Pentecostalism. Arrington, "Dispensationalism," in *The New International Dictionary of Pentecostal and Charismatic Movements*, ed. Stanley Burgess (Grand Rapids: Zondervan, 2002), 584–86.

57. Keir Lieber and Robert Lieber, "The Bush National Security Strategy," U.S. Foreign Policy Agenda: Electronic Journal of the U.S. Department of State 7, no. 4 (December 2002), http://usinfo.state.gov/journals/itps/1202/ijpe/pj7–4lieber.htm.

58. Ibid. Also see Robert Lieber, *The American Era: Power and Strategy for the 21st Century* (New York: Cambridge University Press, 2005), 43.

59. On religious freedom, see *The National Security Strategy of the United States*, September 2002, 3, 4, http://www.whitehouse.gov/nsc/nss.pdf. *The National Security Strategy of the United States of America*, March 2006, 6, 7, http://www.whitehouse.gov/nsc/nss/2006/nss2006.pdf.

60. NSS 2006, 1.

61. Ibid., 5.

62. To get a sense of the backroom bargaining, personal conflicts, and power plays that go into policy formation, see the chapter "Bush Decision-Making: Pre- and Post-9/11," in David Mitchell, *Making Foreign Policy: Presidential Management of the Decision-Making Process* (Burlington, VT: Ashgate, 2005), 174–98.

63. On the disagreements between the State Department and the Defense Department and the fact that "neither faction . . . was particularly religious," see Andrew

Bacevich and Elizabeth Prodromou, "God Is Not Neutral: Religion and U.S. Foreign Policy after 9/11," *Orbis* 48 (2004): 45.

64. In a similar vein, Ross Douthat notes that for these critics there is a tendency to "assume that the most extreme manifestation of religious conservatism must, by definition, be its most authentic expression." Douthat, "Theocracy, Theocracy, Theocracy," *First Things* 165 (2006): 23–31.

65. Ribuffo, "George W. Bush," 49.

66. Quoted in Alice Chasan, "Debunking 'American Theocracy,'" http://www.beliefnet.com/story/192/story_19276_1.html.

67. Quoted in Stephen Mansfield, *The Faith of George W. Bush* (New York: Jeremy P. Tarcher, 2003), 117.

68. Or as Stan Crock puts it, "A president sending political messages to a key constituency isn't the same as a president basing a strategy on a messianic vision." Crock concludes, as I do, that "the Bible itself isn't the basis for his strategy." Crock, "Bush, the Bible and Iraq," *Business Week* Online, March 7, 2003, http://www.pointrichmond.com/peace/bushandbible.htm.

69. Charles Krauthammer, "When Unilateralism Is Right and Just," in Dionne et al., *Liberty and Power*, 95.

70. Or as Leo Ribuffo puts it, "Not only can divergent policy prescriptions be inferred from the Bible and other sacred texts, but also even the theories of interpretation have multiplied as the religious scene has become increasingly complex." Ribuffo, "Religion in the History of U.S. Foreign Policy," 21.

71. Rossing, *Rapture Exposed*, makes this case most forcefully.

72. Bacevich and Prodromou, "God Is Not Neutral," 48–49; Jim Wallis, "Dangerous Religion," *Sojourners* 32 (2003): 20–26. Also see Bruce Lincoln, "Bush's God Talk," *Christian Century*, October 5, 2004, 22–29.

73. Robert Bellah, "American Politics and the Dissenting Protestant Tradition," in *One Electorate under God? A Dialogue on Religion and American Politics*, ed. E. J. Dionne Jr., Jean Bethke Elshtain, and Kayla Drogosz (Washington, DC: Brookings Institution Press, 2004), 63.

74. Bruce Lincoln ("Bush's God Talk") identifies five propositions of "Bush's theology." In accordance with the claims made above, none of these is identifiable as biblical.

75. See Richard John Neuhaus, *The Naked Public Square: Religion and Democracy in America* (Grand Rapids: Eerdmans, 1986); Mark Souder, "A Conservative Christian's View of Public Life," in Dionne et al., *One Electorate Under God?* 21.

CHAPTER 5: THE BIBLE IN POLITICAL RHETORIC

1. I have never been able to find a full transcript of the January 2, 2004, interview, but the incident is relayed in Jodi Wilgoren, "Dean Narrowing His Separation of Church and Stump," NYtimes.com, http://www.nytimes.com/2004/01/04/politics/campaigns/04DEAN.html. Dean had been labeled just a few days earlier, "one of the most secular candidates to run for president in modern history." Franklin Foer, "Howard Dean's Religion Problem," *New Republic*, December 29, 2003, 22.

2. Norman Podhoretz, "A Masterpiece of American Oratory," *American Spectator*, November 2006, 28–35.

3. Such an approach can be see in Michael Knox Beran's "Tongues of Tin: The State of Political Oratory," *National Review*, July 3, 2000, 38–41. On Lincoln's Second Inaugural and the use of the Bible, see Mark Noll, "The Politicians' Bible," *Christianity Today*, October 26, 1992), 16–17.

4. Taken on January 5, 2006, from the Web site http://www.godhatesfags.com, sponsored by the Westboro Baptist Church.

5. Katie Stewart, "What the Bible Says about Abortion," http://www.what saiththescripture.com/Fellowship/What.Bible.Says.Abortion.html.

6. Richard Lowery, "At the Wall: The Bible and Political Speech in America," *Encounter* 59 (1998): 455.

7. Ibid., 456.

8. See, for example, his speech "Remarks at the Dedication of the Oak Cliff Bible Fellowship Youth Education Center in Dallas, Texas," October 29, 2003, http://findarticles.com/p/articles/mi_m2889/is_44_39/ai_111532076?lstpn=article_results&lstpc=search&lstpr=external&lstprs=other&lstwid=1&lstwn=search_results &lstwp=body_middle.

9. George W. Bush, "State of the Union Address," January 20, 2004.

10. On "God's sight" (in the NIV translation), see Gen. 6:11; Luke 16:15; Acts 4:19; Rom. 2:13; 1 Cor. 3:19; Heb. 4:13.

11. Bush ended his speech with this: "We can trust in that greater power who guides the unfolding of the years. And in all that is to come, we can know that his purposes are just and true." "His purposes" appears in Jer. 49:20 and 50:45 (NKJV), and "just and true" appears in Rev. 15:3; 16:7; 19:2 (NIV).

12. Pss. 115:15; 121:12; 124:8; 134:3; 146:6; George W. Bush, "Inaugural Address," January 20, 2005.

13. George W. Bush, "Presidential Address to the Nation, September 11, 2001," in *"We Will Prevail": President George W. Bush on War, Terrorism, and Freedom* (New York: Continuum, 2003), 3.

14. George W. Bush, "Presidential Proclamation Declaring National Day of Prayer and Remembrance for the Victims of the Terrorist Attacks, September 13, 2001," in *We Will Prevail*, 4.

15. George W. Bush, "Remarks by the President from Speech at the National Day of Prayer and Remembrance Ceremony, The National Cathedral, Washington, DC, September 14, 2001," in *We Will Prevail*, 7. Bush seems here to be deviating a bit from standard biblical translations.

16. George W. Bush, "State of the Union Address," February 27, 2001.

17. It was equally unnecessary to prompt listeners with bibliographical specifics at the end of the 2006 State of the Union address. In this speech he intoned, "No one can deny the success of freedom, but some men rage and fight against it," a reference that sounds similar to Dan. 11:11: "The king of the South will march out in a rage and fight against the king of the North." In the same speech he spoke of "inheriting the earth" (Matt. 5:5). George W. Bush, "State of the Union Address," January 31, 2006.

18. On "hidden passages" and cloaking, see Matthew Rothchild, "The Hidden Passages in Bush's Inaugural Address," January 23, 2005, http://www.common dreams.org/views05/0123–05.htm. On "double coding" and "winks and nudges," see Bruce Lincoln, "Bush's God Talk," *Christian Century*, October 5, 2004, 22–29.

19. Rothchild, "Hidden Passages in Bush's Inaugural Address."

20. That this was in fact the strategy used by speechwriters for Christian candidates is confirmed by David Kuo, *Tempting Faith: An Inside Story of Political Seduction* (New York: Free Press, 2006), 60.

21. John Pitney Jr., "President Clinton's 1993 Inaugural Address," *Presidential Studies Quarterly* 27 (1997): 91.

22. William J. Clinton, "First Inaugural Address," January 21, 1993. Clinton included one verbatim line: "The scripture says, 'And let us not be weary in well-doing, for in due season, we shall reap, if we faint not' " (Gal. 6:9 KJV).

23. William J. Clinton, "State of the Union Address," February 17, 1993.

24. 1 Cor. 2:4; 1 Thess. 1:5; 1 John 3:18.

25. William J. Clinton, "State of the Union Address," January 24, 1995.

26. In the same speech, Clinton refers to "we reap what we sow," thus invoking a vocabulary from 2 Kgs. 19:29; Job 4:8; Ps. 126:5; Prov. 11:18; 22:8; Luke 19:21; 2 Cor. 9:6; Gal. 6:7–8.

27. William J. Clinton, "Second Inaugural Address," January 20, 1997.

28. William J. Clinton, "State of the Union Address," January 19, 1999. On the notion of eye lifting, see Pss. 121, 123, and passages such as Isa. 40:26.

29. William J. Clinton, address to Democratic National Convention, Boston, July 26, 2004. On the use of religious themes in the two conventions of 2004 see Wilma Ann Bailey, "The Language of Faith and the 2004 Democratic and Republican National Conventions," *Encounter* 66 (2005): 165–71.

30. See William Bole, "The Democrats' 'Religion Gap' Not Full Story," *Christian Century*, February 24, 2004, 14.

31. This suggestion was made by the Liebermans themselves. Joe and Hadassah Lieberman, *An Amazing Adventure: Joe and Hadassah's Personal Notes on the 2000 Campaign* (New York: Simon & Schuster, 2003), 44.

32. Norman Solomon, "Holy Smoke and Mirrors: Lieberman and the Rise of Centrist Theocrats," August 10, 2000, http://www.commondreams.org/views/ 081000–107.htm. I make no assumptions about the religious affiliation of this author, though his anger at Lieberman is of a kind with what many Jews would say about him. For some examples see Michael Lerner, "Vice President Lieberman?" *Tikkun*, September/October 2000, 5–6.

33. Opinions on the strength and size of secularists in the party vary widely. For Louis Bolce and Gerald De Maio, "Our Secularist Democratic Party," *The Public Interest*, Fall 2002, 3–20, they constitute the majority (7–8). But see the next chapter for an extended discussion of this point.

34. Rod Dreher, "Why Christian Conservatives Like Lieberman, but Won't Vote for Him," http://www.beliefnet.com/story/36/story_3630.html.

35. Joseph Lieberman, *In Praise of Public Life* (New York: Simon & Schuster, 2000), 70.

36. Lieberman, *Amazing Adventure*, 195: "When you think about it, strengthening Medicare and Social Security follows the commandment to honor our fathers and mothers."

37. "Sen. Joseph Lieberman Speaks on Clinton, Sept. 3, 1998," http://www.cnn.com/ALLPOLITICS/1998/09/03/lieberman.

38. Lieberman, *Amazing Adventure*, 37.

39. On Bill Clinton's advice to Lieberman to circulate this speech widely, see Lieberman, *Amazing Adventure*, 28.

40. Lieberman's speech was given on February 3, 2000. It is reproduced in "A Shared Love of God," http://www.beliefnet.com/story/36/story_3698.html. The opening line is slightly adapted from Matt. 21:9; 23:39; Mark 11:9; Luke 13:35; John 12:13; and also Ps. 118:26.

41. Ibid.

42. Quoted in Marc Gellman, "Joe Lieberman as Rorschach Test," *First Things*, December 2000, 9–11.

43. As reported in Brigitte Greenberg, "Lieberman, Bush Embrace Religion," August 28, 2000, http://www.beliefnet.com/story/40/story_4049.html.

44. Lieberman, *Amazing Adventure*, 202.

45. Quoted in Michael Perry, *Under God? Religious Faith and Liberal Democracy* (New York: Cambridge University Press, 2003), vii.

46. "ADL to Senator Lieberman: Keep Emphasis on Religion Out of Campaign," ADL Press Release, http://www.adl.org/PresRele/Rel_ChStSep_90/3629_90.asp.

47. Ibid. Also see "Anti-Defamation League Criticizes Lieberman's Religious Statements," CNN.com, August 29, 2000, http://archives.cnn.com/2000/ALLPOLITICS/stories/08/29/Lieberman.religion/index.html. For Lieberman's response see Carla Marinucci, "Lieberman Defends His Talk of Faith: Candidate Responds to Blast by ADL Chief," SFGate.com, August 30, 2000, http://sfgate.com/cgi-bin/article.cgi?file=/chronicle/archive/2000/08/30/MN67382.DTL.

48. Herb Keinon, "ADL Defends Lieberman Letter, Takes Shas Rabbi to Task," *Jerusalem Post Service*, http://www.jewishsf.com/bk000922/ifoxman.shtml.

49. Marinucci, "Lieberman Defends His Talk of Faith."

50. Dan Gilgoff, *The Jesus Machine: How James Dobson, Focus on the Family, and Evangelical America Are Winning the Culture War* (New York: St. Martin's, 2007), 247; Gilgoff, "Winning with Evangelicals," *U.S. News and World Report*, March 5, 2007, http://www.usnews.com/usnews/news/articles/070225/5excerpt.htm.

51. The data on Vanderslice is discussed in Gilgoff, *Jesus Machine*, 242–67.

52. Ibid., 244.

53. Ibid., 248. This also happened to the director of religious outreach, Brenda Bartella Peterson. See "Democrats' New Faith Outreach Director Quits," *Christian Century*, August 24, 2004, 11.

54. This is Gilgoff's term. See the excerpt of Gilgoff's book in the March 5, 2007, issue of *U.S. News and World Report* for a detailed survey of the immense differences between the campaigns in terms of enlisting religious voters.

55. On Kerry's own acknowledgment of errors in his handling of religion in the campaign, see Amy Sullivan, "Democrats Talk Religion," *Sojourners*, December

2006, 7. Also see John Dart, "Kerry Belatedly Speaks of Faith," *Christian Century*, October 17, 2006, 14.

56. Kerry came to regret this decision. See the articles by Sullivan and Dart cited in the previous note.

57. Kerry's difficulties with Catholics were widely discussed during the election. See William Schneider, "Kerry's Deviation," *National Journal*, June 26, 2004, http://www.aei.org/publications/pubID.20799,filter.all/pub_detail.asp; and "Dear Senator Kerry . . . ," *Commonweal*, August 13, 2004, 5.

58. Gilgoff, *Jesus Machine*, 261.

59. Jodi Wilgoren, "Kerry Evokes the Bible in Appeal for Black Votes," *New York Times*, September 10, 2004, A16.

60. Barack Obama, *The Audacity of Hope: Thoughts on Reclaiming the American Dream* (New York: Crown, 2006), 215–16.

61. "Kerry Quotes Bible; Bush Aide Cries Foul," *Christian Century*, April 20, 2004, 12; "Kerry, Bush Wrangle over Bible Passage," MSNBC.com, March 28, 2004, http://findarticles.com/p/articles/mi_m1058/is_8_121/ai_n6003095?lstpn= article_results&lstpc=search&lstpr=external&lstprs=other&lstwid=1&lstwn=search _results&lstwp=body_middle.

62. Remarks cited in Jill Lawrence, "Kerry Wears Faith Prominently, if Not on His Sleeve," *USA Today*, September 20, 2004, 9a.

63. John Kerry, "Speech to the 2004 Democratic National Convention: Remarks of Senator John Kerry," in *Our Plan for America: Stronger at Home, Respected in the World*, by John Kerry and John Edwards (New York: Public Affairs, 2004), 141.

64. Ronald Reagan was not only a professional actor, but he actually spent time touring the country shilling for GE, where he learned to perfect his oratorical skills (James Humes, *My Fellow Americans: Presidential Addresses That Shaped History* (New York: Praeger, 1992), 247–73. He was thus one of the few presidents in recent memory who could, theoretically, appear credible regardless of what faith position he took.

CHAPTER 6: THE DEMOCRATS, THE BIBLE, AND THE SECULARISTS

1. David Kirkpatrick, "In Ohio, Democrats Show a Religious Side to Voters," *New York Times*, October 31, 2006, 20, http://www.nytimes.com/2006/10/31/us/ politics/31church.html?ex=1319950800&en=f015cb5ceacf154b&ei=5088&partner =rssnyt&emc=rss.

2. See William McGurn, "Bob Casey's Revenge," *First Things* 149 (January 2005): 6–8.

3. Shuler's remark was made in an interview with the Web site redeemthe vote.com, http://redeemthevote.com/heath_shuler.html.

4. John Kerry himself acknowledged errors in his handling of religion in 2004. See John Dart, "Kerry Belatedly Speaks of Faith," *Christian Century*, October 17, 2006, 14.

5. Many of these developments are discussed in Mark Bergin, "Prodigal Party," *World Magazine*, January 27, 2007, http://www.worldmag.com/articles/12612.

6. On Mara Vanderslice making Democrats incorporate "recognizably biblical language into their platforms," see David Kirkpatrick, "Consultant Helps Democrats Embrace Faith, and Some in Party Are Not Pleased," *New York Times*, December 26, 2006, A10.

7. Much has been written about the Democrats' desire to shore up support among religious voters. See, for example, Dan Gilgoff, "The Dems Get Religion: A New Approach for the 2008 Campaign," *U.S. News and World Report*, March 5, 2007, http://www.usnews.com/usnews/news/articles/070225/5evangelicals.b.htm; and Beth Fouhy, "Clinton Calls on Democrats to Find Common Ground with Evangelical Voters," *Associated Press Worldstream*, April 11, 2006, http://www.lexisnexis.com/us/lnacademic/search/homesubmitForm.do (accessed August 15, 2006).

8. "Mike McCurry on Faith and Politics," SBL Forum, April 2007, http://www.sbl-site.org/article.aspx?ArticleId=658.

9. Ibid.

10. For the transcript of the debate where Bush and Dukakis discussed this allegation, see "Debating Our Destiny," http://www.pbs.org/newshour/debatingourdestiny/dod/1988-broadcast.html.

11. The indictments range from Anne Coulter's rather unoriginal association of the party with godlessness, to Edward Klein's more lyrical reference to "soulless, canapé-nibbling, Chablis-sipping, northeastern liberal[s]." Edward Klein, *The Truth about Hillary: What She Knew, When She Knew It, and How Far She'll Go to Become President* (New York: Sentinel, 2005), 241.

12. Louis Bolce and Gerald De Maio, "Our Secularist Democratic Party," *Public Interest*, Fall 2002, 7. On the rise of a similarly radical culture within the current party see John Leo, "The New McGovernites," *U.S. News and World Report*, November 7, 2005, 79.

13. Bolce and De Maio, "Our Secularist Democratic Party," 9. What is interesting about their argument—but not central to our concerns—is the contention that these nonbelievers, *not* conservative Christians, were the true (and unnoticed) instigators of the culture wars. Harboring a "relativistic" worldview and an "antagonism toward traditional values" (7) these secularists implemented a legislative agenda that provoked the rise of a once-dormant Christian right.

14. Strangely, this statistic was often interpreted as an indication of the might of secularists in the Democratic Party. See, for example, "Non-religious Americans Are Increasingly Important for the Democrats' Coalition," USA Today, August 26, 2004, http://www.usatoday.com/news/politicselections/nation/2004-08-26-secular-democrats_x.htm.

15. Stanley Greenberg's claim that "secular warriors" comprise 15 percent of the electorate seems similarly optimistic about the actual political solidity, if not solidarity, of the group in question. See Greenberg, *The Two Americas: Our Current Political Deadlock and How to Break It* (New York: Thomas Dunne, 2004), 128–30.

16. Geoffrey Layman, "Figure 3.1c: Percentage of Secular Democrats," in *The Great Divide: Religious and Cultural Conflict in American Party Politics* (New York: Columbia University Press, 2001), 102.

17. Quoted in "Obama: Time to Reclaim America's Promise," CNN.com, July 27, 2004, http://www.cnn.com/2004/ALLPOLITICS/07/27/dems.obama.transcript/index.html.

18. Amy Sullivan, "The Religion Gap: Can Democrats Bridge It?" *Commonweal,* September 10, 2004, 10.

19. As Mary Matalin, the well-known strategist for the elder President Bush, put it, "Cardinal rule 101 of politics is: *Never let the other side define you.*" Mary Matalin and James Carville, *All's Fair: Love, War, and Running for President* (New York: Random House, 1994), 72.

20. Bolce and De Maio, "Our Secularist Democratic Party." They argue that these journalists, with their blue-state sympathies and anti-fundamentalist sentiments, simply refused to acknowledge the role that secularists had played in the culture wars.

21. See John Green's remarks in the Pew Forum's "Understanding Religion's Role in the 2006 Election," December 5, 2006, http://pewforum.org/events/index.php?EventID=135.

22. See the Pew Forum table (using data from the University of Akron's Fourth National Survey of Religion and Politics) "Table 1. The American Religious Landscape and the 2004 Two-Party Presidential Vote (Arranged by Religious Tradition)," in *2004 Election Marked by Religious Polarization*, February 3, 2005, http://pewforum.org/docs/index.php?DocID=64.

23. Hillary Clinton, *It Takes a Village and Other Lessons Children Teach Us* (New York: Simon & Schuster, 1996), 167.

24. Ibid.

25. Ibid., 159.

26. Hillary Rodham Clinton, *Living History* (New York: Scribner, 2003), 21, 22.

27. Ibid., 22. For more on Jones see Susannah Meadows, "What Are Hillary Clinton's Religious Beliefs?" *Newsweek,* February 12, 2007, http://www.msnbc.msn.com/id/16960621/site/newsweek/.

28. "Sister Hillary," *Economist,* January 29, 2005, 34.

29. Clinton, *Living History,* 117.

30. Ibid., 267.

31. Ibid., 469–70, 480.

32. Michael Tomasky, *Hillary's Turn: Inside Her Improbable Victorious Senate Campaign* (New York: Free Press, 2001), 8.

33. Michael Luo, "For Clinton, Faith Intertwines with Political Life," *New York Times,* July 7, 2007, A1, A8.

34. Susan Estrich, *The Case for Hillary Clinton* (New York: Regan, 2005), 204. Estrich, an experienced Democratic strategist, vouches for the authenticity of Clinton's belief.

35. Nina Bernstein, "Mrs. Clinton Says GOP's Immigration Plan Is At Odds with the Bible," *New York Times,* March 23, 2006, http://www.nytimes.com/2006/03/23/nyregion/23hillary.html?ex=1185249600&en=39bf971a3bd2750a&ei=5070.

36. Raymond Hernandez, "As Clinton Shifts Themes, Debate Arises on Her Motives," *New York Times,* February 1, 2005.

37. Manya Brachear, "Stump Speeches Taking a Page from the Bible," *Chicago Tribune*, June 29, 2007, B2.

38. Michael Sean Winters, "At Home with Religion: Barack Obama, Faith, and the Presidential Campaign," *America*, March 12, 2007, 9.

39. On Obama's religious upside see Winters, "At Home with Religion."

40. Barack Obama, *Dreams from My Father: A Story of Race and Inheritance* (New York: Crown, 1995).

41. David Espo, "Sen. Obama Urges Democrats to Court Evangelicals," Associated Press, June 28, 2006, http://www.ksdk.com/news/elections/election_article.aspx?storyid=99358.

42. Quoted in Mike Dorning, "Evangelicals Open Arms, Wary Hearts Greet Obama," December 2, 2006, *Chicago Tribune* Online, http://www.chicagotribune.com/news/nationworld/chi-0612020256dec02,1,533633.story?ctrack=1&cset=true (accessed May 5, 2007).

43. Barack Obama, *The Audacity of Hope: Thoughts on Reclaiming the American Dream* (New York: Crown, 2006), 39, 221, 218.

44. Barack Obama, "Remarks by Senator Barack Obama at the Opening of the Abraham Lincoln Presidential Library and Museum," April 20, 2005, http://www.barackobama.com/2005/04/20/remarks_by_senator_barack_obam.php.

45. Obama, *Audacity of Hope*, 207.

46. Ibid., 208. On his preconversion doubts, see Obama, *Dreams from My Father*, 286–87.

47. Obama, *Audacity of Hope*, 219.

48. "Full Text of Senator Barack Obama's Announcement for President," February 10, 2007, http://www.barackobama.com/2007/02/10/remarks_of_senator_barack_obam_11.php.

49. Jodi Kantor, "A Candidate, His Minister, and the Search for Faith," *New York Times*, April 30, 2007, A1.

50. Barack Obama, "Dr. Martin Luther King Jr. National Memorial Groundbreaking Ceremony," November 13, 2006, http://obama.senate.gov/speech/061113-dr_martin_luthe/.

51. Obama, *Audacity of Hope*, 222.

52. Ibid., 224.

53. See Kantor, "Candidate, His Minister."

54. Obama, *Dreams from My Father*, 93.

55. See Gary Wolf, "How the Internet Invented Howard Dean," *Wired*, January 2004, http://www.wired.com/wired/archive/12.01/dean.html.

56. The two bloggers in question were Amanda Marcotte and Melissa McEwan. Marcotte's profession of atheism can be gleaned from her post, "More Thoughts on Meanie Atheism," April 22, 2007, http://pandagon.net/2007/04/22/more-thoughts-on-meanie-atheism. I had a difficult time identifying a clear statement of nonbelief from McEwan, but this seems evident from her blog, Shakespeare's Sister, at http://shakespearessister.blogspot.com.

57. Both of these quotes appear in David Ingram and Mark Johnson, "Edwards Chastises Staffers for 'Intolerant Language' on Their Blogs," *Charlotte Observer*,

February 8, 2007, http://infoweb.newsbank.com/iw-search/we/InfoWeb?p_action=
doc&p_docid=11757C131D4295AB&p_docnum=1&p_queryname=2&p_product=
AWNB&p_theme=aggregated4&p_nbid=J50B53AJMTE4OTEwMjY0OS4xMTA4
Nzc6MToxNDoxNDEuMTYxLjQzLjE2Nw.

58. "John Edwards Hires *Two* Anti-Catholics," press release, Catholic League
for Religious and Civil Rights, February 6, 2007.

59. The campaign's deliberations are reported in Alex Koppelman and Rebecca
Traister, "Edwards Campaign Rehires Bloggers Marcotte and McEwen [*sic*],"
Salon.com, February 8, 2007, http://www.salon.com/news/feature/2007/02/08/blog-
gers_rehired/index.html.

60. All of these remarks can be found in John Edwards, "Statement on Campaign
Bloggers," February 8, 2007, http://blog.johnedwards.com/story/2007/2/8/113651/
4503.

61. Lindsay Beyerstein, "Why I Refused to Blog for Edwards," Salon.com, February 26, 2007, http://www.salon.com/opinion/feature/2007/02/26/beyerstein/.

62. They issued statements on the same page as "Statement on Campaign Bloggers" cited above. On the perspective of Melissa McEwan, see her "My Life as
Right Wing Target," February 16, 2007, *Guardian Unlimited*, http://commentisfree
.guardian.co.uk/melissa_mcewan/2007/02/my_life_as_a_rightwing_target.html. For
Marcotte's remarks see her "Announcement," February 12, 2007, http://pandagon
.net/2007/02/12/announcement; and her "Why I Had to Quit the John Edwards
Campaign," February 16, 2007, http://www.salon.com/news/feature/2007/02/16/
marcotte.

63. For articles about the story see John Broder, "Edwards' Bloggers Cross the
Line, Critic Says," *New York Times*, February 6, 2007, A16; and Kathryn Jean Lopez,
"Unholy Hire," *National Review* Online, February 6, 2007, http://article.national
review.com/?q=MjYzN2FiZjFmOGIwZDcyZDQ1NzM1MDU5OGM2MzljZTE=.

64. David Kuo, "John Edwards: 'My Faith Came Roaring Back," Beliefnet,
http://www.beliefnet.com/story/213/story_21312.html.

65. This point was made in an article examining Edwards's actions in the after-
math of the Virginia Tech massacre. Mike Allen, "Edwards Rises to the Moment,"
Politico.com, April 23, 2007, http://dyn.politico.com/printstory.cfm?uuid=118
FD743–3048-5C12–002C9CEC5306C8A2.

66. Kuo, "John Edwards."

67. Edwards seems to have softened his position. Compare his interview with
the Interfaith Alliance on December 3, 2003, http://www.interfaithalliance.org/
atf/cf/05044A38–9516-4831–9AA2-E10AFAB8886A/q3edwards.pdf. My surmise
is that his remarks in this interview reflect his actual position and the softer approaches
adumbrated above are employed for purposes of engaging religious voters.

68. Steve Koehler, "Edwards Talks Moral High Road" *Springfield News-Leader,*
April 20, 2006, http://www.johnedwards.com/news/headlines/springnl20060420/
index.html.

69. Ibid.

70. John Edwards, "Time to End Poverty," *Sojourners*, September–October
2005, 7.

71. Kuo, "John Edwards."

72. "A 2002 survey by the Pew Forum on Religion and Public Life suggests that 27 million Americans are atheist or agnostic or have no religious preference" (Daniel Dennett, "The Bright Stuff," *New York Times*, July 12, 2003, 11). Dennett was basing this claim on question 18 in the survey conducted in March 2001 by the Pew Forum, which asked about religious preference. One percent of the respondents claimed to be atheists, two percent agnostics, and eight percent "no preference." Dennett arbitrarily conscripted the "no preference" category into the Bright army and thus came up with an inflated estimate of their power and possibilities in American politics.

73. The argument that there are 63 million nontheists is made on the Web site of the Secular Coalition of America, http://www.secular.org/constituency.html. This claim is based on a Harris Interactive poll in which 9 percent "believe there is no God" (note that this latter number appears to include persons who self-identify themselves with a religious group) and 12 percent are "not sure whether or not there is a God." The poll was conducted from September 16 to 23, 2003, and posted on October 15, 2003. See "Table 1: Belief in God and Certainty of Belief," http://www .harrisinteractive.com/harris_poll/index.asp?PID=408. Once again, the error lies in consolidating two highly dissimilar categories.

74. The impetus for this approach comes from Barry Kosmin, Egon Mayer, and Areila Keysar, "American Religious Identification Survey," 2001, Graduate Center of the City University of New York. http://www.gc.cuny.edu/faculty/research_ studies/aris.pdf. The authors write: "In sharp contrast to that widely held perception, the present survey has detected a wide and possibly growing swath of secularism among Americans. The magnitude and role of this large secular segment of the American population is frequently ignored by scholars and politicians alike." As noted in a footnote below, the authors are not speaking of nonbelief when they speak of secularism but people who have "no religion." Thus the secular segment is not composed of atheists and agnostics, but those who are unaffiliated—a rather different type of cohort. These distinctions have been lost on nonbelieving activists as well as journalists. A similar claim for growing secular numbers is made in the Editorial of the *Charleston Gazette,* May 1, 2007, 4a.

75. The difficulties demographers face in defining this term and doing survey data are discussed by John Benson, "Beyond Belief: Looking at the Less Religious," Public Opinion Pros, 2005, http://www.publicopinionpros.com/features/2005/jan/ benson_3.asp.

76. Take, for example, the 1996 Pew Religion Survey in which "atheist or agnostic" combined for one percent of the population and those with "no preference" for religion were at 15.3 percent. Thus, if we combine the two groups—only one of which could plausibly be described as a group—we would misleadingly conclude that "secularists" comprised 16.3 percent of the population. This figure would make them larger than, let's say, Baptists, who are at 13.6 percent according to the same survey. See Andrew Kohut, John Green, Scott Keeter, and Robert Toth, "Table 3–1: Belonging: Religious Traditions," in *The Diminishing Divide: Religion's Changing Role in American Politics* (Washington, DC: Brookings Institution, 2000), 18. The American Religious Identification Survey of 2001 conducted by CUNY has atheists,

agnostics, humanists, and secularists *combined* as comprising a little less than two million people, and little less than one percent of the population. Conversely, the category "No religion" has 27.5 million people comprising 13.2 percent of the population. Barry Kosmin, Egon Mayer, and Areila Keysar, "American Religious Identification Survey, 2001," http://www.gc.cuny.edu/faculty/research_studies/aris.pdf. It emerges from this that demographers and political scientists will need to define the term "secular" in much more precise terms.

77. As John Green points out, not all unaffiliated people are atheists or agnostics. Most are "simply indifferent to religion . . . not hostile to it, just indifferent." Pew Forum, "Understanding Religion's Role." Green goes on to discuss the problems inherent in assuming the unaffiliated are nonbelievers. Thus, when some place the unaffiliated into the camp of nonbelief they are mixing apples and oranges.

78. Stanley Greenberg's claim that "secular warriors" comprise 15 percent of the electorate seems similarly optimistic about the actual political solidity, if not solidarity, of the group in question. Greenberg, *The Two Americas: Our Current Political Deadlock and How to Break It* (New York: Thomas Dunne, 2004), 128–30.

79. The figure of atheists and agnostics as comprising 3 percent is suggested by the 2002 Pew Forum survey discussed above.

80. On this point see John Green's remarks in the Pew Forum's "Understanding Religion's Role."

81. The observations about the difficulties in organizing nonbelievers and their election-day performance are discussed by John Green in Richard Ostling, "Non-Religious Americans Are Increasingly Important for Democrats' Coalition," NCTimes.com, April 24, 2007, http://www.nctimes.com/articles/2004/08/26/special_reports/religion/21_45_198_25_04.prt.

CHAPTER 7: REPUBLICANS AND EVANGELICALS

1. "Giuliani, McCain Lead among Evangelical Republicans," April 2, 2007, Pew Forum, http://pewforum.org/docs/?DocID=188. The survey was conducted again on the same site on June 18. Giuliani placed first among evangelicals, followed by the unannounced Fred Thompson.

2. Alison Mitchell, "Musing on Religion, Giuliani Extols His Vision of Tolerance," Nytimes.com, April 21, 1994, http://query.nytimes.com/gst/fullpage.html?res=980CE7DA1231F932A15757C0A962958260&sec=&spon=&pagewanted=print.

3. Andrew Kirtzman, *Rudy Giuliani: Emperor of the City* (New York: William Morrow, 2000), 4. The remark about the "priestlike" Giuliani is made by Fran Reiter in Deborah Strober and Gerald Strober, *Giuliani, Flawed or Flawless? The Oral Biography* (Hoboken, NJ: John Wiley & Sons, 2007), 267.

4. Mitchell, "Musing on Religion."

5. Wayne Barrett, *Rudy! An Investigative Biography of Rudy Giuliani* (New York: Basic, 2000), 52.

6. Kirtzman, *Rudy Giuliani*, 264.

7. Fred Siegel, *The Prince of the City: Giuliani, New York, and the Genius of American Life* (San Francisco: Encounter, 2005), 249.

8. "Mayor Faults Firing of Teacher over Prayer," *New York Times*, June 21, 1998, http://query.nytimes.com/gst/fullpage.html?res=9F07E1DC143CF932A15755 C0A96E958260.

9. Elisabeth Bumiller, "Mayor Unfairly Using Religion, First Lady Says," *New York Times*, February 10, 2000, http://query.nytimes.com/gst/fullpage.html?res= 9400E7D6133EF933A25751C0A9669C8B63.

10. For extended discussions on these themes, see Barrett, *Rudy!* and Kirtzman, *Rudy Giuliani*.

11. See Howard Kurtz, "In 1993 Memo, Giuliani Staff Gave Harsh Assessment of Flaws," *Washington Post*, February 14, 2007, A3.

12. Both the remark of Land and Giuliani are quoted in "Transcript: Rudy Giuliani on FNS," May 14, 2007, http://www.foxnews.com/story/0,2933,271917,00.html.

13. See Sheryl Henderson Blunt, "The Giuliani Choice," *Christianity Today*, May 5, 2007, http://www.christianitytoday.com/ct/2007/june/13.20.html.

14. Strober and Strober, *Giuliani*, 298.

15. Marc Santora and Adam Nagourney, "Giuliani Takes on G.O.P. Orthodoxy on Social Issues," *New York Times*, May 12, 2007, A1, A12.

16. See Jacques Berlinerblau, *The Secular Bible: Why Nonbelievers Must Take Religion Seriously* (New York: Cambridge University Press, 2005); and Berlinerblau, "Secularism in the Elimination Round," *Chronicle Review*, June 1, 2007, B6–B9.

17. "McCain Says Roe v. Wade Should Be Overturned," MSNBC.com, February 18, 2007, http://www.msnbc.msn.com/id/17222147.

18. Terry Neal, "McCain Softens Abortion Stand," *Washington Post*, August 24, 1999, A4.

19. David Brody, "McCain Says He Needs Evangelicals to Win," *CBN News*, March 19, 2007, http://www.cbn.com/CBNnews/122005.aspx.

20. Dena Ross, "John McCain on Character and Heroism," Beliefnet, http://www.beliefnet.com/story/180/story_18040.html.

21. John McCain, "Statement on Marriage Protection Amendment," June 6, 2006, http://mccain.senate.gov/press_office/view_article.cfm?id=34. The conservative pro-Romney commentator Hugh Hewitt notes that McCain failed to vote yes on the Federal Marriage Amendment and that the Arizona version he supported actually failed to pass. Hewitt, *A Mormon in the White House: 10 Things Every American Should Know about Mitt Romney* (Washington, DC: Regnery, 2007), 121.

22. John McCain, "McCain Statement on Stem Cell Research," July 18, 2006, http://mccain.senate.gov/press_office/view_article.cfm?id=108.

23. The church in question is North Phoenix Baptist Church, and it is discussed in David Van Biema, "McCain's Faith: 'I Pray Regularly,'" *Time*, March 13, 2000, http://www.time.com/time/magazine/article/0,9171,996351,00.html.

24. Matt Stearns, "McCain Reaching Out to Christian Conservative Base," McClatchy Newspapers, June 10, 2007, http://www.mcclatchydc.com/homepage/story/16589.html.

25. John McCain, *Faith of My Fathers* (New York: Random House, 1999), 331, 332.

26. Ross, "John McCain on Character and Heroism."

27. McCain, *Faith of My Fathers*, 206, 253.

28. Van Biema, "McCain's Faith."

29. "Sen. John McCain Attacks Pat Robertson, Jerry Falwell, Republican Establishment as Harming GOP Ideals," February 28, 2000, http://transcripts.cnn.com/TRANSCRIPTS/0002/28/se.01.html.

30. Frank Bruni, "McCain Apologizes for Characterizing Falwell and Robertson as Forces of Evil," *New York Times*, March 2, 2000, http://query.nytimes.com/gst/fullpage.html?res=9B02E3DE1E39F931A35750C0A9669C8B63&sec=&spon=&pagewanted=print.

31. Dan Balz, "McCain Reconnects with Liberty University," *Washington Post*, May 14, 2006, A4.

32. Brody, "McCain Says." Confirming that the rumors did indeed come from the Bush camp is David Kuo, *Tempting Faith: An Inside Story of Political Seduction* (New York: Free Press, 2006), 129.

33. John McCain, *Worth the Fighting For: The Education of an American Maverick, and the Heroes Who Inspired Him* (New York: Random House, 2003), 136–37.

34. "McCain Courting Christian Conservatives," Associated Press, *Washington Post*, January 17, 2007, A2; "McCain Says He Hopes to Mend Ties with Christian Leader," Associated Press, *Washington Post*, January 17, 2007, A2.

35. See McCain, *Worth the Fighting For*, 327–65.

36. See Dan Gilgoff, *The Jesus Machine: How James Dobson, Focus on the Family, and Evangelical America Are Winning the Culture War* (New York: St. Martin's, 2007).

37. Mitt Romney, *Turnaround: Crisis, Leadership, and the Olympic Games* (Washington, DC: Regnery, 2004), 7.

38. Robert Rudy, "Public Views of Presidential Politics and Mormon Faith," Pew Forum. May 16, 2007, http://pewforum.org/docs/?DocsID=213.

39. The figure of 66 percent is discussed in Cathleen Falsani, "A Mormon President?" *Chicago Sun-Times*, April 20, 2007, 36. A variety of recent polls are gathered together in Howard Berkes, "Faith Could Be Hurdle in Romney's White House Bid," http://www.npr.org/templates/story/story.php?storyId=7245768.

40. Carol Costello, "Romney: Sharpton Remark on Faith Was Bigoted," CNN.com, May 10, 2007, http://www.cnn.com/2007/POLITICS/05/09/sharpton.romney/index.html. On Christopher Hitchens's book, *God Is Not Great: How Religion Poisons Everything* (New York: Twelve Books, 2007), see my "Secularism in the Elimination Round," *Chronicle Review*, June 1, 2007, B6–B9.

41. Amy Sullivan, "Mitt Romney's Evangelical Problem," *Washington Monthly*, September 2005, http://www.washingtonmonthly.com/features/2005/0509.sullivan1.html.

42. Stephanie Simon, "For Them, Faith Trumps Works," *Los Angeles Times*, June 16, 2007, A1.

43. Adam Nagourney and Laurie Goodstein, "Mormon Candidate Braces for Religion as Issue," *New York Times*, February 8, 2007, A1.

44. Quoted in Howard Berkes, "Faith Could Be Hurdle." A poll cited in Hewitt, *Mormon in the White House*, suggests that 33 percent of South Carolinians could not vote for a Mormon (172).

45. Evan Lehmann, "Romney, in Heart of Bible Belt, Asks Christians to Trust Him," *Sun* (Lowell, MA), May 6, 2007.

46. Quoted in Hewitt, *Mormon in the White House?* 221.

47. Many quotes to this effect can be found in John J. Miller, "Evangelicals for Romney? A Major Question of the Coming Period," *National Review*, December 18, 2006, http://nrd.nationalreview.com/article/?q=YWNjMzE2MGMzZGFlZmNjZG ZiNDA3YjYyMmFjOWY1NTc=.

48. R. W. Apple Jr., "The 1994 Campaign: Massachusetts; Kennedy and Romney Meet, and the Rancor Flows Freely," *New York Times*, October 26, 1994, http://query.nytimes.com/gst/fullpage.html?res=9F07E6DB153FF935A15753C1A96295 8260&n=Top%2fReference%2fTimes%20Topics%2fSubjects%2fD%2fDebating.

49. On some of Romney's notable policy shifts, see Terry Eastland, "In 2008, Will It Be Mormon in America?" *Weekly Standard*, June 6, 2005, 16–22. Also see Jennifer Rubin, "Mitt Romney's Conversion: His Pro-Life Turn Is More Recent than You Think," *Weekly Standard*, February 5, 2007, 17.

50. Quoted in Hewitt, *Mormon in the White House?* 103.

51. Ibid., 130–34. Here his statement before the Senate Judiciary Committee is quoted at length.

52. "Mitt Romney Wants to Re-Tool Washington: Mike Wallace Interviews the Contender for the GOP Presidential Nomination," May 13, 2007, http://www.cbsnews.com/stories/2007/05/10/60minutes/main2787426.shtml.

53. Jim Rutenberg, "Romney Favors Hubbard Novel," April 30, 2007, The Caucus: Political Blogging from the *New York Times*, http://thecaucus.blogs.nytimes.com/2007/04/30/romney-favors-hubbard-novel.

54. Sridhar Pappu, "The Holy Cow! Candidate," *Atlantic Monthly*, September 2005, 108; Hewitt, *Mormon in the White House?* 222.

55. Pappu, "Holy Cow! Candidate," 116.

56. "Winners and Losers in Republican Presidential Debate?" *Anderson Cooper 360 Degrees*, June 5, 2007, http://transcripts.cnn.com/TRANSCRIPTS/0706/05/acd.01.html.

57. Quoted in Rachel Zoll, "Romney to Robertson's School to Court Conservative Christian Vote," Associated Press, May 4, 2007, http://www.boston.com/news/local/massachusetts/articles/2007/05/04/romney_to_robertsons_school_to_court_conservative_christian_vote/ .

58. Kent Jackson, "The Sacred Literature of the Latter-Day Saints," in *The Bible and Bibles in America*, ed. Ernest Frerichs (Atlanta: Scholars Press, 1988), 163, 164.

59. "Mitt Romney: The Complete Interview," *ABC News*, February 18, 2007, http://www.abcnews.go.com/ThisWeek/Politics/story?id=2885156&page=1.

60. Quoted in Nancy Gibbs, "Romney's Mormon Question," *Time*, May 10, 2007, http://www.time.com/time/magazine/article/0,9171,1619552,00.html.

61. Quoted in Berkes, "Faith Could Be Hurdle."

62. As one writer aptly put it, "Romney makes a very unlikely dangerous fanatic. One doesn't usually make a couple of hundred million dollars as a venture capitalist on the basis of blinkered irrationality." Rich Lowry, "A Mormon First?" *National Review* Online, May 15, 2007, http://article.nationalreview.com/?q=NzY5NTUw ODQxMTIzNDg2ODExM2Y3Yzg0MTE4NjdmYzg=.

63. Quoted in Daniel Burke et al., "With the Help of a Dozen, Democrats 'Get Religion,'" *National Catholic Reporter*, October 27, 2006, 12–15.

64. Pappu, "Holy Cow! Candidate," 116.

CONCLUSION: THE SYMBOL AND THE SEPARATION

1. See "Pastors Name the New International Version as Their Favorite Bible," http://www.ellisonresearch.com/ERPS%20II/release%209%20versions.htm; and Ron Sellers, "Survey: Protestant Ministers Rate 12 Different Bible Versions," http://www .lifeway.com/lwc/article_main_page/0%2C1703%2CA%25253D157025%252526M %25253D200915%2C00.html.

2. Martyn Percy, "Whose Time Is It, Anyway? Evangelicals, the Millennium, and Millenarianism," in *Christian Millenarianism: From Early Church to Waco*, ed. Stephen Hunt (Bloomington: Indiana University Press, 2001), 32.

3. Christian Smith, *American Evangelicalism: Embattled and Thriving* (Chicago: University of Chicago Press, 1998), 129.

4. Richard Kyle, *Evangelicalism: Am Americanized Christianity* (New Brunswick, NJ: Transaction, 2006), 3.

5. See Bruce Barron and Anson Shupe, "Reasons for the Growing Popularity of Christian Reconstructionism: The Determination to Attain Dominion," in *Religion and Politics in Comparative Perspective: Revival of Religious Fundamentalism in East and West*, ed. Bronislaw Misztal and Anson Shupe (Westport, CT: Praeger, 1992), 83–96.

6. Alan Wolfe, "Faith, Freedom, and Toleration," in *One Electorate under God? A Dialogue on Religion and American Politics*, ed. E. J. Dionne Jr., Jean Bethke Elshtain, and Kayla Drogosz (Washington, DC: Brookings Institution Press, 2004), 224.

7. Alister McGrath, *A Passion for Truth: The Intellectual Coherence of Evangelicalism* (Downers Grove, IL: InterVarsity Press, 1996), 17.

8. Randall Balmer, *Thy Kingdom Come: How the Religious Right Distorts the Faith and Threatens America: An Evangelical's Lament* (New York: Perseus, 2006), 23.

9. See my *The Secular Bible: Why Nonbelievers Must Take Religion Seriously* (New York: Cambridge University Press, 2005); and "Secularism in the Elimination Round," *Chronicle Review*, June 1, 2007, B6–B9.

10. See Christopher Hitchens, *God Is Not Great: How Religion Poisons Everything* (New York: Twelve Books, 2007); Richard Dawkins, *The God Delusion* (Boston: Houghton Mifflin, 2006); and Sam Harris, *The End of Faith: Religion, Terror, and the Future of Reason* (New York: Norton, 2005).

11. Quoted in Martin Marty, "America's Iconic Book," in *Humanizing America's Iconic Book: Society of Biblical Literature Centennial Addresses 1980*, ed. Gene Tucker and Douglas Knight (Chico, CA: Scholars Press, 1982), 9.

12. Mark Noll, "The Politicians' Bible," *Christianity Today* 36 (1992): 17.

13. Marcy Kaptur, U.S. Cong. House, *In Honor of Sgt. Keith Kline,* 110th Cong., 1st sess. (July 13, 2007: E1510; http://frwebgate.access.gpo.gov/cgi-bin/getpage.cgi?dbname-2007_record&page=E1510&position=all.

Index of Scripture
and Other Ancient Sources

Index of Names and Subjects